On Teaching and Learning in College

Reemphasizing the Roles of Learners and the Disciplines

Paul L. Dressel
Dora Marcus

On Teaching and Learning in College

Jossey-Bass Publishers
San Francisco • Washington • London • 1982

ON TEACHING AND LEARNING IN COLLEGE
Reemphasizing the Roles of Learners and the Disciplines
by Paul L. Dressel and Dora Marcus

433 California Street
San Francisco, California 94104
&
Jossey-Bass Limited
28 Banner Street
London EC1Y 8QE

Library of Congress Cataloging in Publication Data

Dressel, Paul Leroy, 1910-
On teaching and learning in college.

Bibliography: p. 221
Includes index.
1. College teaching. I. Marcus, Dora.
II. Title.
LB2331.D73 1982 378'.125 82-48077
ISBN 0-87589-543-3

Manufactured in the United States of America

The paper in this book meets the guidelines for permanence and durability of the Committee on Production Guidelines for Book Longevity of the Council on Library Resources.

JACKET DESIGN BY WILLI BAUM

FIRST EDITION

Code 8232

The Jossey-Bass Series in Higher Education

Preface

As a prelude to writing this volume, I reflected upon my experiences as both student and teacher over a period of some sixty-five years spent in elementary, secondary, college, and postgraduate schools. My general intent was to identify those teachers who stood out as decidedly good or bad and then attempt to explain why. I found that, although I could recall many individual elementary and secondary school teachers by name and subject taught, none stood out as having provided an extraordinarily stimulating learning experience. Indeed, the only episode of my elementary school experience I recalled vividly was one in which a teacher of arithmetic insisted (reinforced by the textbook used) that in working problems of the type, if 3 percent of a number is equal to 24, what is the number?, one must proceed as follows: If 3 percent of the number equals 24, then 1 percent of that number equals 8, and 100 percent of that number equals 100 times 8 or 800. My observation that if the 3 percent were written as .03 and divided directly into 24 the result achieved was obviously 800 and all intervening steps were subsumed was met by the threat that unless the correct protocol was followed, the answer would be declared incorrect. From that example, I was led to recall many other incidents in classrooms over the years in which teachers utilizing procedures originally developed to expedite understanding, so used them that they routinized education. The net recollection, especially of my elementary and secondary educational experiences, was that teaching emphasized memorization of specific procedures and correct answers but seldom provided opportunity for or rewarded original or creative thought and insight.

From my undergraduate years, I recalled only two teachers outstanding in stimulating my interests and learning. The first was a teacher of mathematics who was perhaps the worst classroom performer I ever saw. But he was wise enough to encourage and even require me to work through a calculus textbook on my own and report my progress to him only occasionally. Freed of the boring classroom experience, I accomplished a great deal. In particular, I developed an independence of teachers which, in some measure, every undergraduate student should achieve. The second outstanding teacher of my undergraduate years was a history professor. He was very demanding but won my admiration by forthrightly stating that remembering the particular names and facts to be covered in the course was of minor importance. The real purpose of the experience he defined as arriving at some understanding of the difficulties of writing history, and of the inevitable fallibility of history due to incomplete or fallacious records and the unfathomable motivation of historical figures. In that professor's course, I was led, by reading, writing, and recurring explication and comment, to see that history is a creation of man and an imposition of that creation on a period and series of events. As a result of the experience, I have continued to read history with pleasure and benefit.

From my years as a graduate student, again I was able to identify only two outstanding teachers, both in mathematics. One was a man who continually nudged his students (usually by hints rather than overt direction) to redefine problems or to find some unusual and creative way to solve them. The praise and recognition for seeking and communicating distinctive insights provided an incentive in each class session. My respect was marvelously increased when I learned much later that the professor himself had almost invariably worked out at an earlier time some of the intriguing approaches that he encouraged his students to explore. The other memorable professor of my graduate years was one who engaged himself to demonstrate his research approach before a small group of advanced students and faculty members. He undertook to do his research on a blackboard and to restrict it to that while the group was together. Striving to put into words the thoughts going through his mind, he thereby provided insights into the working of the mind of a research mathematician such as are never revealed by the final written account. In some cases, nothing of significance was covered in the hour-and-a-half or two-hour seminar. In a few cases, the material tentatively developed in the previous seminar was destroyed or modified or declared obvious by some unverbalized later insight. The unusual individual who engages in such a demonstration is the direct antithesis of the professor adept at covering materials he or someone else has repeatedly polished. Knowledge and thinking in the raw have a character different from the well honed. Strangely enough, knowledge can often be better understood when viewed as it develops than when polished to impress.

I found these reflections a useful basis for pulling together many other observations and readings on the process of teaching and learning. I would urge those concerned with improving their teaching to engage in that same kind of critical reflection and then go on to review the impact of their own classroom teaching practices, assignments, and evaluations on students. One conviction that may emerge is that the individual teacher is far less important in a student's development than many teachers are inclined to think.

In moving to a more abstract level in my reflections on teaching and learning, I shortly concluded that the major weakness of most of the teaching (including some of my own) that I had experienced was that the teacher had given too much attention to the classroom and to the teacher's activities in that classroom. Judging from my own student experience, most classroom sessions were largely a waste of time. They were useful only when they provided some direction and motivation for learning outside of the classroom. Learning is, after all, a very personal thing, and some of the most profound aspects of it are at a level of ideation and mental manipulation that goes far beyond the words, sentences, and principles that provide the primary fodder in the classroom. Understanding is more than a matter of memorizing and recalling verbalization; it requires time and effort.

The second significant insight that came out of this summary reflection was that the strong and narrow disciplinary orientation of most teaching I had known at the undergraduate level was a major deficiency in cultivating the type of learning related to the problems of human existence and to deriving some satisfaction from that existence. I concluded that it was not that the disciplines in themselves represented an undesirable way of organizing knowledge, but rather that teachers, having become so immersed in these disciplines, no longer viewed them in relationship to the basic problems and concerns of mankind. Hence they could not grasp and interpret to learners the essential nature of their discipline. In teaching, the concepts and modes of thought of the several disciplines must be interrelated and applied if they are to be meaningful to the student who moves from the classroom to the complicated reality in which we all live.

As a result of this reminiscing on my own experiences, extensive reading of the views of others about the nature and objectives of college teaching, and some prior attempts to express my own views about college teaching, I have come to a set of assumptions or convictions that is always implicit and often made explicit in this volume. These assumptions deserve prior statement here so that the reader may be warned in advance of my convictions and values.

1. I strongly disagree with those who regard the good teacher as one who knows students well and sees close interaction with them as an opportunity to direct and to enhance their personal development. My dissent is based upon several considerations. First of all, I do not believe that people looking to a career in college and university teaching are generally suited for or motivated toward developing personal relationships with students in which the teacher is to be viewed as a pal, a therapist, or an ideal model. The pri-

mary qualification of a professor is a depth of knowledge in a particular discipline and sufficient continuing interest in that discipline to maintain an awareness of disciplinary developments and their implications for curriculum and instruction. The only purpose of instruction is to enable students to learn, and the individual who engages in teaching without stimulating others to learn cannot be considered an effective member of the teaching profession.

2. I do not believe, as many professors argue, that it is essential for an undergraduate college teacher to be involved in frontier research devoted to expanding the discipline. However, extensive reading and some synthesizing scholarly investigations to keep the teacher aware of recent developments and to provide some basis for revising courses and stimulating the students are essential. Furthermore, I doubt that it is wise to take up much time of the able researcher in the instruction of undergraduates. Teaching, well done, is tremendously time consuming. Researchers will usually, and quite understandably, give inadequate time to teaching and to evaluating student work.
3. College or university teachers should not assume that they are members of an elite that society is obligated to support in semi-luxury to do as they wish. Teaching is a social service occupation, and the administrators who manage a social service, whether designated as a service bureau or as a college or university, have an obligation to account to society for the expenditure of the funds provided. This is true in all public and private service, but in the case of the college and university, each teacher is presumably a professional and must, in deference to that professional status, collaborate with the administrators and associates in providing evidence of the continuing commitment to the task at hand and full accountability in performance of it.
4. The obligations of a professor to a student neither require nor justify intimate and dominating relationships, but anyone who presumes to be a teacher has an obligation to become familiar with the students' backgrounds and with their hopes and aspirations. Too often I have witnessed pro-

fessors teaching even the introductory courses as though every student ultimately sought a Ph.D. in the discipline. At one time, professors in each discipline were expected to develop courses especially designed for students in particular fields. I recall being involved, in the early 1930s, in teaching mathematics for agriculture students, mathematics for science students, mathematics for business students, and mathematics for engineers, as well as mathematics for prospective mathematicians. If one believes, as I do, that the search for meaning requires some grasp of the essential nature of each of the major disciplines and some appreciation of its possible role in a variety of life issues and problems, then some reasonably clear path must be found between disciplinary courses taught for students building a career in that field and those courses offered to cover a smattering of ideas in current use. Every college or university teacher should be concerned with knowing the interrelationships in objectives, methods, concepts, and structures between his or her discipline and other disciplines. Every teacher also needs to be aware of general course requirements and some of the more common patterns of course experiences prevalent among students so that these can be drawn upon in the development of a particular course.

5. My awareness of human frailty makes it impossible for me to assume that a professor should have complete autonomy in development of courses, the means and processes by which they are offered, or the grading of students who take them. There are many pressures from many directions on every citizen in a democratic society. Professors are not exempt. When these pressures emphasize research, it is only human nature to weight one's activities in that direction unless there is a counterbalancing force toward other academic functions. If there are subtle pressures (or obvious rewards) for passing athletes, it is inevitable that some professors will thereby be induced into iniquity, with resulting inequity to other students and teachers.
6. I have grave doubts about the recurrent enthusiasms of a

novel gimmick or gadget as a promoter of learning. Clowning in the classroom, computer-assisted instruction, individually programmed instruction, case studies, games, field studies, travel—these all have, no doubt, validity with some students for some kinds of learning, but any one carried to an extreme is unlikely to survive long. One highly deviant course cannot resolve the problem of providing high-quality education, and it can detract from the worth of other courses and educational experiences.

7. Ultimately, the provision of a learning environment and a set of principles must be buttressed by a system of rewards so distributed as to make clear to everyone that an institution desires, supports, and rewards good teaching. Governing boards should demand regular accounting from administrators and faculty on the character and quality of teaching and on the satisfaction of the students with their experiences, and should create a system of rewards that ensures the continuance of good teaching.

It will become clear to the reader of this book that I have no simple prescription for good teaching. Ultimately, the good teacher must want to be a good teacher. Then that individual must become objective and continually self-critical in seeking feedback from students and peers, as well as evidence in student performance that his or her teaching is indeed effective in stimulating learning. It should be equally clear to each professor in a college or university that those who do not commit themselves to good teaching but continue to perform will be assigned to other necessary and well-performed activities or be let go. In some sense, a college or university ought to model some of the ideals of living in a democratic society. Students know more than we think about the productivity and quality of performance of faculty members, and they see in the operation of the reward system some values and their application that are hardly in accord with what higher education should exemplify.

The major weakness in college teaching is that too many teachers operate as though teaching a particular segment of a discipline (content) constitutes a fixed and constant assignment regardless of time, place, students, programs, or other factors. *The essence of good teaching is to adapt it to the particular context in which it is provided in such manner as to promote the student's inevitable search for meaning.* The purpose of this volume is to point out the significant elements in the context based upon a concern for stimulating meaningful learning.

As usual, in the preparation of this book I have drawn upon the ideas of many others. In some cases, where these ideas are particularly significant or have been specifically stated, I have made direct acknowledgment. On the whole, however, I see little new in the last fifty years in the writings about either college teaching or curriculum, and I decline to make special recognition of individuals unless their particular phraseology is unusually apt or rich in its connotations. I have, however, provided some suggestions for further reading at the end of each chapter and an extensive bibliography for readers who wish to explore supporting or contrasting views about college teaching and learning.

As has been the case for many years, I am indebted to a number of people for their assistance and encouragement in this task. I would recognize particularly Laura Bornholdt, vice-president of the Lilly Endowment, with whom I have shared many conversations on these matters. I would also express appreciation to E. Alden Dunham of the Carnegie Corporation, who was instrumental in having some funds made available to me to view and comment on the developments in the Doctor of Arts degree for college teaching. Many of the ideas in this volume were supported, if not originated, by experiences in review of these Doctor of Arts programs. My doctoral students were generally a continuing source of stimulation. I would mention especially Nellie Hardy, whose dissertation dealt with the teacher typologies discussed in Chapter One.

My coauthor, Dora Marcus, has, as a former student and a friend and constructive critic over several years, helped to clarify my thinking and to expand it by elaborating her own ideas, which I find remarkably consonant with mine. She was ably assisted by Shari Cisco, who was of invaluable help in expediting an early typed draft. Special credit is due Katherine McCracken for her expert editing and revising of the entire manuscript in its early stages.

Finally, I would mention Ruth Frye, who has been my assistant for many years. Through her devotion to the task of providing many copies of parts of this book at various stages and her excellent assistance in the preparation of special charts and forms and in editing and proofing, she enabled this book to come to final form.

East Lansing, Michigan Paul L. Dressel
July 1982

To the Reader

Any reader of this volume should be forewarned that it does not contain recommendations or solutions ensuring good teaching that the reader can directly apply to his or her own teaching. Through the years, as we have had opportunity to review new methods of teaching and new types of courses, we have concluded that overenthusiasm about any single approach to teaching is the road to a stereotyped performance that will ultimately produce poor teaching. There can be no one model of good teaching that will suit the variety of teaching roles and differing objectives of undergraduate teaching. Thus good teaching must be adapted to the particular *context* in which it takes place and appraised by the learning that results. An understanding of the nature of the disciplines and their relationship to education, life, and work is essential to contextual teaching.

A teacher's commitment to learning and a sense of excitement in pursuing that commitment must be accompanied by an abiding awareness that, in the long run, it is what the learner does rather than what the teacher does that really counts in teaching. Accordingly, we are concerned that each reader be stimulated to think seriously and in depth about the nature of learning, both as a process and as a result. Then, we hope, the reader will be led to a state of mind in which teaching practices and materials are continually reviewed, revised, and rejected in keeping with teachers' special obligations to stimulate scholarship in their students' lives.

This volume is divided into three parts, each of which can be read more or less independently of the others. Part One reviews much that has been said about teaching in the past but is organized around our four prototypes of teaching and the interplay between teaching and learning. In particular, we contend that the primary role of education is humanizing rather than disciplinary mastery. Part One reflects our recognition of the pervasive role of the disciplines and their interrelations in good teaching and meaningful learning.

Part Two arises out of our perception in recent years that those who regard education largely as personal development have ignored the tremendous resources in knowledge, methodology, and values that have evolved within the various disciplines over the centuries. Part Two attempts to show that the disciplines are not so distinctive as they sometimes seem, although the totality of knowledge is so vast that it cannot be dealt with in a unitary fashion. The various disciplines represent ways of investigating the totality of knowledge and the means used to acquire and to organize it. The teacher should never forget that disciplines are artifacts of man's search for meaning—they are means of arriving at meaning. For effective teaching and learning, teachers must acquire knowledge of these characteristics of the disciplines and the complex interrelations among them.

Part Three may be read in the context of relevant sections of the senior author's *Handbook of Academic Evaluation* (1976) and *Improving Degree Programs* (1980). It suggests some of the implications of contextual teaching both for curricular organization and the preparation and selection of college teachers. These implications come as close as we believe to be compatible with the need for each person to work out his or her own salvation as a teacher. We do give some explicit suggestions on deciding and preparing to be a teacher and occasionally offer critical judgments of some existing practices.

If, having completed this volume, readers criticize us for not providing definitive solutions to the problems discussed, allow that they have been forewarned. If they gain a new conception of the interplay between teaching and learning and the relevance of the disciplinary context, and are motivated to incorporate this conception into a lifelong professional commitment, we will have been effective teachers.

Dora Marcus
Paul L. Dressel

Contents

The Authors

Paul L. Dressel is professor emeritus of university research at Michigan State University in East Lansing. He received his bachelor's degree in mathematics from Wittenberg College (1931), his master's degree in mathematics and physics from Michigan State (1934), and his doctoral degree in mathematics from the University of Michigan (1939).

Since 1932, when he first joined the mathematics faculty at Michigan State University, Dressel has served in various capacities and was often the first person assigned to a particular responsibility. In 1936 he began coordinating the orientation program for new students, which led gradually to developing a testing program, remedial services for students, and a counseling center that he directed for over a decade. For several years he was chairman of the Board of Examiners, which was empowered to grant, by any appropriate means, credit in any course offered in the institution. The Board eventually became the Office of Evaluation Services and was charged with designing and carrying out numerous studies on educational issues. From 1949 through 1952, Dressel was director of the Cooperative Study of Evaluation in General Education sponsored by the American Council on Education; results of the study were reported in *General Education: Explorations in Evaluation* (1954), coauthored by Dressel and Lewis B. Mayhew. In subsequent years, Dressel's staff was expanded to conduct educational research and related studies at

Michigan State, and in 1959 he became the first person to head the newly created Office of Institutional Research.

Dressel has served as a consultant to numerous colleges and universities. He was long active in accreditation with the North Central Association of Colleges and Universities and served on the executive board of the Commission of Institutions of Higher Education, 1966-1970. For over ten years he has been chairman of the Illinois Commission of Scholars, which reviews and recommends or denies all new doctoral proposals from Illinois state-assisted higher education institutions. He was president of the American Association of Higher Education, 1970-71, and has been involved in studying Doctor of Arts programs, resulting in the publication of *The New Colleges: Toward an Appraisal* (1971); *Blueprint for Change* (with Frances DeLisle, 1972); *College Teaching: Improvement by Degrees* (with Mary Magdala Thompson, 1974). He also was involved in critiquing nontraditional graduate programs as reported in *A Review of Nontraditional Graduate Degrees* (1978) and *Problems and Principles in the Recognition or Accreditation of Graduate Programs* (1978).

Dressel has received awards for research from the American Personnel and Guidance Association (with Ross Matteson, 1950) and from the American Educational Research Association (the E. F. Lindquist Award, 1980). He was granted an honorary Doctor of Laws degree by Wittenberg University in 1966.

Dora Marcus is assistant professor at Michigan State University in East Lansing. Her early training was in the social sciences; she received her bachelor's degree in sociology from Wayne State University (1954), her master's degree in sociology from the University of Michigan (1956), and more recently her doctoral degree in administration and higher education from Michigan State University, specializing in evaluation research.

For twelve years, 1955-1966, Marcus conducted organizational research as a staff member of the Institute for Social Research at the University of Michigan. She is coauthor with Philip M. Marcus of an article on control in organizations, which has been selected by *Public Administration Review* as a prototypic statement and has been reprinted widely. For several years, Marcus served as an assessor in personnel selection for the State of Michigan. She has also had extensive experience conducting assessment programs in colleges and universities, particularly as an evaluator for the Northwest Area Foundation.

Since joining the faculty of Michigan State University in 1973, Marcus has conducted research on curriculum for the Office of the Provost and has served as a program evaluator for a competency-based degree program sponsored by the Ford Foundation and housed at Justin Morrill College. During her years with this program, Marcus has taught courses in higher education and group decision making, and has managed the program's assessment center. Currently, she coordinates a new residence instruction program in her role as assistant to the dean in the College of Social Science at Michigan State.

On Teaching and Learning in College

Reemphasizing the Roles of Learners and the Disciplines

1

Teaching Styles and Effects on Learning

The heart of a college or university, with the exception of a few primarily graduate and research-oriented institutions, is the undergraduate program. Undergraduates and the programs in which they enroll justify much of the operational budget, the facilities, and consequently, the curriculum and faculty. In turn, the character and quality of an undergraduate program depend upon the professors and the teaching that they provide. Hence whether one discusses administration, finance, curriculum, or evaluation, some attention to teaching is essential.

In the process of writing an earlier volume, *Improving Degree Programs* (Dressel, 1980), which dealt with program and curriculum development and evaluation, the senior author found it necessary to consider the nature of the teaching process. This chapter, which draws freely on that earlier work, will further elaborate the conception of college teaching and learning expounded there, but with changes in order and emphasis to accommodate to the central themes of this volume. In particular, the discussion of teacher prototypes or orientations of classroom behavior should prove useful to teachers as a way of clarifying their own teaching performances and as profiles of possible alternative teaching styles.

Teacher Prototypes

After extensive discussion with teachers and educators, Hardy and Dressel identified and defined the following four teacher orientations (Hardy, 1976):

1. In discipline-centered teaching, the content and structure of the discipline are rigidly determined and in no way modified to meet the requirements, needs, or special concerns of either the teacher or learner.
2. In instructor-centered teaching, the teacher is the expert and the main source of knowledge in both the particular subject matter and the discipline. The instructor, around whom all class activity revolves, is the focal point in the teaching-learning process. The student is a passive recipient rather than an active participant.
3. In student-centered cognitive teaching, intellectual development is held to be the most important outcome of the teaching-learning process. Both content and teaching practices are selected and adjusted to accommodate the cognitive growth of the student toward teacher-specified objectives.
4. In student-centered affective teaching, the personal and social development of the student is the focus of the teaching-learning process. Both the content and the teaching practices are adjusted to foster the total development of each individual. The individual is expected to develop idiosyncratically rather than to adapt to content or to the demands of the teacher.

These prototypes are not empirically based. Rather, they represent a conceptually derived resolution of a complex of teachers' characteristics and a composite of teachers' thoughtful but highly subjective reactions. Teacher responses to the orientations were useful in producing a large number of statements indicative of the views and behavior that individuals related to the various orientations. These responses were added to the already extensive collection acquired from other studies and from teacher rating scales. Drawing upon all these materials, Hardy and Dressel then further developed the four orientations into a form to be used by teachers wishing to review and organize their views about teaching.

Additionally, an attempt was made to accommodate to recurring faculty reservations about the use of orientations or prototypes, such as the following:

- The use of prototypes is demeaning and ignores the uniqueness of individual professionals.
- Widely used typologies are likely to have values attached to them by administrators or others that lead to inequities in the appraisal of individual teachers.
- There will never be unanimity in definition of teaching types; hence typologies confuse and mislead rather than help.
- Any set of categories is a set of abstractions, whereas individuals are not merely composites but adapt their views and practices to changing circumstances.

There is some validity to these objections, but accepting them entirely would not only rule out any characterizations of teaching but would also discourage evaluation of individual teachers. Furthermore, the approach actually used here effectively answers some of the objections, as later discussion will demonstrate.

We do not regard these proposed teacher types as ones to which every teacher could be readily assigned. Rather, the intent has been to define each orientation by typical views and practices which teachers might identify or contrast with their own practices and thus arrive at a profile across the orientations. The individual teacher might then reflect upon this profile, evaluate, and possibly undertake to reinforce or to alter it. We do not value either consistency or rigidity in adherence to a typology. In fact, we prefer the term *orientation* rather than typology, suggesting a tendency toward the use of certain teaching behaviors rather than a rigid commitment to them. Although each of the orientations could be so defined as to be internally consistent and thereby imply a philosophy of teaching or education, most teaching styles are eclectic—not by formal choice, but by unconscious or conscious imitation of former teachers and colleagues and influenced by fortuitous circumstances and various institutional pressures.

Following is an elaboration of each of the four teaching prototypes or orientations. An exhibit of the composite results in Table 1 points up the differences among the orientations.

Discipline-Centered Teaching. In discipline-centered teaching, the course content and the structure of the discipline are rigidly defined and are not modified or rearranged to meet the requirements, needs, or special concerns of either the teacher or learner. The professorial obligation is to assure that each segment of the discipline covered by the course is presented in a sound scholarly manner. Learning is the obligation of the student. The *course content* includes those concepts, methods, theories, and materials that seem to present best that segment of the discipline as defined by scholars in the discipline. The specification of content is facilitated and reinforced by the selection of a text and of supplementary references. The preferred *method* of instruction is a series of lectures (perhaps supplemented by a text and references) planned to cover the specified content systematically and according to a fixed schedule.

The *classroom setting* tends to be formal, with emphasis on scholarly authority and objectivity. *Interactions of students and of students with the professor* deal almost exclusively with issues arising out of the classification of course content. Students are given the same or very similar assignments to be pursued through use of the text and standard reference materials. Students are *evaluated and graded* on specific skills and items of knowledge and on traditional or standard ways of presenting them. The professor's *self-image* is that of an authority in the discipline or certain of its subphases. The professor is responsible for presenting a defined segment of that discipline to students, each of whom is assumed to be motivated to acquire an understanding of it. Students are regarded as prospective majors in the discipline or in a field to which the discipline has direct relevance. Course coverage and teaching methodology are the same for all classes, regardless of heterogeneity or size. Neither *individuality* nor *creativity* is sought because *objectivity* is prized, and standards of mastery imposed by expert judgment do not accommodate student idiosyncrasies.

Teaching in the disciplinary mode may be very effective with students who are vitally interested in the course and the discipline, and especially so with graduate students. Teachers so oriented may be vital, warm human beings interested in those students who share an interest in the discipline and demonstrate potential for success in it. Such professors are frequently found in mathematics and sciences, but not solely there.

Instructor-Centered Teaching. In instructor-centered teaching, the teacher selects and develops the ideas presented to students. Students are expected to adjust to the professors and to learn more from them than from reading, discussion, or critical thought. *Students* are regarded as an admiring audience and as a source of acolytes. *Course content* is based upon personal preferences and may include practical applications or interrelations with other disciplines that the professor finds interesting and complementary (also complimentary) to his or her personal insights and scholarship. The instructional procedures are chosen to highlight the teacher's personality and eccentricities. *Classroom discussions,* which may exhibit the instructor's humor, critical facilities, and versatility, focus upon and clarify the instructor's views. *Assignments* likewise reflect the instructor's interests and points of view. The instructor (perhaps without consciously so doing) evaluates and grades students on their ability to imitate, reflect, and elaborate on professorial perspectives, conceptions, and formulations.

The professor's *self-image* is that of scholar and teacher of stature—a recognized authority. The professor may make conscious or unconscious adaptations to an audience, but the adaptations are based on affective rather than cognitive concerns. The professor radiates self-confidence and expects applause—and may deserve it. The instructor-centered teacher may not give much thought to adaptation to individual students or student groups and may even, without fully realizing it, ignore or resent student *originality* or *creativity* as competition. The *standards* of instructor-centered teachers tend to be highly personal and idiosyncratic. *Subjectivity* and *objectivity* are not always distinguishable, and they are roles of the moment rather than consistent stances. Within this instructor-centered category, there are identifiable subtypes. Some teachers consciously entertain and titillate rather than educate. Some simply and uninhibitedly express their natural personality. And some have had such a range of experiences and are so talented in communicating them that, without conscious intent, they become the course. These talented types are those whose names recur in the advice (sometimes good) given to students by other students, graduates, and professors: "Be sure to take a course from Professor X." This instructor-centered orientation is found in some of the best and most inspiring teachers and also in some of the worst. An overweening ego may make the reputation of a professor, but it may not result in good teaching.

Student-Centered Cognitive Teaching. In student-centered cognitive teaching, the intellectual maturation of the student is regarded as the goal of the teaching-learning process. Both content and teaching techniques are chosen to foster the cognitive development of the student. Emotions (affect) are not ignored but are expected to be controlled and directed by intellect. The cognitively oriented teacher regards students as individuals who are becoming self-reliant and capable of self-direction. The knowledge that they will acquire and the ways they will use it are not predictable by the teacher. This cognitive emphasis is conjoined with an awareness that affect often directs and controls cognition. Affect, then, is to be recognized and brought under control to achieve more rational behavior. It may also be acknowledged that, in the nature of the human being, there are moments in which affect reigns supreme. There is joy in scholarship and intellectual performance.

Course content is chosen to be interesting, stimulating, and productive of student intellectual growth. *Teaching methods* or learning experiences, chosen primarily to encourage or even force students to think, may include student discussions, Socratic dialogue, experiments, lectures, demonstrations, exhibits—any experience that stimulates curiosity, thought, and understanding. The *classroom atmosphere* may be exciting and yet relaxed, encouraging participation of students and stimulating them to become creative, analytical, and logical in their thinking. *Student discussions and interactions* are used as processes to encourage understanding and application of concepts and principles. However, the teacher, always focusing on cognitive development, may intervene and redirect discussion whenever it strays from the point. *Assignments* are designed to require and develop cognitive abilities and to motivate the student toward self-reliance and intellectual maturity. Students are *evaluated and graded* on their ability to define and solve problems that require new resources and strategies.

The teacher's *self-image* is that of one who both models effective thinking and encourages student emulation. Accordingly, the teacher's role is to develop the students' capability in inquiry rather than to present an organized body of knowledge. The cognitively oriented teacher undertakes to foster in students the ability to generalize the mode of inquiry and to extend it well beyond the course content to problems more typical of those that occur in life. In so doing, the teacher finds *individualization and adaptation* desirable, both as motivation and as providing real problems for which neither the means of solution nor the answers are readily available in the text. The teacher encourages *objectivity* while recognizing that complete separation of cognition and affect is neither possible nor desirable. *Standards* are high but harder to define than in a discipline-based course because the objectives and the tasks are broader and more inclusive. Furthermore, as students are encouraged to move toward defining their own standards, uniform appraisal procedures may become impossible. The cognitively oriented teacher is less concerned with covering a specified body of content than with fostering students' interest in learning as well as their understanding and ability to use what they have learned.

Student-Centered Affective Teaching. In student-centered affective teaching, the personal, social, and intellectual development of the individual is the primary goal of the teaching-learning process. Moreover, affective and social development, as a composite, is taken to be a prerequisite to significant intellectual development. Both course content and educative activities are selected and adjusted to accommodate this goal. Education is seen as therapeutic, and intensive interaction of individuals in groups is, therefore, regarded as an essential part of it.

In this orientation, *content* is secondary and is selected (or indistinguishably merged with activities) to help students mature and to confirm to them their emerging status as adults. The preferred *instructional methods* encourage student involvement, with emphasis on discussion sessions led by students or instructors (or perhaps simply convened with no leadership). Informality, frankness, and student *interaction* characterize the sessions. Since students are encouraged to work toward self-expression and self-determination, formal *assignments* are seldom evident. Students are evaluated or evaluate themselves on the basis of participation, self-expression, affective development, and personal satisfaction. Grades in the traditional sense are not used. The students' remarks tend to be highly objective and personal, although subject to group discussion and appraisal. In this mode, it is uncertain whether students become objectively subjective or entirely subjective by decrying objectivity. The affective orientation is found most commonly in the social sciences (sociology or psychology), occasionally in the humanities (literature or philosophy), and rarely in mathematics and the natural sciences. This distribution reflects distinctions among the disciplines and differences among the individuals attracted to them.

In Table 1, the major characteristics of the four teacher prototypes or teaching orientations just discussed are displayed in such a manner as to facilitate comparison and contrast.

Cognitive Versus Affective Orientation

Student-centered teaching may be focused on cognitive development, on affective development, or on the complex but natural commingling of affect and intellect that characterizes all human beings. Some people would regard this conception of teaching as based upon a humanistic point of view. Since we believe that cultivation of the intellect is the primary concern of higher education, we doubt the validity of teaching that is completely affective in orientation. This is not to say that affective outcomes are inappropriate, that they are not learned, or that they do not involve knowledge and reflection. Though self-insight, self-acceptance, and a start toward self-realization can be deeply educational experiences, such experiences, even when successful, are not necessarily accompanied by acquisition of skills and the ability to use them. The individual experiencing such affective development may be happier and better able to cope with life, but there seems to be no more reason for granting credits or degrees for this than for giving credits or a degree in medicine to someone who has recovered from infectious hepatitis.

At the other extreme, pure cognitively oriented teaching is impossible. Both teachers and students, whether or not they realize it, come to an educational experience with biases and value commitments. For example, most teachers attempt to communicate to students both the values and preconceptions of the discipline and the satisfaction that accompanies knowing and using ideas, concepts, and methods that characterize it. Nevertheless, it is possible to approach teaching (especially in mathematics, logic, and the natural sciences) as though the disciplines taught are purely intellectual and theoretical enterprises. Some teachers appear not to have recognized any other view, whereas others have recognized affective potentials but have consciously striven to avoid them in their teaching. This conscious avoidance of affect is in itself an affective commitment, although not always so recognized. With some people, that avoidance results from profound convictions and deep-seated biases.

The distinction between cognitive orientation and affective orientation may be theoretically possible, but the complete separation of cognition and affect in actual teaching and learning is artificial, if not impossible. The difference between the two orientations is more one of intent and emphasis than it is a

Table 1. Characteristics of Four Teaching

Components	*Discipline-Centered Teaching*	*Instructor-Centered Teaching*
Course content	Based on disciplinary concepts, principles, theories, and methods.	Based on teacher's preferences and perceptions.
Method of instruction	Lectures and standard text, with systematic coverage of the body of knowledge.	Lecture or teacher-dominated discussion highlighting teacher's personality.
Classroom setting	Emotion free, with emphasis on scholarly objectivity.	Teacher dominated and controlled.
Student-faculty interaction	Familiarity and intimacy with students discouraged.	Discussions with students focused on clarifying lecture points.
Assignments	All students in course given the same assignment.	Reflect the teacher's interests and views of the discipline.
Objectives and evaluation	Students judged and graded by comparison with mastery standards.	Students judged and graded on ability to imitate professorial approaches, perspectives, and formulations.
Professorial self-image	Identifies with the discipline rather than with teaching role.	Has strong ego and radiates self-confidence.
Students	Viewed as would-be majors and graduate school candidates.	Viewed as an audience or a source of acolytes.
Adaptation to or in student groups	Course coverage standard for all sections.	Some adjustments made for different audiences.
Originality or creativity	Students encouraged to use the standard way of solving pre-structured problems.	Originality in student responses acceptable if it does not clash with teacher's views.
Individualization	Assignments designed to help students master materials presented.	Students expected to adapt to teacher's interests rather than develop their own.
Source of standards	Standards of mastery set for each unit of learning by experts in the field.	Teacher standards based upon acceptance of his or her views.
Objectivity	Expression of opinion in the classroom minimized.	Teacher's seeming objectivity actually highly subjective.

Note: This table was modified from one that appears in Paul L. Dressel, *Improving Degree Programs: A Guide to Curriculum Development, Administration, and Review* (San Francisco: Jossey-Bass, 1980), pp. 127-129.

Orientations, by Components.

Student-Centered Teaching (Cognitive Approach)	*Student-Centered Teaching (Affective Approach)*	*Components*
Composed of materials interesting to students and productive of cognitive outcomes.	Secondary—used to help students in maturation.	Course content
Discussion, with special lectures to focus on important issues.	Emphasis on student involvement and interaction as a means of personal and social development.	Method of instruction
Somewhat relaxed but intellectually stimulating.	Highly informal, encouraging free student expression of feelings and concerns.	Classroom setting
Interactions planned to be intellectually stimulating to students.	Interactions in groups, with instructors acting as moderators.	Student-faculty interaction
Geared to cultivate the desire to move toward intellectual maturity.	No formal assignments—students encouraged to work toward self-expression.	Assignments
Students judged and graded on tasks that require new resources and strategies.	Students evaluated (perhaps by themselves and their peers) on participation and self-expression.	Objectives and evaluation
Developer of student's ability to analyze, reason, use language effectively, and solve problems.	Counselor and "resource person."	Professorial self-image
Regarded as individuals who must become self-reliant in using their knowledge.	Viewed as individuals who must achieve self-insight and accept full responsibility for their own behavior and goals.	Students
Emphasis on the *how* and *why* of knowledge.	Group interaction used to motivate students to learn.	Adaptation to or in student groups
Originality in thinking encouraged.	Each student expected to achieve self-realization.	Originality or creativity
Students encouraged to develop their own analytic abilities.	Allows individuals to develop and acquire new resources and new ways of organizing ideas.	Individualization
Students expected to develop and use high standards in their own work.	Standards individually derived and self-imposed.	Source of standards
Analytical, objective, and logical instructional methods.	Understanding and acceptance more prized than objectivity.	Objectivity

complete dichotomy. Similar arguments could be made for the interdependence of all four orientations. For example, an otherwise discipline-oriented teacher may be sensitive to individual differences and adapt assignments to them in reference to either ability or interest.

In fact, our observations and experiences to date with these four orientations suggest that most teachers fall athwart all four rather than into any one, and they may shift in emphasis from one to another as they deal with different content, course levels, and students. This is facilitated by the fact that the four orientations are related in pairs. The disciplinary orientation and the student-cognitive orientation can be regarded as extremes on an objective disciplinary continuum. At one extreme, the emphasis is on presenting the discipline as an organized body of knowledge, with some attention to modes of inquiry. At the other extreme, the emphasis is on developing student cognition by assimilation of the modes of inquiry. The instructor orientation and the student-affective orientation present a continuum along which the human element takes precedence over the discipline. Some teachers who find themselves preferring one continuum may have an eclectic disciplinary or human (personal or student) orientation rather than any extreme position. Other teachers may combine an instructor-centered orientation with either an orientation to a discipline or a student-cognitive and student-affective orientation. The one combination that seems unlikely (from observations of teachers and their responses to this structure) is that of discipline orientation and student-affective orientation. But even this composite may characterize some teachers in psychology or sociology.

We point out these possible combinations to emphasize, once again, that we do not claim that the four orientations are discrete types or that each teacher will perfectly fit one category. The four orientations are the result of observation and the logical analysis of tendencies rather than of statistical analysis seeking independent types. The whole intent has been to develop a pattern of orientations that might be useful to teachers in self-analysis. We personally favor the student-cognitive orientation and question (at least at the undergraduate level) the extreme positions on the student-affective, instructor-centered, and discipline-centered orientations. But effective and stimulating teaching based upon any of these orientations or composites is surely possible for some teachers in selected courses and disciplines and with appropriate students.

These teacher orientations have value as a way to improve teaching and learning by making teachers more conscious of their stances and the relevance of these stances to their objectives, courses, and students. Teaching practices and their underlying values are thereby brought to the teachers' attention, and the tendency unthinkingly to imitate others or to fall into rote patterns may be overcome.

Emphasis on Learning

If learning is embraced as the criterion of effective teaching, however, much of the emphasis on teaching may be misplaced. The verb *teach* may be either transitive or intransitive, but the intransitive usage implies nothing about the nature of teaching. The sentence "Jones teaches" states only that Jones engages in activities designated as teaching, whether by self-characterization or the judgment of others. The statement conveys no information about what Jones does or about the attendant circumstances. In its transitive form, *teach* indicates that someone learns something as a result of the activities of a teacher. A learner may be self-taught. The statement that Jones teaches history uses *teach* as a transitive verb, but it is no improvement over saying that Jones teaches. A disciplinary attachment is indicated, but the learner, the object of the teaching, is not. The sentence suggests that Jones does something to history, although history surely does not change significantly because of Jones's teaching. In fact, we should say that Jones teaches students *about* history rather than that he teaches history to students.

The success of teaching must then be determined by whether and what the students learn, not by what the teacher does or asks students to do, and most certainly not solely by the scholarly precision and verve with which Jones presents the historical materials. This is not to say that the materials, content, and forms of presentation are unimportant or irrelevant; rather, it emphasizes that these are subject to choice by the teacher guided by a concern for their effectiveness in promoting learning by students. Teaching and learning must always take place in some context and involve some content.

The term *content* evokes such words as discipline, knowledge, subject matter, values, abilities, and skills. But closer examination reveals that these are by no means equivalent terms. A discipline is both an organized body of knowledge and an organized mode of accumulating and ordering knowledge. As such, it includes disciplinary methods, skills, strategies, concepts, principles, structural elements, value commitments, and analytic and synthesizing modes of thought. Knowledge, understanding, and mastery of the methods, skills, and strategies are not taught so much as they are exemplified by the teacher and the materials used. Students emulate, assimilate, and learn in individual ways and often in ways not well understood by either the teachers or the students.

Content connotes what is in or what is covered by a course. As Table 1 indicates, content may be determined by a teacher or predetermined by the course description. The content of a course has much the same sense as the contents of a book. The term indicates the substantive material of the course without any implication of how, why, or where the material will be presented. Content and subject matter are often used interchangeably, but this ignores an important distinction. We prefer to regard subject matter as external to the discipline, referring rather to the problems or aspects of reality around which the discipline developed or to which its methods are being applied. This distinction is a significant factor in the teaching orientations. For example, the disciplines of physics and mathematics can be directed to the making of musical instruments, the building of bridges, or the analysis of human behavior. The application of a discipline to a distinctive subject matter involves values, abilities, and skills that are often ignored when a discipline is regarded solely as an organized body of knowledge. Subject matter is the problem or immediate focus of human concern, whereas course content involves the study of a subject matter by use of one or more disciplines. The problem approach to development of course content encourages, if it does not actually necessitate, interdisciplinary teaching.

To the extent that knowledge, values, abilities, and skills are acquired by students as intended consequences (objectives) of teaching, these outcomes justify the costs of education. These outcomes have personal, esthetic, social, economic, and political implications that are, by nature, interdisciplinary or supradisciplinary. The individual who acquires knowledge, values, abilities, and skills achieves some immediate personal satisfaction and develops the capacity for a more pleasurable and productive life. Society benefits both qualitatively and quantitatively from the presence and contributions of these educated individuals. The nation also benefits from their contributions to goal setting and political decision making. Teaching is supported because of these benefits, and these same benefits provide much of the satisfaction of those teachers whose vision of their roles extends beyond their interest in and commitment to their disciplines. For these reasons, we are convinced that the cognitive orientation, as earlier defined, is the most appropriate for undergraduate college teachers in a democratic society.

The concept of Jones teaching students about history resolves some of the previously noted ambiguities of the teaching task. However, teachers are generally well trained in their disciplines but are relatively uncertain about appraising and adjusting to differences in students or in program purposes. Hence teachers may confuse communication with teaching. The scholarly readers of a definitive research report become, at that moment, students of the writer, but at a very different level of specificity and understanding from that expected of college freshmen. Sensitive teaching, especially in a democratic society, must recognize and adjust to audience differences in sophistication and purpose. The concept *student* must be qualified by reference to the reason for and the nature of the learning sought. Is the student a graduate or undergraduate, a major or nonmajor? Each of these may have distinctive reasons for taking a course. The part-time adult student of age thirty to sixty and the full-time freshman of seventeen or eighteen bring sharply different backgrounds and purposes to the learning situation. If the teacher accepts responsibility for the students' learning, these differences among students must be taken into account. Learning objectives, instructional materials, and teaching methods should be adapted to individual differences in motivations and goals. Ever present should be the concern that the learner acquire increased independence in and motivation for pursuit of further learning.

One of our major assumptions is that class activities should motivate and direct learning inside and outside the classroom. Only if the teacher accepts and meets this responsibility is the role of the teacher as motivator and director of learning fully realized. But many professors think of teaching merely as appearing before a selective and relatively homogeneous student audience in a classroom for a specified period of time and at specified intervals to administer a carefully predetermined dose of information. This conception of teaching may produce learning for certain students, but such a teaching model is not the best for most undergraduate courses or for any other level of learning.

In only a very limited sense is teaching either an administratively imposed or a self-assumed role and responsibility. When one person learns from another, the latter has become a teacher, whether or not he or she realizes it. Being in the same room or living in the same age is not necessary for learning to be motivated by a teacher and achieved by a learner. Most of the difficulty with defining and evaluating good teaching lies in our lack of understanding of how individuals learn and in our inability or unwillingness to specify that which is most desirable to learn. In subsequent chapters, we shall focus upon student learning and ways of defining what is to be learned and the means of facilitating the learning process.

Suggestions for Further Reading

Anderson, J. "The Teacher as Model." *American Scholar,* 1961, *30,* 393-398, 400-401.

Axelrod, J. *The University Teacher as Artist: Toward an Aesthetics of Teaching with Emphasis on the Humanities.* San Francisco: Jossey-Bass, 1973.

Baird, L. L. "Teaching Styles." *Journal of Educational Psychology,* 1973, *64 (1),* 15-21.

Eble, K. E. *Professors as Teachers.* San Francisco: Jossey-Bass, 1972.

Eble, K. E. *The Craft of Teaching: A Guide to Mastering the Professor's Art.* San Francisco: Jossey-Bass, 1976.

Green, T. F. "The Concept of Teaching." In D. Vandenberg (Ed.), *Teaching and Learning.* Urbana: University of Illinois Press, 1969.

Hardy, N. T. "A Survey Designed to Refine an Inventory of Teaching Styles To Be Used by Individuals Preparing for College Teaching." Unpublished doctoral dissertation, Michigan State University, 1976.

Hyman, R. T. *Ways of Teaching.* Philadelphia: Lippincott, 1970.

Layton, D. (Ed.). *University Teaching in Transition.* Edinburgh, Scotland: Oliver and Boyd, 1968.

Pullias, E. V., Lockhard, A., and others. *Toward Excellence in College Teaching.* Dubuque, Iowa: Brown, 1964.

University of London Teaching Methods Unit. *Improving Teaching in Higher Education.* Leicester, England: Cavendish Press, 1976.

2

Learning: The Goal of Teaching

There is a vast amount of writing and some research about college teaching. Much of the latter is practically oriented, focused upon the behavior of teachers in the classroom. The respective merits of such "methods" as lecture, discussion, and seminar, and the efficacy of various components of a vast technology have provided the basis for innumerable essays and many books. It is doubtful, however, that student learning has been improved thereby either in quality or amount. The reasons for this are extensive, beginning with the immediately obvious one that relatively few college teachers read or heed critiques of college teaching. More significant reasons are that the focus is on teaching instead of on learning and that there is no agreement about how and what students learn or should learn.

The early colonial college provided a sequentially organized common required experience for all students. Students progressed through the four-year (originally three-year) program in a lockstep monitored primarily by tutors who were themselves often only a year or two removed from student status. These early programs were both content oriented and student oriented, and the task of the tutor-teacher was that of helping or even forcing the student to cover the prescribed content. We need neither approve nor regret the demise of this pattern of education to recognize that in it the responsibility of the teacher was the facilitation of student learning. Furthermore, the common required program was sequential, thus providing students with a sense of progress. A tutor, by teaching the same group of students at each stage of their progress, provided a concrete example of the anticipated educational product. Whether or not these tutors adequately modeled the disciplinary emphasis implied by training the "muscles of the mind," it is evident that the ultimate objectives in those early programs were cognitive powers and value commitments rather than knowledge of some specific content. However, there is no valid evidence that these objectives were actually achieved by the recipients of degrees.

Over time, the emphasis in higher education has shifted from learner to teacher and to a narrow conception of teaching that focuses upon specific knowledge rather than the ability to organize and apply it. The factors supporting this change in emphasis are:

- an increase in the number of disciplines and departments
- program and major options for students
- program, major, and general education requirements
- electives both in majors and in general education
- inclusion among the undergraduate options of vocational and professional programs
- interdisciplinary courses and programs
- faculty specialization within the disciplines

These seven factors are interrelated and reinforcing, thereby generating a continuing (disciplinary and course) expansion based largely on faculty interests and abetted by faculty-primed or faculty-supported program requests from students and external groups. The curriculum has become either a wasteland or a utopia of rich, varied, and delightful experiences, depending upon the point of view and the values of the beholder. It has not always been understood or acknowledged by those supporting the cafeteria conception of degree programs that degree requirements have been subtly transformed from achievement of a standard (however ill-defined) of knowledge to accumulation of a specified number of courses or credits. The granting of a degree for completion of 40 three-credit courses (120 credit hours) ought to be based upon an assumption about the quality of these courses and their cumulative impact upon the student. Moreover, even in the unlikely event that all forty courses were well taught (whatever that may mean), the requirement does not assure an educated individual. Emphasis in higher education currently focuses upon teaching and credit accumulation rather than upon learning and validated accomplishment.

If our concern in an educational program is with the education acquired by individuals, *good teaching can be defined and appraised only in the context of what, how much, and how many students learn.* At their best, teachers only encourage and facilitate learning. At their worst, they may pervert or destroy it. Teachers who make excessive demands upon students unfairly divert efforts from other courses and teachers. They also sacrifice learning to memorization and rote recall. Time-consuming "busy work" is easy to prescribe but is unlikely to yield significant learning.

Learning and Teaching Compared

Semantically, the distinction between learning and teaching was blurred in earlier English and the verb *learn* referred to both processes. This use of *learn*—as in "That'll learn you!"—still survives in substandard and dialectal English.

A learner is an entity that acquires knowledge or skill through experience. In this sense, a computer can learn. The learning experiences, and hence the resultant learnings, may be fortuitous (unfocused) or may be directed by personal interests or by societal problems, and they may or may not be so organized as to have cumulative impact. Ability to retrieve and to apply knowledge and skills is not automatic but, rather, results from learned associations and the motivation and ability of the learner to make these meaningful associations. In fact, the learner may follow a personally devised sequence of learning experiences and thereby become both teacher and learner. An alert, reflective, and critical individual can also learn much from fortuitous experience.

Learning is a process in which the learner attends to surrounding circumstances and is changed by exposure to them. Learning in a meaningful context is aided by the expectation and intent that what one learns has extrinsic as well as intrinsic value. Learning involves:

- something to be learned (facts, principles, skills, modes of thought, values)
- experiences that permit or foster learning by using appropriate processes, materials, and structures for organizing the experiences, and environments in which the experiences are provided
- acquiring knowledge, skill, attitude, or value orientation

An individual is not a learner until learning is taking place. Most individuals exposed to attention-arousing experiences learn something in some context, but what is learned may not be desired by the learner, anticipated by the teacher, or relevant to those contexts in which it might be useful. The verb *learn* is primarily transitive. Used as an intransitive verb, it is meaningless unless the acquisition of knowledge or skill and some purpose is assumed. An individual learns something for a reason or purpose. Learning is apparent only as the learner displays the ability to apply learning or to relate it in meaningful ways to other learning.

Education, regarded as a societal function, refers to the provision of planned purposeful experiences for developing (drawing or leading out) each individual and, through the influence of these educated individuals, an improved society. Although much education takes place in unplanned, informal circumstances, the specific nature and worth of the learning in these unplanned educational experiences may be either good or bad, depending upon the experiences and what and how individuals learn from them. Planned, purposeful learning based upon the expectation that the learners attain useful and significant knowledge, skills, abilities, and values is facilitated by teachers—professionals charged by society with the responsibilities of:

- recommending the content, subject matter (issues and problems), and objectives upon which learning is to be focused
- developing or selecting the processes, materials, and structures to be used
- participating in defining and forming the environment for learning
- motivating individuals to learn and fostering the development of ways of learning applicable in all life experiences

Viewed in this way, the verb *teach* is also primarily transitive. If individual *A* becomes a learner only in learning something, so too does individual *B* become a teacher only when someone (*A* perhaps) is learning something through *B*'s efforts. If whatever a professor has done has not resulted in at least one student learning something of value, the professor's behavior has been totally ineffective. Effective teaching is always in a context, and at least one learner is an essential component of that context. Effective teaching is to be evaluated by the number of those who learn as well as by the extent, nature, relevance, and quality of what is learned. The effectiveness of teaching is always contingent upon what is learned, who learns it, and the increased range and level of competent behavior of the learners. Effectiveness may be increased by careful selection and possible adaptations of materials, methods, organizing principles, and environment.

The teacher is primarily a facilitator of learning. Viewed in this manner, the obligations of the teacher include:

- motivating individuals to learn by providing both intrinsic and extrinsic incentives

- selecting and organizing learning experiences, using materials of intrinsic worth, and so structuring the materials and experiences as to encourage sequential, cumulative learning that promotes integration across disciplines and application (extrinsic worth) to both timely and timeless problems
- adapting learning materials, experiences, and delivery system to the particular problems, context, and students in order to enhance learning while minimizing risk
- individualizing experiences by reference to student learning ability, stage of maturity, past learning, aspirations, and learning characteristics or styles
- exemplifying or modeling thought processes that students are to develop
- evaluating learning progress and developing learner independence in motivation, career and program planning, and evaluation of competence

The precise meanings of *intrinsic* and *extrinsic* in the preceding statements are not evident, but their significance is implicit and sometimes explicit in subsequent discussions.

The words *course* and *curriculum* are derived from the Latin verb *currere* "to run." *Curriculum* (literally, "a little run") referred to a running or a race course. Accordingly, the curriculum and its component courses can be viewed as a structure (an imposed context) through which the learner is guided by a process of instruction or teaching. A specific degree or certificate program may be designated as a *course of study*, thereby restricting *curriculum* to the composite array of courses at institutional or departmental levels.

Instruction (see Table 2) implies providing a structure for learning and has many synonyms: (1) catechization, coaching, schooling, teaching, tutoring (Briggs, 1970; Bruner, 1966; Davis, 1976); (2) conditioning, inculcation, drilling, indoctrination, rehearsing, training (McKeachie, 1963); (3) pedagogy (literally "child-guiding" in its Greek origins), didactics; (4) eduction, education, guidance; (5) exemplifying, modeling. Groups 1 and 2 emphasize teachers' activity, suggesting processes yielding memorization or rote learning. Group 3 suggests a systematic or scientific approach to instruction. Group 4, in contrast with in-

Table 2. Conceptions of Instruction and Learning.

Instruction	Learning
1. catechization or tutoring	assimilation or memorizing
2. conditioning or inculcation	practicing or studying
3. pedagogy or didactics	psychology of learning
4. eduction or education	discovery or self-directed learning
5. modeling or exemplifying	imitation and internalization

struction, implies the influencing of learning by motivation and suggestion. Group 5 presents the teacher as a model or exemplar for the learner.

As indicated in Table 2, *learning* (the goal of instruction) also has numerous synonyms (Claxton and Ralston, 1978; Gagné, 1970): (1) assimilation, absorption, cramming, memorizing; (2) studying, practicing, drilling, mastering; (3) learning psychology; (4) self-directed learning, ascertaining, determining, discovering; (5) imitation and internalization. As Table 2 implies, these several conceptions of instruction and learning are related. However, whereas attention to instruction places priority on teacher activity, attention to learning immediately raises the issue not only of *what* the learner does but also *how* and *in what* context he or she learns.

Learning is dependent upon motivation, direct sensory experiences, activities conducive to learning, and the ability to use an abstract symbolic language. The purpose of instruction can then be seen as facilitating learning by planning, directing, modeling, and evaluating appropriate experiences while recognizing that a rigid prescriptive pattern of instruction is unlikely to be effective with all learners. Learning also depends upon past learning, the stage or level of development (knowledge, conceptualization, abstraction) of the learner, the nature of the material or skills to be learned, and the characteristics of the individual. Individual characteristics include interests, aspirations, attitudes and value commitments, ability, and learning skills. Differences among learners in these factors complicate the task of sequencing and assure that no structure can be found that will be equally stimulating, intelligible, or useful to all.

If the view is accepted that teaching is directed to the facilitation of learning, then good teaching is an activity depending upon systematic and contingent transactions between learners and teachers. Teaching must be based upon the context in which it takes place and upon the contexts in which the subsequent learning is to be used. The prospective learners are the most significant aspect of that context since many other aspects of that context (both for immediate learning and ultimate use) result from the characteristics of the student body of the institution and the particular segment of it taking a course. However, since a course as the unit of instruction is often determined by the departmental and disciplinary context, the teaching of a course tends to be specific to course content. In contrast to this limited conception, significant learning transcends content and is the composite result of learning from the entire array of courses taken by a student. An individual course and its teacher, or even the student's major and the staff charged with teaching courses in that subject, are only a small part of that total experience.

Significant learning has taken place when an individual has grown, developed, or matured in a number of respects that have relatively little relationship to specific courses and content. The following statements characterize this conception of learning.

1. Significant learning has taken place when the learner displays independence, initiative, and originality in interpreting and reacting to problems and questions. Whereas much of the learning structured by courses and teachers aims at producing specific responses to specific stimuli (objective test questions, for example), the ultimate expectation is that the individual interpret the stimulus in reference to an immediate context and to personal goals and values and react accordingly.
2. Significant learning has taken place when an individual not only knows but is also able to interpret, understand, and use words, concepts, and symbols to facilitate his or her own thought processes and judgments.

3. Significant learning has taken place when an individual can effectively communicate with others (whether of less, similar, or greater sophistication) about issues or ideas and about personal commitments, activities, and plans in reference to them. This and the preceding statement recognize that language is not only a medium of communication but also a tool for ordering and understanding the environment and human activity currently evident in it.
4. Significant learning has taken place when the concepts, symbols, and ways of manipulating them have been internally assimilated into a structure that enables the individual to analyze and organize the universe and immediate environment in a personally meaningful way. It is desirable that this structure correspond at major points with that held by other educated persons, and the individual should retain control over the structure (rather than become controlled by it) so that flexibility, adaptation, and fundamental adjustments are possible. In many respects, as with scientific hypotheses and theories, it is less important that the structure and its inherent explanations be "right" than that they be useful in: (a) simplifying, understanding, organizing, and recalling information; (b) integrating and reinforcing knowlledge; (c) synthesizing knowledge—the old with the new and the elementary with the advanced; (d) generating new ideas and explanations; and (e) applying or transferring knowledge to new problems and circumstances. Since the total body of knowledge and that portion of it in the possession of any one individual is always undergoing expansion and adjustment, the structure of the body of knowledge—whether in toto, in a discipline, or in an individual—is always and inevitably relative, optional, and developmental rather than absolute. Otherwise, education only replaces one set of biases and rigidities by another perhaps more timely but ultimately no less confining.
5. Significant learning has taken place when the student comes to regard a teacher as only one of many contextual resources available to help make learning easier. Systematic and contingent interaction or transaction between teacher

and learner better describes the role of teacher than does the delivery system with the teacher as producer and student as recipient. The mature learner becomes his or her own teacher.

6. Significant learning has taken place when an individual exhibits the ability to adjust to multiple, perhaps even conflicting, demands by appraising their relative importance and assigning to them personal priorities based upon a recognized and internalized set of values.

The preceding six criteria of significance obviously could be rephrased as objectives or as competencies. They do indeed transcend the content and coverage considerations from which most courses, outlines, or syllabi are devised. Their attainment requires personal growth or development over time. Nevertheless, any course or teacher that does not foster development along these lines has a very limited and dubious perspective. These learning outcomes are far more important criteria of undergraduate education of high quality than are the specific knowledge and skills accruing from specific college courses and teachers. It is not unreasonable, then, to regard a course and the content covered by it as less important than the learning experiences provided and the relevance and effectiveness of these experiences in promoting growth in respect to the specified criteria. Courses, content, and teachers are obviously only means rather than ends in themselves. Yet the significance of an individual step in a stairway is enhanced rather than depreciated by recognizing that the collective contribution of the steps is that of moving an individual from one level to another over a space not readily covered in a single leap.

Philosophical Commitments in Teaching

A spate of philosophical views—rationalism, realism, idealism, humanism, neohumanism, eclecticism, instrumentalism—reflects various efforts to undergird college teaching and the curriculum with a coherent and consistent set of values. But these labels have remained unknown to teachers engrossed in developing introductory departmental courses and major programs. In any case, the labels and associated views would seem, and probably would be, irrelevant to most teachers. Yet, implicit in college program developments and teaching orientations, there are five distinctive philosophical views:

theocentric—makes divine sovereignty and glory the central truth, with all other truth dependent upon or emergent from that ultimate source

ideocentric—emphasizes the worth of the accumulated knowledge in the disciplines

sociocentric—places individual service to society (or to the nation) at the center of education

idiocentric—assumes that a democratic society requires maximal individual development

eccentric—highlights the individual instructor as a model for emulation

Bible colleges and other institutions operating in the context of fundamentalist religious commitments tend to be theocentric. The professor who asserts that his sole objective as a teacher is "to do God's will to the best of my ability" well exemplifies this position. Liberal arts colleges committed to majors and distribution requirements are predominantly ideocentric. Programs dominated by the social sciences and by interdisciplinary problem courses often operate from a sociocentric viewpoint. Programs committed to individual (idiocentric) development tend to result from faculty commitments to humanistic psychology. The eccentric conception emphasizes professorial rather than student idiocentricity. An eccentric may be erratic, odd, or simply unusual and offbeat. The number of really excellent teachers on most campuses is small, and thus they are indeed atypical, unusual, odd, offbeat, and eccentric. Efforts to base an educational program on outstanding teachers quickly founders because outstanding teachers are scarce if objective criteria and standards are applied, and well-nigh universal if self-judgment is accepted.

These five philosophical commitments result in the assignment of quite different priorities to such matters as disciplinary content, core requirements, physical education, foreign languages, communication and mathematical skills, performing arts, and career development. However, actual program requirements and the curriculum as a whole emerge from the complex interactions of many additional factors. The influences of students, faculty, administrators, academic traditions, and educational philosophies are aided or negated at various times by pressures from society, professional organizations, employers, donors, politicians, laws, accrediting agencies, and governing boards. Whatever is in the curriculum at any moment is an artifact of diverse circumstances seldom fully recognized, yet so ensconced that threat of major alteration generates unified resistance. The needs of students and the implications of these needs for revising educational objectives and experiences are easily ignored in the resulting turmoil.

The five philosophical views also imply differing conceptions of learning and teaching. In the *theocentric* commitment, man is but one manifestation of Divine Will. Worship and service to the end of achieving salvation may be the ultimate concern of individuals and of education. Intrinsic worth is then assigned to Truth and all mundane uses of knowledge are extrinsic. In the remaining four philosphic commitments (ideocentric, sociocentric, idiocentric, and eccentric), there is obviously much in common with the four teaching orientations presented in Chapter One. The disciplinary orientation is *ideocentric.* Intrinsic worth is assigned to ideas of great significance, so adjudged because perceptive and knowledgeable individuals agree in this appraisal. Specific knowledge or intellectual ability, whether of immediate practical significance or rendered important by social whim, is of lesser or extrinsic worth. The use of extrinsic rewards to encourage the acquisition of intrinsic values may be regarded as inappropriate and debasing motivation—akin to bribery. Adulation of the unusual personality (teacher-centered orientation) obviously corresponds to the *eccentric* philosophical commitment. The *idiocentric* and *sociocentric* commitments, both the student-centered (cognitive), on the one hand, and student-centered (affective), on the other, are more complexly related. At the extreme, the affective orientation may view the social constraints imposed on individuals as antithetical to the fullest individual development. The disciplinary organization of knowledge is regarded as one of those constraints. The individual becomes the measure of the worth of everything. Intrinsic value is an individual judgment.

The student-centered (cognitive) orientation is more responsive and responsible to human society than the student-centered (affective), or indeed than the disciplinary or the idiocentric and eccentric orientations. In the context of education directed to assisting individuals in living a satisfying and productive life in society, the significance of the distinction between intrinsic and extrinsic merit becomes one of little or no interest, since the values that motivate human behavior can seldom be unambiguously identified or discriminated. In the following chapters, most of the discussion focuses upon expansion and clarification of the student-centered (cognitive) teaching orientation as a combination of the ideocentric, sociocentric, and idiocentric philosophical commitments. In this orientation, the current disciplinary structures play a large role because they represent the composite efforts of mankind in becoming more truly human by seeking for the explanations, meanings, and purposes of human existence. Education is ultimately a humanizing agency and process.

Suggestions for Further Reading

Ausubel, D. P. "Cognitive Structure and Transfer." In N. Entwistle and D. Hounsell (Eds.), *How Students Learn.* Readings in Higher Education, 1. Lancaster, England: Institute for Research and Development in Post-Compulsory Education, University of Lancaster, 1975.

Beard, R. *Teaching and Learning in Higher Education.* Harmondsworth, England: Penguin Books, 1972.

Bloom, B. S. *Human Characteristics and School Learning.* New York: McGraw-Hill, 1976.

Bloom, B. S., and Broder, L. J. *Problem-Solving Processes of College Students.* Chicago: University of Chicago Press, 1950.

Briggs, L. J. *Handbook of Procedures for the Design of Instruction.* Monograph No. 4. Pittsburgh: American Institutes for Research, 1970.

Bruner, J. S. *Toward a Theory of Instruction.* Cambridge, Mass.: Harvard University Press, Belknap Press, 1966.

Claxton, C. S., and Ralston, Y. *Learning Styles: Their Impact on Teaching and Administration.* AAHE-ERIC/Higher Education Research Report No. 10. Washington, D.C.: American Association for Higher Education, 1978.

Clayton, T. E. *Teaching and Learning–A Psychological Perspective.* Englewood Cliffs, N.J.: Prentice-Hall, 1965.

Davis, J. R. *Teaching Strategies for the College Classroom.* Boulder, Colo.: Westview Press, 1976.

Entwistle, N., and Hounsell, D. (Eds.). *How Students Learn.* Readings in Higher Education, 1. Lancaster, England: Institute for Research and Development in Post-Compulsory Education, University of Lancaster, 1975.

Gagné, R. M. *The Conditions of Learning.* (2nd ed.) New York: Holt, Rinehart and Winston, 1970.

Hill, W. F. *Learning Thru Discussion.* Beverly Hills, Calif.: Sage, 1972.

McKeachie, W. J. "Research on Teaching at the College and University Level." In N. G. Gage (Ed.), *Handbook of Research on Teaching.* Chicago: Rand McNally, 1963.

Perry, W. G., Jr. *Forms of Intellectual and Ethical Development in the College Years: A Scheme.* New York: Holt, Rinehart and Winston, 1968.

3

Education as a Humanizing Experience

The object of instruction is to make learners or problem solvers self-sufficient both, individually, within appropriate limits and, collectively, in those matters that involve broad societal issues. To achieve this stage, the individual needs to acquire competency in the use of language as a tool for communication and thought and some understanding of how knowledge is stored, organized, and retrieved. The individual also needs to acquire insight into social organization and to learn how to cooperate and collaborate with others in defining, analyzing, and resolving social issues. Every person seeks recognition, security, and affection, and an understanding of self, others, and the world. The significance of death becomes a major preoccupation with advancing age. On these fundamental human needs the motivation to learn is grounded. They also provide a basis for stating transcendent educational objectives that give direction to teaching by indicating the nature of the learnings desired and suggesting the characteristics of relevant learning experiences. This chapter will examine the humanizing forces among mankind, the organizing and learning tools acquired by the educated person, and different modes of structuring learning. Finally, six humanizing competencies and their accompanying experiential elements will be presented.

Education, in a formal and extended sense, is a relatively late arrival in the development of civilized man. Our present conception of the educational process is a result of the existence of a number of humanizing forces that appeared early in the development of the human species and differentiated it from other animals. The understanding and strengthening of these forces are fostered by well-founded educational experiences, but we need always to remember that our conception of formal and extended education should rest upon uniquely human potentials and characteristics. Furthermore, education, viewed as a humanizing agency, must also be regarded as a socializing agency and as a process for fostering the development of unusual human potential. Not everyone in the cast of a play can be a star, but the fullest success of the play depends upon the commitment of the supporting cast and the stagehands as well as upon that of the leads.

A modest, reasonable, and yet highly significant goal of education is that it help people to lead lives satisfying to themselves and those around them while contributing to the attainment of peace, justice, beauty, and truth for all mankind. Within the broad spectrum implied, there will be those veering to one extreme who would sacrifice society to achieve their own selfish ends, whereas others will sacrifice themselves for their perception of the higher good. The distinctions of the extremes are not always evident, for they may differ more in personal rewards sought than in actual impact on others. However, the tendency—perhaps the right—to err in either intent or accomplishment is part of being human. The gift of innate perfection or the existence of an educational program producing it would destroy the humanity of mankind.

Humanizing Forces Among Mankind

In the absence of sound and accepted theological, philosophical, psychological, or sociological evidence documenting the humanizing forces present among mankind, any characterization of them must be arbitrary and subject to discussion. Following is one possible list of the humanizing forces operative among mankind:

1. a long period of dependence for both maturation (infancy and childhood) and decline (senectitude and senility)
2. a complex social organization involving specialization, interdependence, and collaboration
3. the possession of self-awareness and an attendant capacity for self-criticism in context
4. a capacity to make and to use tools, both those for thought (mathematics, logic, language), and those for manipulation (technology)
5. the development and use of language as a tool for thinking and for expression of the process and results of thought
6. the purposeful modification and use of the environment to supply the basic needs of food, clothing, shelter, security, health, and affection and to indulge other desires and aspirations
7. an urge to explain the world and human presence in it
8. an awareness and commitment to values transcending basic needs and aspirations
9. an ideological transcendence of time and space, including awareness of the past and concern for the future
10. the capacity to engage in abstract, value-free thought and to reach value-based judgment

These ten forces or abilities are so interrelated that the number could readily be condensed to four or five. The long period of dependence is a major factor in the social structure and makes possible a formal program of education. Tool making and using could be interpreted to include language development since language itself is a tool. Language, in turn, permits and encourages abstract thought, including thinking about values. Transcendence of time and space depends upon language, upon means for encoding and decoding it, and upon the urge to explain the world and man himself. Only gradually has man come to realize that extravagant use of the environment reflects both dubious values and infringements upon the rights of others, including future generations.

A humanistic view of higher education includes a commitment that every higher education program should help people to recognize, reinforce, and integrate these humanizing forces. By participating in these programs, learners achieve their individual human potential in greater measure and contribute more significantly to human society than would otherwise be the case. This view recognizes that equality of ability and equality of opportunity and perfectibility are unattainable because of those very factors of variability that provide individuals with potentials capable of great success or abysmal failure.

The single objective of acquiring knowledge within or across disciplines is not an adequate interpretation of this humanistic educational responsibility, although an understanding of the nature and role of disciplinary-based thought or the development of human consciousness is an essential aspect of humanistic education. This understanding is unlikely to be generated by a few required courses in the humanities. The required-course approach may even be contraindicated by the repeatedly demonstrated fact that humanities courses tend to focus on items of knowledge regarded as important artifacts of individual strivings in the long and continuing effort of mankind to become *human*. The knowledge of names, works, and even of ideas has little to do with being human in the fullest sense. Moreover, all disciplines are part of the human effort and heritage; collectively, they constitute the humanities. It is more important to understand and be able to internalize, adapt, and apply the essential nature and procedures of the disciplines in life experience than to acquire and file isolated information that is difficult to recall, possibly no longer true, and often irrelevant to contemporary or future concerns.

Models as Means and Ends of Learning

Perhaps the central task of humanizing education is to help each learner develop or acquire a model of the world and of life in it, whether or not entirely accurate, that provides a basis for coping with living in that world. Language is learned, not inherited, and it is imposed upon rather than simply mirroring reality. The learner internalizes an image or vision of reality by various experiences in and with that reality.

Much, perhaps most, of the initial learning about reality is nonverbal. For example, the person who observes someone else putting a small steel ball in an opening at one end of an opaque box and, by intricate manipulation, moving that ball so that it comes out at the other end may want to try it. The box and ball can be taken in hand with no words exchanged, and the box examined closely. No characteristic other than the entry and exit holes can be seen. After the ball is put in the first hole, a series of initially random manipulations are engaged in. The definition of the task will tend to direct the moves. If that task is looked upon as getting the ball through the box once, random moves will suffice. If the task is looked upon as getting the ball through the box in the shortest time, trial-and-error learning and habituation will be adequate. If the task is seen as describing accurately the internal structure of the box, then the likely pattern is systematically collecting evidence and formulating hypotheses to be tested. After successive slow trials, cautious adjustments, and careful listening to the ball's movements, the internal structure of the box will be conceived. With that conception, the individual may then be able to run the ball through the box with no wasted motion even though the conception may not be precise. The conception, or image, can be reduced to a drawing that can be exhibited to others, thereby expediting their mastery of the task—again without a word. The mental image can be validated by cutting the box open. The mental image, even when functional in solving the problem, may deviate somewhat from the actuality. To communicate the knowledge gained to others by means other than observation and manipulation, the concept *maze* may be introduced and a set of instructions written that specify the various steps in positioning and manipulating the box.

Many tasks, such as riding a bicycle or skating, are initially grasped by observation, followed by trial and error, perhaps with mechanical aids (double-runner skates) or physical support by another person, all without need for words. We learn a series of operations that achieve a desired result. This *enactive* type of learning involves doing, learning forms of behavior, and getting the habit of them. The transition to a perceptual organization of the task depends upon visual, tactile, or other sensory evidence that is then summarized into mental images or graphics (iconics). Production of the written instructions, put together with the mental image and its validation, allows the box-and-ball learner a mastery of the immediate task and generates a degree of assurance in tackling similar tasks that far surpasses that in purely trial-and-error learning. Such learners may solve the problem with the written instructions, but it is unlikely that such instructions would be fully meaningful to them unless they saw such a box, tried or observed manipulation, and became aware in some manner (by a blueprint or sketch) of the maze within. Language is an imposition on physical reality, a means of creating abstractions, and a tool for relating and thinking about both; it does not do away with exploratory action and image formation.

Much learning proceeds in the fashion illustrated by these three stages. We see others successfully manipulate a variety of tools or engage in sequential, purposeful activity. We imitate, but we often find that until we achieve a perceptual organization or a mental image, our imitations are not markedly successful. At the next stage, when concepts or principles are introduced and phrased as propositions, the possibilities of specifying relationships and restructuring our statements generate new insights into the task and admit of generalizations and application not readily possible before. As we become more sophisticated in the use of a language, we can introduce abstract concepts or state hypotheses and then investigate their relationship to understanding, explaining, or manipulating reality.

Organizing and Learning Tools

As a learner accumulates knowledge, he or she finds it necessary to organize this knowledge in a manner that expedites its recall and use. The recall of the names of the external parts of the human body is assisted by relating the names to the parts of one's own body. Recall of the internal organs and structures is assisted by an actual drawing or mental image of a partially dissected body and its several layers of tissue, vessels, fibers, and organs. Knowledge of the functions carried on and of their synchronization or sequence requires greater insight and introduces another level of organization.

A learner may use a *mnemonic* (either created or appropriated) to assist recall. Thus memorizing the diagram

	tangent	
sine		secant
cosine		cosecant
	cotangent	

in conjunction with several rules assists in learning and recalling numerous relationships among these trigonometric functions. The rules are:

1. Each function is equal to the product of the two adjacent functions.
2. Each function is the reciprocal of the diagonally opposite function.
3. Each function is equal to the ratio of an adjacent function to the function immediately beyond, proceeding in the same (clockwise or counterclockwise) direction.

In words, these rules and diagram appear formidable, but many people have successfully used the mnemonic without memorizing or understanding the rules. The derivation of these relationships from definitions of the functions has much less to do with their recall and use than many mathematics professors incline to believe.

In music, the learner who associates the key designation and number of sharps by use of "*g*o *d*own *a*nd *e*at *b*reakfast *f*irst" may keep in mind that the key of D# has two sharps but lack any understanding of the intervals or steps in various scales (major, minor, etc.) or of the role of sharps (and flats) in defining them. But with fuller insight, the learner will no longer find the mnemonic needful or useful.

The next stage is one of *symbolism.* Words, hieroglyphs, or symbols are arbitrarily assigned to some aspect of a task. Actions and images are encoded into statements or propositions that, in their formation and manipulation, are subject to the rules of the transformational apparatus of grammar. The use of words in many new tasks is only an extension of action: verbal reference replaces pointing, touching, or eye movement. Words involving distinctions or characteristics not experienced or understood will generally have limited meanings that must be expanded by experience. Thus the learner who is introduced in algebra to such concepts as the

associative law: $(a + b) = (b + a)$,

distributive law: $a(b + c) = ab + bc$,

commutative law: $ab = ba$

is likely to learn these by rote and regard them as rather silly. After all, it is obvious that five multiplied by three is equal to three multiplied by five! The laws have no associations and no meaning because the learner has had no experience with systems in which these abstract laws are violated. Although filling a pail of water (A) followed by (plus) emptying it (B) is not the same as emptying a pail (B) followed by (plus) filling it (A), it is unlikely to occur to the student to extend the association law to that circumstance, and, even if the idea did occur, it might seem irrelevant to both teacher and student. A highly sophisticated level of learning is required before abstract concepts (unrelated to experience) can be accepted, understood, and used. And when that stage has been arrived at, the concepts are no longer complete abstractions—they are tools for thinking. This use of language for thinking is a stage well beyond that of use for expression. This fact, indeed, is one reason why many educators hesitate to use the word *mastery.* The concept of mastery, if used at all, must always be regarded as relative to a limited meaning in a particular context.

Language, mathematics, statistics, and logic are commonly regarded as disciplines and, in the context of formal schooling, as areas in which an educated person must have some mastery. Alternatively, these disciplines may be regarded as tools, in that proficiency in the use of their symbols and processes provides the basis for organizing, interrelating, and understanding ideas in all phases of human's interactions with each other and with the environment. These disciplines also provide the means for the expansion of knowledge by enabling people to formulate and then to investigate the utility and validity of various explanatory or organizing concepts, principles, hypotheses, and relationships. Integrative theories, expressed in words, numbers, and symbols, become possible, as does the communication of these to others.

Any discipline can be regarded as a tool if it is used as a basis for expanding that discipline, exploring relationships with other disciplines, or understanding or resolving problems generated out of people's interaction with others and with the physical and biological environment. Disciplines and the knowledge and skills intrinsic to them are tools for understanding, for communication with others, and for expansion of knowledge, not only within a discipline and among disciplines but also in regard to the problems and aspirations of mankind and the universe.

There are also auxiliary tools that require skills and knowledge if they are to be used effectively. In computer parlance, these tools constitute the hardware and disciplines provide the software. Before the development of the printing press, knowledge was relatively slowly committed to and stored on stone, slate, papyrus, or tablets of baked clay. Dissemination of knowledge by painstaking and error-prone copying was the rule. The printing press and the printed page are early examples of tools that had a marked impact on education, both on the process and on the outcomes anticipated. Both writing (the expression of ideas by recording them on paper) and penmanship became subjects for the school. The typewriter or word processor shifts the emphasis from penmanship to other recording and processing skills. The retrieval of information stored in a computer requires skill both in storing and in retrieval, as well as the knowledge and intellectual ability to retrieve that stored information in some meaningful, useful, organized form.

Many tools, such as telescopes, microscopes, spectacles, surgical instruments, computers, levers, steam engines, and bicycles, are amplifiers or extenders of the sensory or motor capacity of mankind. They enable people to accomplish a task faster, easier, or better than previously and perhaps with less waste and expense (although assessment of the full costs in depletion of resources has seldom been undertaken). A pencil sharpener sharpens a pencil faster than a knife, does it with less physical effort, and makes for a more attractive and sharper pencil. The electric pencil sharpener is no doubt easier to use than a hand-cranked one. Comparative costs have probably not been determined.

Gestures, megaphones, drums, smoke signals, telegraph, telephone, radio, and television represent a sequential development in the transmission of sounds and pictures over distances. The slide rule, calculating machine, and computer are also successive landmarks in the development of tools. The first permitted quick calculations that facilitated problem solving. The second provided greater accuracy and permitted more convenient multiple-valued statistical operations. The computer actually facilitates and extends human thinking capacity by providing for complex analyses and computations that would otherwise take many years or be practically impossible. It has become possible to define and deal with problems that formerly were unrecognized, ignored, or simply avoided. However, none of these tool developments has eased the task of reaching decisions in the face of people's biases or conflicting values. The implications of alternative analyses, interpretations, and values may be made clearer, but the intrusion of affect while defining a problem and attempting a resolution remains a highly prevalent human obstacle.

Instruction, Learning, and Teaching

It is uncertain how much the learning process is helped by the development of a theory about it. Yet insofar as a theory, a design, or a set of assumptions helps a learner or teacher give a rationale for a sequence of interesting and goal-directed learning experiences, some formal statement is desirable. A theory, whether of learning or of instruction, need not be prescriptive. In view of the variations in people's interests, motivations, abilities, and goals, it seems unlikely that any specific rules for acquiring or encouraging the acquisition of knowledge or skill will hold for all learners and teachers.

It seems equally unlikely that teaching and learning can be normatively defined. It is certainly possible, as seen in Chapter One, to develop a profile of practices and points of view that are evidenced by teachers and learners as they engage in educational activity. Yet the particular combination of the many variables involved, and especially the affective considerations and interactions of teacher and learner, make it doubtful that erecting normative practices will provide a clear or useful model to any teacher or learner. Perhaps the most abysmal aspect of much of college and university education is the common routine (the norm) found in so many classrooms, with neither teachers nor students showing any great enthusiasm in class or out of it.

There is some point, however, in analyzing the range of possible activity involved in teaching and learning and in providing a rationale for a consistent and coherent pattern that makes the educational experience more purposeful. In this process, it is essential that the discussion deal with both the teacher and the learner. The term *instruction,* as noted earlier, has some implication of implanting a structure in an individual, although it is not clear whether that structure is that of the learning itself or one to promote learning. If, however, one accepts the view that the major obligation of a college teacher initially is to motivate the student, then it follows that the teacher's role is that of providing experiences that develop in the learner a commitment to and a desire for learning, both in general terms and in a particular course.

This requires on the part of the learner an expectation that the experience in a course can be interesting and useful. It requires a willingness to attend to what is done in the course, and it includes an expectation that the teacher will initiate the course by providing personal answers to such questions as: Why is the material and the experience in this course important and worth the expenditure of your time to learn it? What can you as a learner do with it? What more can you do and what can you do better and more effectively if you acquire, in reasonable measure, the knowledge, abilities, and skills included in this course? It is appropriate that the teacher deal not only with the long-run implications but also with immediate ones. What is the relationship of this course and the experiences provided in it to other courses commonly taken at the same time? How is the discipline here interrelated with other disciplines? What problems make up the subject matter for this discipline? What other disciplines must be drawn upon to make this subject matter more fully understood?

A Structure for Learning

A college teacher is also obligated to provide early in any course a structure or organization that will help the learner conceive the relationship of various pieces of the course, the relationship of the course to other courses in the same discipline, and the relationship to other disciplines. The structure provided may be based upon a variety of considerations, and it may take on many different forms.

Even the structure of a discipline, as will be seen in Chapter Five, is not an absolute. Scholars in a discipline will differ markedly on the specifics of the disciplinary structure, and most will see that structure as developing rather than fixed. In some disciplines, such as literature, there may not even be a commonly accepted structure, although such concepts as literary forms, functions of literature, and role of literary study are readily identified. The structure for learning a discipline may differ from the structure that has become the standard way of thinking about the discipline. For example, the formal proofs of geometry do not closely follow the development of the insights and reasoning necessary to establishing the proofs as finally presented. The structure for learning how to apply a discipline may be quite different from the structure for learning the discipline. The mathematical modes of analysis and solution introduced into physics, engineering, mathematics, or economics to deal with particular types of problems found there may differ in form and notation from related materials used in courses for mathematics majors. Structures may also be of a personal character. Just as no two people are likely to see a work of art in exactly the same way, no two are likely to organize the structure of their learning and all of its associations in the same manner.

There are a variety of modes of structuring. Use of major concepts, such as mass, weight, similarity, and continuity, involve an approach to learning in which the major ideas or concepts selected apply across many disciplines but may take on special meanings in particular disciplines. A categorical approach to structuring involves the establishment of a set of classes and a set of criteria for sorting ideas or objects into these classes. The earlier description of four teacher orientations represents a categorical approach. One trouble with categories is that there is usually a degree of ambiguity in the classification of particular ideas or objects that have characteristics that cut across categories or are marginal to one or more of them. Physical characteristics, such as size, weight, and density, can also be viewed as categorical. Many courses in the social sciences (particularly history) are organized chronologically or temporally. Here the structure corresponds, to a considerable extent, to the sequence of occurrence. But chronology does not always provide the best approach to understanding recurring events that may occur at different times and places in various cultures and yet possess a high degree of commonality. Structuring by sequential development is another type, one more dependent upon the immediate characteristics or objects studied than is structuring by chronology. Structuring according to complexity, which deals with the number of variables and the complications of their interrelationships, is still another way to organize experience. Structuring according to nearness or remoteness is another mode, with both extremes affecting emotion and motivation. Treating problems of immediate significance to some learners is not likely to be especially effective for cognitive learning. When emotions run high, habit, bias, or prejudice tends to dominate cognition. Looking at problems of other peoples, remote in time or place, may be more productive—if they can be introduced in a way that makes the experience meaningful to the learner.

In developing a structure for learning, the teacher is faced with the fact that the long-term human desire to achieve coherence, order, continuity, uniformity, consistency, and integration may be at odds with the motivations and experiences of individual learners, the risks involved in them, the difficulty of the ideas or methods, and the control or lack of control over the direction and nature of the learning process and what is to be learned. With learning, there is a need to give attention to such matters as the speed of learning, the resistance to forgetting, the applicability or transferability of what is learned, the strain or difficulty involved in learning, and the attitudes that may thereby be created. Besides, it is important to take into account the significance and wider applicability of the representational mode or form used (action, imaging, or symbolization) and its power for further learning and for reinforcement of what has been learned before.

Among the psychological considerations—particularly related to motivation—there are several distinctions useful in planning a learning sequence. When something to be learned is directly related to something an individual desires, there is a direct, internal, and immediate motivation for that individual to learn. When the ideas or skills to be learned have no immediate significance to the individual, relate to problems considered irrelevant, or may have significance only at some later point in life, learning is harder because gratification is deferred; and indirect motivations, such as grades, rewards of tangible nature, or a desire for respect and praise, may become operative.

In arriving at a structure suitable for a specific course and group of students, the teacher should make a distinction between what knowledge is of interest to and significant for the scholar in the discipline and what is appropriate to the student. Obviously, where that distinction is drawn depends upon the student's level, interests, and aspirations. The graduate student in a discipline may share with the scholar an interest in a certain problem that is virtually meaningless to the learner for whom an experience in the discipline may be largely a matter of broadening of horizons or applicability in another field.

Obviously, there are many ways in which course content and program experiences can be structured and ordered. The natural tendency of the individual teacher in a particular course is to allow course title, content, and number indicating a level or sequential position in a program to predetermine course structure, with minimal attention to the long-term development of the learner. This is the natural, almost inevitable, consequence of viewing a course entirely in reference to content coverage. We are convinced that the single most important factor in structuring a course must be a statement of educational objectives that reflects the humanizing function of education and thereby transcends courses—and, to a considerable extent, also transcends particular majors and degree programs. Whether a student's major is mathematics, science, sociology, literature, or philosophy little alters the humanizing obligation of a liberal arts college and its faculty. Programs in business, teaching, and health specialties are not exempt from that obligation. Indeed, since the vocational focus and its impact on society is more obvious there, the humanizing function of education becomes even more important. Hence objectives that capture this humanizing obligation transcend particular courses and programs. For some programs of a social service nature, such objectives may be made so specific as to signal competency levels essential for professional performance.

The remainder of this chapter sets forth six objectives and their competency implications that reflect the humanizing obligation of higher education and provide the single most important source for planning degree programs, courses, and teaching and learning within them.

Six Humanizing Competencies

1. *An educated person should be able to acquire knowledge and use it.*

This competency is consistent with an emphasis on understanding the nature of the discipline of knowledge and on developing the ability to engage in inquiry. Although a student should acquire some knowledge during college, he or she also should acquire the abilities, motivations, and insights that enable one to expand and apply the knowledge. The person must be able not only to master new concepts and new patterns of thought but also to inquire into and use new modes of inquiry.

Clarification: "Acquiring knowledge" includes using and evaluating source material, firsthand observation, analyzing and interpreting data, experimentation, interviews, discussion. Using knowledge includes evaluating the accuracy and relevance of evidence, solving problems, explaining events, analyzing possible courses of action, prediction.

Range of application: This competency applies to problems in all areas of activity (vocational, social, personal).

Relevant learning experiences: These include independent study, community services, team learning, study of current problems, special projects, writing requirements.

Evidence of accomplishment: The learning experiences provided should offer opportunity for assessment of competency through observation of the process of analysis of the result (paper, laboratory report, art object, and so forth). This assessment may be viewed at three levels: (a) determination of whether and to what extent individuals have had experiences appropriate to the development of the competency; (b) study of participation in each such experience to see whether it requires and contributes to the development of the competency; (c) assessment of the extent to which individuals demonstrate the competency. If neither (a) nor (b) occurs, then any results found as part of (c) are fortuitous.

The assessment required in (c) necessitates a clear definition of the competency. For example, the report of an independent study project may be read to determine whether it reveals use of sources, observation, experimentation, and so forth. It may also be read to determine how the knowledge gained was applied.

If the range of learning experiences is too limited or too theoretical, comprehensive assessment may require some additional task from which evidence of competency can be collected. Since this competency is too complicated for satisfactory assessment in an hour or two, it is desirable to review the evidence before the student's last quarter in school so that any additional task could be incorporated into that final quarter rather than being added as part of a final comprehensive examination. A senior thesis or a senior independent study project might provide a significant part of the evidence required.

2. *An educated person should have a high level of mastery of the skills of communication.*

The ability to read, listen, and acquire additional information is a corollary of the first competency. The individual should be able to express ideas orally or in writing so that they may be understood, judged, and applied by others. Although the individual may display the greatest versatility in use of communication skills in areas of concentration in college study, he or she should be able to communicate intelligently about any problem that arises in the roles of worker, citizen, and parent.

Clarification: "Having a high level of mastery" includes being perceptive in acquiring information and assessing attitudes, accurate in using technical vocabulary, facile with the grammar of the discipline, adaptable to audiences, flexible in style, constructive in criticism. "Skills of communication" include reading with facility and critically both popular and scholarly materials, listening in formal and informal situations, speaking to large assemblies and discussing in small groups, writing formal research papers and critical essays.

Range of application: This competency applies to problems centering around communication associated with nonacademic and vocational activity as well as with the academic program.

Relevant learning experiences: These include reading (analysis and evaluation of newspapers, magazines, and scholarly or research papers), listening (lectures, interviewing, and small group discussions), speaking (reading a formal paper, class recitations, small group discussions, debates, and dramatics), writing (technical reports, classroom papers, critical analyses).

Evidence of accomplishment: People are always communicating with themselves or others by reading, listening, speaking, or writing. Hence evidence of accomplishment must be gathered at various times and under many different conditions. (a) How many significant points can an individual recall from a lecture he or she has just heard? (b) How accurate are the data he or she gets from observation or from an interview? (c) How reliable are personal perceptions of phenomena, of attitudes of speakers, of interviewees, and of peers? (d) How well organized and how clear is the individual's formal expression? (e) In how many different situations is the individual able to accomplish (a) through (d) at a high level?

Many opportunities arise for observing communication

skills. Perhaps the identification of specific activities in residential colleges can be made and then related to the desired communication skills. The specific conditions of observation need to be stated, and some new activities may have to be developed. It should be noted that the nature of the communication pattern is important in revealing the quality and amount of communication and in providing evidence on all of the five other competencies that can be observed and assessed only as the individual communicates them by word or action.

3. *An educated person should be aware of his or her own values and value commitments and realize that other individuals and cultures hold contrasting values that must be understood and, to some extent, accepted in interaction with them.*

This competency may be revealed in several ways. In conversation and in analysis of issues, an individual will demonstrate awareness of the values and conflicts of a democratic society. He or she will recognize value differences among individuals, nations, and cultures and will accept that these value differences cannot always be resolved satisfactorily. The individual should recognize that values underlie every action and should support personal convictions through advocacy and action.

Clarification: This statement assumes that most individuals have a set of values (even if only those of currying favor and avoiding difficulty by accepting, or appearing to accept, the values of those with whom they are in contact at the moment) but that they are not always conscious of their values because these either have been assimilated as behavior without being recognized as values or have become habitual because of precept and prescription without consideration of alternatives. It also assumes that (a) values are largely culturally determined, (b) there are no absolutes, (c) meaningful interactions among individuals and cultural groups require a degree of understanding and acceptance rather than mere tolerance.

"Being aware of" means being conscious of, willing to attend to, and concerned about. "Values" refer to the bases, considerations, or points of view (conscious or unconscious) given priority through actual choice or action in situations where differing values dictate differing choices or actions. "Understood" means that the contrasting values are known, these alternative values are recognized as contrasting, the implications of these values for thought and action are sensed, at least in part, and the origin, development, or justification for these alternative values is grasped. "Accepted" means that the values of other individuals and cultures are not rejected out of hand as untenable or wrong because they differ from our own, and respect is accorded to the individuals and the culture in which these values are embedded, even though some of the values themselves are regarded as unacceptable. "Interaction" refers to reading or writing in which the individual confronts or is confronted by the need for sympathetic and rational treatment of the views, customs, and actions of individuals with contrasting values, discussion in which there is face-to-face contact and verbal interchange, mutual cooperation, and assistance.

Range of application: This competency applies to all activities engaged in by the individual. This does not mean that individuals should become so self-conscious and introspective about their reactions and thoughts as to become incapacitated for action. It does mean that the constraints and sanctions of the individual's immediate associations often generate views, attitudes, or behavior without his or her conscious attention to the values they support or are interpreted by others as supporting. Adherence to the social mores and personal habits are efficient and often permit time for more significant thought and pursuit of deeper meaning. Yet the life that is unexamined in detail may become unexaminable in any fuller, more complete sense. Accepting value differences also opens the way to valuing the worth and dignity of the individual and his or her originality and creativity which, along with critical inquiry, are basic value commitments of higher education.

Relevant learning experiences: The range of application of this competency is limitless. Any experience, whether in or out of class, on or off campus, can have relevance. Some experiences will be more effective than others, however, because they confront the individual with a situation in which the values revealed are so different that the implications and impact of value differences cannot be ignored. With some individuals, differences in speech, food, dress, esthetic standards, use of leisure time, politics, religion, and so forth, such as those found among individuals from various parts of the country, will serve as the initial stimulation. For others, some probing into the rationale for personal views and those of other students and professors may be required. In order to sense fully the importance of value commitments, an individual may require something of a "culture shock," such as is attainable only by attempting to live in a community of a very different pattern from that to which one has become accustomed. Although courses and other structured experiences may be expected to make some contribution to value consciousness and motivation analysis, community service, team-learning experiences, and study abroad are likely to have even more effect. Activity involving the cooperation and interaction of individuals with differing value commitments may contribute significantly to this competency.

Evidence of accomplishment: The learning experiences provided should offer opportunity for assessment of the competency through observation of the process or analysis of the result (paper, laboratory report, art object, and so forth). The assessment should include determination of whether the individuals have developed awareness of their values, awareness of value differences and conflicts among their immediate associates, knowledge of cultures with greatly contrasting values, a concern that their own actions support values they believe in, ability to recognize and take account of differences in values as a basis for understanding the views and behavior of others, acceptance of and willingness to be exposed to value differences, concern for and recognition of originality and creativity both in themselves and in others.

4. *An educated person should be able to cooperate and collaborate with others in studying, analyzing, and formulating solutions to problems and in taking action on them.*

In research and instruction within the college or university, in the involvement of citizens in community, state, national, and international affairs, and in the activity of individuals in business, industry, government, and the home, the consideration and solution of problems require close collaboration among individuals and extensive cooperation in larger groups. The college experience should educate a person to operate effectively both as a participant and a leader.

Clarification: This competency is closely related to the first one, which puts the emphasis on the individual's ability to acquire and use knowledge and to relate it to problems. That does not bar the individual from seeking the help of others or collaborating with others but demands that he or she have attained that competency. This fourth competency, however, is explicitly concerned that the individual, having achieved that competency in some measure, also has the ability to cooperate and collaborate with others. This is important because the very nature of a democratic society and its associated technology puts more and more emphasis on the ability of individuals to relate themselves effectively to others and to realize instead of obliterate themselves in so doing. This competency is also closely related to the second competency (communication) and the third (values). Effective communication is essential to and evidenced by cooperation and collaboration. Effective cooperation and collaboration depend upon valuing other individuals and capitalizing on the individuality and creativity of each.

"Cooperating" implies joint action, concurrence, agreement, personal contribution, and compromise. "Collaborating" means working together, acting jointly, agreeing upon a division of labor and the procedure for combining individual efforts into a single product. "Cooperate" and "collaborate" are both used here with the view that collaboration involves more active participation in accepting the worth of group effort and in contributing to it than does mere cooperation, which may involve only relatively passive acceptance of what is done by others. "Study" connotes the acquiring of knowledge by some systematic investigation, involving more than rote knowledge. It includes continuing concentration to the point of understanding and accepting some concern for application or use. "Analysis" as here applied to problems involves not only the separation of the problem itself into its constituent elements—that is, the isolation of the central issue and related ones and the identification of assumptions, factors, and possible causes—but also the recognition of opinions, relevant facts, materials, and principles that may be called upon in understanding and developing solutions to the problem. "Action" has a wide range of meanings, depending upon the nature of the problem and the range of persons or factors involved in it. If the problem is one that concerns only those investigating it, the necessary actions may be very clear and emerge almost immediately from the fact that a solution has been agreed on. If the problem involves a larger group, it may be incumbent upon those that determine a solution to engage in the necessary interpretation and political activity to persuade the larger group to accept the solution.

Range of application: This competency applies to collaborative activity on vocational, social, and personal problems that arise in preparation for courses in the college, in the laboratory, in the determination of college policies, in the residence hall, or in the society at large.

Relevant learning experiences: These include team or group projects and reports, committee assignments in college or residence hall, community service projects, seminars involving divisions of labor in study and analysis of a problem, surveys.

Evidence of accomplishment: The learning experiences provided should offer opportunity for assessment of the competency through observation of the process or analysis of the result. The result here, however, is a composite of the contributions of several individuals rather than the work of one. It may not be possible to determine the extent and nature of a single individual's collaboration in the final product. Therefore, assessment will need to include (a) determination of whether and to what extent individuals have had experiences appropriate to development of the competency; (b) study of student participation to see whether it actually uses and strengthens the competency; (c) observation, self-appraisal, or group appraisal of the extent to which individuals contribute to the group effort substantially and dynamically.

Since this competency emphasizes cooperation and collaboration, the primary concern is with the individual's ability to facilitate group deliberation, task allotment, and synthesis of the individual skills involved. In the first competency, individual skills are involved. Here the concern is with the effective pooling of individual resources to accomplish a task that either could not be performed by an individual or would not be done as efficiently or effectively on an individual basis.

5. *An educated person should have an awareness of, concern for, and a sense of responsibility about contemporary events, issues, and problems.*

Today few colleges and universities are ivory towers. Administrators and faculty members are usually involved in community, state, and national affairs. They serve as consultants to government, business, and industry, as well as teaching and doing research on the campus. Much of this activity, however, is not evident in the classroom, and a student's college experience concentrates on the acquiring of additional knowledge without relating it to current events. Many are disturbed by this lack of relevance and feel that education should generate concern and obligation for constructive action. Moreover, the student who is encouraged for four years to ignore what is going on in the world and to refrain from involvement in it may continue doing so. Those who are aware of issues and problems off and on campus are often regarded as dissidents or troublemakers by other students, as well as by the faculty and administration. A college education should make a difference in individuals, and one essential difference is the increased ability to understand, accept responsibility for, and take action on contemporary problems. Civic responsibility is an important goal of a college education and should be incorporated into the college experience.

Clarification: "Awareness," "concern," and "sense of responsibility" indicate successive and cumulative levels of attention. "Awareness" simply connotes knowledge that events are occurring or have occurred, or that certain issues or problems exist. "Concern" involves conscious direction of attention to these events and some degree of regard, solicitude, or anxiety about the implications or outcomes. "Sense of responsibility" indicates acceptance of some personal obligation for assessing the implications of events and contributing to the resolution of issues or solution of problems.

"Events," "issues," and "problems" indicate a range of matters requiring attention to and involvement in society. No one can be aware of all events, but the educated person must be aware of those that have significant implications for society and his or her successful performance in it.

Politics, sports, catastrophes, and developments in medical science are all relevant. Issues are frequently timeless, but events generate new issues or new aspects of issues. What are the moral and legal implications of human organ removal and replacement? Problems likewise may be current (open housing legislation) or timeless (equality and justice for all).

Range of application: This competency is applicable to problems of all types but does not imply that everyone is expected to be equally aware of and concerned with all. The range of concern probably indicates the extent to which an individual's education is perceived as relevant to his or her role as a person.

Relevant learning experiences: Awareness, concern, and responsibility are not readily inculcated by learning experiences specifically developed and directed to those ends. Rather, they result from (a) projection of a program or college image that attracts students more concerned with problems than with mastery of a discipline; (b) faculty that demonstrates, in and out of class, that they are alert to and concerned about events outside academe, and that education is viewed as useful only as it is relevant to and contributes to the improvement of the life of the individual and society; (c) viewing all experiences, decisions, and actions in reference to their ultimate results and the values they appear to support; and (d) a continuing mental and physical oscillation between the disciplines and individual concerns, between ideas and theories and the problems or issues they serve to illuminate or explain, between the isolated item of data or discrete fact and the essential but elusive unity and interrelationship of all knowledge in the life of the individual.

Almost any learning experience can provide opportunity for development of this competency if it is a continuing and conscious concern of the professor who insists that it also be a continuing and conscious concern of the student. Group discussions of contemporary issues will assist in this development by encouraging individuals to express concerns and permitting them to examine the implications of these issues personally as well as socially.

Evidence of accomplishment: The nature of the relevant experiences suggests that what is taken as evidence of accomplishment may have to depend largely on observation and subjective appraisal. It would be possible to administer a test of contemporary affairs or a specially prepared current events test; but knowledge, although it indicates awareness, does not demonstrate either concern or responsibility.

This competency also is related to all of the preceding ones. Concern and responsibility will be evidenced to the extent that an individual acquires and uses additional knowledge about an event, issue, or problem, develops and exchanges his or her views with others, cooperates and collaborates with others in study and in action, identifies the values involved in various views about results of events, issues, or problems, and relates these values to his or her own. Thus the most significant aspect of the fifth competency is that it requires the other competencies to be related to the contemporary scene. Evidence of accomplishment, then, is to be sought by (a) appraisal of the extent to which the total college program promotes attention, in class and out, to contemporary events, issues, and problems; (b) determination of the extent to which the individuals engage spontaneously in communications and actions about issues and problems; and (c) determination of the extent to which individuals demonstrate awareness and concern and have taken some responsibility for formulating a personal point of view and acting on some issue or problem.

6. *An educated person should be able to relate his or her development of competencies into a coherent, cumulative,*

and somehow unified experience and to apply these competencies to further development as an individual and to the fulfillment of obligations as a responsible citizen in a democratic society.

A student's college program should be structured in relation to these six competencies and the student should continually try to relate experiences to these competencies. Living and learning must be related within the college experience if continuing learning is to be a part of adult life after college. The student's passive fulfillment of rules and requirements to get a degree must be replaced by active involvement in planning a cumulative experience climaxed by tangible evidence of accomplishment. These competencies can determine the type and pattern of experiences to be provided in college.

Clarification: The length of, concepts used in, and the reflexive nature of this statement in relation to the preceding competencies make it evident that this is a complex capstone competency, the central significance of which lies in its integrative implications. "Coherent" implies cohesiveness, consistency, interrelatedness, connectedness. It emphasizes that college experiences—at least those planned, organized, or generated by the college—are congruous with each other and mutually complementary rather than inconsistent and conflicting. "Cumulative" means that experiences are additive and integrative, that earlier experiences provide the foundation for later experiences, which simultaneously build upon and bind together the earlier experiences in the achievement of new levels of insight and competency. "Somehow unified" suggests that the desired unity or integration is, in great part, an individual accomplishment that is neither fully predictable nor describable.

In sum, this competency implies that the individual finds a sense of accomplishment and satisfaction in his or her progressive increase in competencies that are seen as ever more relevant, both to scholarship and to life. Thus college experiences in these competencies accumulate and produce a unity peculiar to the individual that provides self-confidence for the work ahead.

Range of application: If this competency is to be attained, it must be a concern in each and every aspect of the learner's experience. College life in its entirety must be examined stage by stage, retrospectively and especially prospectively, if the individual is to sense progress and see an essential unity in his or her cumulative experience. Perception of incongruence and inconsistency becomes a challenge to seek for coherence rather than a disheartening discontinuity in experiences.

Relevant learning experiences: Periodic self-evaluation of progress will help in organizing experiences and assessing their impact. Advisers may assist in this process. The expectation of such self-evaluation will encourage planning and conscious selection of experiences, and attention to this contribution to development.

Involvement as individuals and in groups in evaluating the impact of the college will also focus attention on this competency.

Evidence of accomplishment: The individual who raises questions about relationships between current studies and past ones or who seeks to apply knowledge to current problems displays a tendency to exercise this competency. Conversations, papers, and actions can all be examined to see to what extent a wide range of relevant ideas or concepts is brought to bear on a problem and the extent to which there is awareness of the values involved.

Some such statement of competencies and an analysis of conditions producing them are essential if education is to be a humanizing experience. The competencies are so interrelated that the experiences appropriate to fostering one of them are very likely to be appropriate for others. To bring some greater cohesion into the task of selecting and planning these experiences, the following discussion suggests a set of experiences essential to a balanced undergraduate program seeking to develop these competencies.

Experiences Essential to a Humanizing Program

The nature of each of the six competencies suggests relevant educational experiences. These experiences have, in part, already been suggested in the analysis of the competencies, but their specific features have not been indicated. Twelve different, although not independent, experiences for students are listed here with some remarks on their significance and relevance to the attainment of these competencies.

1. *The student should have sustained contact with at least two different disciplines or areas of study.*

The phrase "sustained contact" is used rather than "major" because an interdisciplinary or problem-oriented concentration can be as demanding as the usual departmental major. Sustained contact should be distinguished from supportive study of a discipline. Limited work in a number of related disciplines is often necessary for full understanding of any discipline. Any extended study of the physical sciences or certain of the social sciences requires work in mathematics. In this case, mathematics is supportive or contributory unless the study is expanded into sustained contact. Allowing for such supportive work, sustained contact with two disciplines would seem sufficiently demanding, although certain combinations might justify or demand a third. A student interested in Russian studies might maintain contact throughout four years with the history, literature, and language of Russia. Sustained contact replaces the superficiality of the breadth requirement and the narrowness of the departmental major with a composite experience in two or more disciplines that contribute to a central theme or concern.

This requirement encourages the learner to define a pervasive theme that justifies the choice. The student must plan his or her own program rather than select from ready-made departmental majors. The adviser or tutor must concentrate on the individual's personal interests and concerns rather than on the department's disciplinary demands and convenience. Finally, it forces both individual and adviser to relate the disciplines to each other and to some central theme or issue.

The sustained contact with two or three disciplines should touch on different divisions of knowledge, but this may not always be possible. Disciplines such as history (which combines the humanities and social sciences) and psychology (which is both a science and a social science) lend themselves to such interdivisional combinations. Mathematics and statistics are related to almost every other discipline. History and philosophy can apply to science and mathematics. Such combinations encourage breadth and discourage overspecialization at the undergraduate level.

2. *The student should have an opportunity to explore the historical, philosophical, and cultural backgrounds and implications of the disciplines studied.*

Courses in these areas might be offered in departments of history, philosophy, sociology, or anthropology, if the departmental professors are sufficiently competent in other disciplines to develop the courses in a meaningful way. However, especially in the sciences, these elements would probably be best developed by scientists who are familiar with the history or philosophy of their field, or by scientists in collaboration with professors from the social science or humanities departments. Students whose concentrations are in the humanities or social sciences also benefit from study of the ways in which scientific methodology or technology contributes to these disciplines.

These experiences add an element of breadth to the student's program. They allow the student to recognize the inherent relationships among the humanities, social sciences, and sciences. These experiences also provide deeper insight into the nature and methods of inquiry of the individual disciplines.

3. *The student should confront several current problems directly affected by the disciplines studied.*

Such an experience might be provided in courses but, since problems tend to be interdisciplinary, a seminar or special interim term program that includes a heterogeneous group of students and faculty may be required. If the problems have scientific, social, and political implications, they might help the individual both to explore the relations of the disciplines and to understand the interdisciplinary approach to the study of problems. From this one experience, the learner might obtain a practical problem-solving experience, collaborate in team investigation, and derive insight into contemporary events and issues. He or she will use the knowledge and methodological skills gained from this study of the disciplines and, by communicating with others, will demonstrate and consolidate the mastery of that knowledge and skill.

4. *The student should confront a distinctively different culture and value system.*

Study or travel, such as a year abroad, or work or service

in an underdeveloped country or with a deprived group in one's own country, might effect such a confrontation. It might also be accomplished, to some extent, through literature and contact with foreign students. Such an experience should span the four years rather than be limited to one particular semester or year. It should also be related to disciplinary studies. For example, a science student, using a cultural confrontation with a Spanish-speaking group, might comment on some science textbooks used in Mexico, Spain, or South America. That person might also read current Spanish newspaper or periodical articles on scientific developments. Ideally, the program would be organized so that the individual develops competency in the language, works with people who speak the language, studies or travels in a country where the language is spoken, and then, upon his return, continues to use the language in particular areas of concentration. If this extended use of the language cannot be arranged, it may be wiser to concentrate on reading knowledge and appropriate related experiences, or to discard the language requirement in favor of an experience with a culturally different English-speaking group. For some students, the college experience itself is a confrontation with a new culture and a new set of values.

5. *The student should be introduced early to independent study and continue this in increasing scope through the entire program.*

   In later years, independent study should culminate in two experiences: a study in depth in one or both of the disciplines of sustained contact, and a study of a problem that involves all prior study and additional reading in fields not studied. The former would be an experience in depth; the latter, an experience in breadth and in depth. Independent study can be related to experience with current problems or with a different culture, as well as to sustained contact with specific disciplines.

6. *The student should have a practical experience that has a significant relationship to the disciplines he or she has chosen to emphasize.*

   For some learners, this practical experience might require one or several regular semesters. Others might have a series of summer work experiences. The experience might be on the campus and involve working with a professor on a research project, preparing instruction on tutoring individuals, or teaching a freshman course. In any case, those individuals should achieve a true work experience and should not see themselves as full-time students picking up pin money by part-time employment.

For some, this experience may have direct vocational implications, such as service in a social work agency or community program, or a job in business or industry. For those in teaching or in medical technology, interning would meet this requirement. This practical experience allows students to apply their knowledge, helps them to make the transition from college to the world of work, develops awareness of contemporary problems and issues, and provides opportunities for working with people who are not members of an academic community. This experience, too, should teach students the practical value of the disciplines studied.

7. *The student should have team experiences in learning and problem solving.*

Much current research requires the cooperation of people with various talents and knowledge. The solution of community problems brings together people with diverse interests and talents. Most problems are so complex that no one person has the time or the capacity to explore all the relevant factors and possible solutions. By working with a team, possibly under the guidance of a faculty member, students can examine their own methods of problem solving and approaches to learning and can compare and contrast these with others. Students learn not only how to work with others in analyzing and solving a problem but also how to improve their own learning and problem-solving competencies. This experience should take place at various levels and might be combined with several of the other experiences. For example, the third experience (confrontation in depth with several current problems) could readily use a team approach. Confrontation with a different culture, independent study, or practical work could also use a team approach. If these experiences are closely related, they will reinforce one another and unify the student's total educational experience.

8. *The student should have the experience of living and working in a community of educated people, an experience that provides a model for the kind of living pattern higher education hopes to encourage.*

A community of scholars implies more than respect for knowledge and pursuit of knowledge. It means living with a group of people who share common experiences, concerns, and goals. It includes experience in self-government, in resolving the problems of daily living, and in developing policies and regulations that encourage scholarly pursuits. Thus students should be members of a small community for an extended period of time so that discussion of policies and problems has real significance for the future. There should be no imposed compartmentalization of responsibility, such as the distinction between student personnel, residence hall management, and academic staff. Community living will not provide the experience and responsibility desired if the compartments are predetermined and the policies are imposed by external authorities. The student should solve the problems of developing a congenial environment appropriate to an institution of learning.

9. *The student should have continuing experiences in studying and discussing current events.*

This should be done in all courses, including the natural sciences. An alert instructor can often refer to current national and international developments and demonstrate his or her own awareness of them while encouraging students to do likewise. The instructor will also encourage interest in a discipline by demonstrating its relevance to life. Students can be asked to read and to report on current news articles after interest is aroused. They should follow current events, examine the implications of these developments for their field of study, and consider what solutions to current problems their field offers. In the study of these events, foreign language may be used to include the points of view of other nations and cultures. This area of experience is closely related to the confrontation in depth with current problems, and it can be related to several other areas of experience.

10. *The student should have continuing experiences in organizing and presenting ideas in speech and writing.*

The attempt to express one's own point of view in speech or writing is one of the best learning experiences possible. It is easy to mistake casual familiarity with words and phrases for real mastery. Until an individual tries to work out his or her ideas succinctly and clearly in order to convey them to others, inaccurate knowledge, incoherent expression, and fuzzy thinking will not become fully apparent. Collaborative experiences with others, independent study reports, and conferences with faculty members provide situations where clear and precise communication can be fostered.

11. *The student should have a continuing contact with one or more faculty members who are interested in his or her long-term development as a person.*

This faculty member might help the learner to structure his or her program of studies in relation to goals that they, together, continually define and refine. The possibility of relating these experiences sequentially and cumulatively to the desired competencies depends, to some degree, on the learner but, to a greater degree, on the faculty member's familiarity with the learner's needs and problems. This individuality of planning is essential, for any attempt to structure students' college experiences in such detail as to provide unity and integration for all would almost certainly substitute rigidity and compartmentalization for flexibility and unity.

12. *The student should have continuing experience with a broad evaluation program that is future oriented and provides detailed information about his or her progress toward the desired competencies.*

This evaluation program should include some culminating experience in which the student is asked to demonstrate his or her competency. This experience must be so clearly related to prior experiences that the learner cannot doubt the relevance of or appropriateness of the final evaluation. The adviser or tutor should contribute to both the continuing and culminating evaluation. Evaluation is a vital part of learning and a means of directing learning, not solely a means of determining whether an adequate amount of learning has taken place. Evaluation becomes particularly important when it is recognized as a means of establishing the independence of the learner. Teaching is, after all, a temporary state that achieves full effectiveness only when the learner or problem solver becomes self-directed and self-sufficient in many, though certainly not in all, respects. Humanization involves both personal and social responsibilities and development.

Relation of Competencies to the Disciplines

The disciplines of knowledge are the result of the several humanizing forces operative in human beings. They also constitute the means for arousing and fostering humanization in each new generation, but the cumulative accomplishments of mankind cannot be applied as poultices to individuals, drawing to a head in a few years the insights and benefits of thousands of years of human striving. Somehow, each individual must sense and assimilate human drives, aspirations, and forces and participate in that accomplishment. The knowledge now organized by disciplines will be acquired (if at all) by rote unless learning is motivated and assisted by organizing principles and values transcending the disciplines. We shall return to this in Part Two.

Suggestions for Further Reading

Astin, A. W. *Four Critical Years; Effects of College on Beliefs, Attitudes, and Knowledge.* San Francisco: Jossey-Bass, 1977.

Bell, D. *The Reforming of General Education.* New York: Columbia University Press, 1966.

Bowen, H. R. *Investment in Learning: The Individual and Social Value of American Higher Education.* San Francisco: Jossey-Bass, 1977.

Bruner, J. S. *The Process of Education.* Cambridge, Mass.: Harvard University Press, 1962.

Bruner, J. S. *Toward a Theory of Instruction.* Cambridge, Mass.: Harvard University Press, 1966.

Chickering, A. W. *Education and Identity.* San Francisco: Jossey-Bass, 1969.

Curwin, R. L., and Fuhrmann, B. S. *Discovering Your Teaching Self: Humanistic Approaches to Effective Teaching.* Englewood Cliffs, N.J.: Prentice-Hall, 1975.

Dressel, P. L. *College and University Curriculum.* (2nd ed.) Berkeley, Calif.: McCutchan, 1971.

Grant, B. M., and Hennings, D. G. *The Teacher Moves: An Analysis of Non-Verbal Activity.* New York: Teachers College Press, 1971.

Greene, T. M., and others. *Liberal Education Reexamined: Its Role in a Democracy.* New York: Harper & Row, 1943.

Handlin, O., and Handlin, M. F. *The American College and American Culture: Socialization as a Function of Higher Education.* New York: McGraw-Hill, 1970.

Institute of Society, Ethics, and the Life Sciences. *The Teaching of Ethics in Higher Education.* Hastings-on-Hudson, N.Y.: The Hastings Center, 1980.

4

Enriching Learning Through Technology

Chapter Three considered the nature of education as a humanizing experience and ended with a discussion of the various types of educational experiences required. This chapter pursues that thought further by considering the range and significance of the various types of educational experiences appropriate to our available technology and the nature of the learning desired, and by proposing a new conception of the teacher's role in relation to that technology.

The teacher, educated in a discipline and viewing competency in that discipline as the major requirement for effective teaching, may react negatively to the use of educational technology, forgetting, for the moment, that pencils, pens, paper, and books are part of that technology. Even teachers in the fields of drafting, engineering, and chemistry, who regularly use equipment of one kind or another in their workrooms or laboratories, may still regard discussions of educational technology as implying the development of machines, instruments, or procedures that will displace the teacher. Teachers in philosophy, mathematics, literature, and other disciplines of the liberal arts, accustomed to almost complete reliance on textual materials, oral presentations, and oral or written responses from students, may doubt that other experiences are desirable. A major reason for this reaction is a lack of understanding about what educational technology is and a suspicion that it is merely time-consuming gadgetry introduced to enliven the classroom or to replace it.

Viewed in its broadest sense, educational technology is simply an attempt to apply technological know-how to improve education. Ideally, this effort starts with an analysis of the learning desired, determination of the experiences that are likely to be effective in helping students learn, and development and use of these experiences, followed by an evaluation to determine whether they have indeed been effective. Teaching has, for years, used a more and more extensive educational technology, but the development has been so gradual that most teachers have not been fully aware of it.

Before a spoken language evolved, teaching must have been by demonstration and imitation. At a later point, much of teaching was, and had to be, oral, simply because writing developed much later than speech. History reports that the financial officers of some of the early English kings kept their records by means of notched sticks. Obviously, people had to learn how to use and interpret this rather simple form—technology—of record keeping. Even today, we may use a stick to draw a picture or figure in the sand or soil or on a place mat at lunch to illustrate a point. Marks on clay tablets unearthed in the Near East indicate that they must have been used by students learning how to write in cuneiform. Where baked clay, papyrus, and slates were used in the past, today chalkboards and easels with paper pads are used for writing and for the temporary exhibition of materials to be assimilated by students.

In the days before printing was developed, materials were written out in longhand and laboriously copied (usually with many errors) in order to make them available to others and to preserve them for later generations. And for many years, these copies (a rather primitive educational technology) formed the major source of knowledge for teachers and students. When printing first came into use, it is said that many masters were outraged because their lectures could now be made generally available. This availability constituted a threat to the professorial role of lecturing that had formerly been the only way anyone could get the benefit of the professor's learning. In the present day of sound and visual recording and rapid copying, we have effective means of educating people without having to bring large groups together in a single classroom dominated by a professor. Indeed, as some wit has pointed out, a professor's tape recorder could deliver a lecture to the students' tape recorders, with neither professor nor students present.

But these are by no means the whole of educational technology. The development of spectacles, telescopes, and microscopes effectively extended the vision of man and thereby vastly expanded the range of phenomena to be investigated. And, in turn, these instruments became essential for the educational process. These extensions of vision, conjoined with the camera, the x ray, and, more recently, the making of holographs that incorporate three dimensions, have provided ways of recording expanded vision and enriching the classroom and laboratory learning process as never before possible. Man has long since learned to make sketches, drawings, paintings, and rubbings that preserve the essence of certain visual experiences and permit them to be transferred to others. The development of photography allowed even more accurate reproduction. Black-and-white film permitted the recording of motion, and color film added to this the preservation of the color components of the objects in motion. More recently, videotapes have enabled us to unite sound, color, and motion and to present them to others at different places and times. What we once could experience only by being present at an event or by traveling to the site of a building or picture is now readily transferred (in great part, although not completely) in time and space to enrich the education of students.

For many years, man has engaged in the accumulation of collections of objects, art works, and the like in museums, libraries, parks, art galleries, planetariums, horticultural gardens, zoological gardens, and county, state, and world fairs. The educational experience possible in each of these is, in many respects, far richer than that provided in most schools, but the costs of travel or reproduction and the time thereby consumed have forced many teachers and schools to underuse or to ignore them. Collections of rocks, insects, and animals have also provided at least a visual enrichment beyond pictures in textbooks, but the tendency for these mounted specimens to deteriorate wth time and handling had greatly limited their use in student learning. Although embedding objects in plastic can prevent such deterioration, it makes impossible the tactile experiences that are desirable in some circumstances and for some people.

Models, mock-ups, and diagrams have been effectively used in museums to bring out interrelationships among objects and to present the third dimension clearly. Assembled models of planes, steam engines, and cars—particularly if the parts are movable—provide an experience in understanding these technological developments far beyond what a picture can supply. The military student who has at hand plastic soldiers, horses, guns, and models of all the accouterments of war can lay out and sense strategy and tactics far better than he can with a map with dots and crosses on it. If, further, a model of the terrain is provided, the visual components of learning are expanded to the point where reliance on the verbal is reduced greatly. Graphs, diagrams, maps, and globes also constitute ways of presenting data or aspects of reality so that students may grasp ideas not well understood before. The use of a globe and a light source to represent the sun can enable a child to understand the reason for night and day more easily than can any verbal statement or two-dimensional picture.

In the average school of even twenty years ago, teachers were already surrounded by an extensive technology. The technology that teachers use most readily, if not effectively, is that which they experienced as students. Accordingly, there has been a great reliance on listening as the principal mode of learning, and on reading, writing, and viewing along with it. Other than with exotic foods and drinks, taste has been largely ignored, although people learning to cook find that taste is an admirable check on whether the ingredients have been well chosen and mixed in the right proportions. Taste is sometimes used as a partial means of identifying various substances. Touch is seldom used except in the education of the blind, although the sense of touch is an excellent way of learning something about the texture of cloth, metal, or rocks, or of determining how paint has been applied to obtain certain effects in a picture. Smell is almost totally ignored, although a sensitivity to odors can be useful in cooking, cleaning house, identifying plants, or working in the laboratory. These remarks about the sensory aspects of learning suggest that one of the major purposes of educational technology should be to make known the sensory realities of those substances students confront in the learning process.

Certain forms of educational technology have long been used in education. Indeed, some are employed so widely that they are not recognized as adaptations of technological development to educational use. At present, technological developments provide for a much wider range of educational usage than is apparent in most classrooms. Cost and availability are part of the problem, although the costs of science laboratories have long since been incorporated into educational budgets. Most programs are not flexible enough, and facilities and equipment needed are not yet widely available. Relatively few teachers have as yet experienced as students the fullest educational potential of these developments, and usually they have neither the time nor the opportunity to explore them adequately. Besides, many institutions have neither the appropriate facilities nor the technical assistance sometimes required for the use of such new technology. Tightly scheduled programs and lack of cooperation may forbid the use of off-campus facilities such as museums and art galleries. The failure to use existing technology certainly cannot be blamed on the teachers alone.

Purposes and Uses of Educational Technology

From our observations of the use of available educational technology, we conclude it is still highly underemployed. For example, many history classrooms have an extensive range of excellent maps; yet in some classrooms, the maps are seldom used and then for a very limited purpose, such as locating a city. At the other extreme, there are teachers so enthusiastic about the gadgetry of educational technology that they use it to the point of creating confusion, having not really considered how this technology can best be employed to broaden, deepen, or stimulate learning. Much of computer-assisted instruction turns out to be little more than drill on vocabularies, definitions, principles, and simple problem solving. Many teachers, indeed, have apparently not given careful attention to the effective use of textbooks and library resources. Although many course syllabi contain an extensive list of resources, the list frequently seems appended more to impress fellow teachers than to encourage students or to ensure that they have a planned sequence of encounters with the best writers and researchers in the field.

It is fitting to open a discussion of the purposes and uses of educational technology by identifying the wide range of educational experiences and opportunities it can provide. Quite obviously, the first comprehensive purpose in the use of technology would be to improve and extend learning or understanding. Increasingly, motivation, interest, convenience, and realism of experience are also purposes; and they are meritorious purposes, though they should be subsidiary to the major ones. No matter how well chosen are the words describing a building or the comfort achieved in an automobile by the use of a new spring design, words will never provide the insights that seeing the building or riding in the automobile will readily yield. A textbook picture or a slide of the building cannot provide an equivalent of the experience available through the use of film or videotape in which the movement through or around the building is thoroughly and insightfully commented upon by a person accompanying the cameraman. Film, videotape, computer-assisted instruction, laboratories, work-sample kits, and other educational technologies offer an enormous range of learning experiences well beyond those of the lecture or recitation in a classroom. It is important to understand that this increase in range of experiences, even when available, may only increase the insights and understanding achieved by students about concepts and principles initially presented in textbooks and lectures. The student is provided with a wider range of sensory involvement and a better sampling of materials and experiences but uses them only to master traditional objectives largely limited to acquiring factual knowledge and the simpler skills.

Educational technology can be used to extend the range of educational objectives by bringing into the student's environment much more potent—deeper, richer, more complex, more realistic—experience than could otherwise be had. A Shakespearean play can be read in a classroom over a period of weeks accompanied by lectures by the professor and the reading of various commentaries. If it happens that the play is being presented on television with an excellent cast, watching that broadcast, preceded by some introduction and followed by some discussion, should be a richer experience than simply reading and discussing the play. It is also a more realistic approach in that reading a play is never quite the same as seeing it performed.

Various forms of educational technology also provide the possibility of preserving peak and unique experiences. These would include films or videotapes of the performances of great musicians, of surgeons, or of natural events that are unusually picturesque or cataclysmic. Technology can also make learning much more individualized. Some slides used in the typical classroom situations are exhibited for only a few seconds, others for lengthy intervals. The exhibit time may be more than adequate for some students but grossly inadequate for others; it depends largely on what is said about the slide. Lectures, too, are given in a certain span of time, and people vary in how far they are able to capture the essence of these in notes. Computer-assisted instruction provides the opportunity for individuals to work through various programs repeatedly or to accelerate their learning. Unfortunately, this very flexibility runs into difficulty with professors, registrars, and business officers who schedule lectures and classes and collect fees according to a rigid calendar pattern.

Educational technology has numerous advantages in facilitating and motivating learning. The non-English-speaking person who hears a television commercial in English about the comfort of a new car may have learned nothing from the statement, but after riding in the car for ten minutes (an enactive experience), he will have arrived at a conclusion about its comfort. By direct experience using other senses than hearing, this person will have easily learned how comfortable the car is, although perhaps not why.

Educational technology may also provide learning experiences that are more pleasant and convenient than the traditional lecture, textbook, or classroom discussion. For example, educational television can bring significant learning into the home. Without time-consuming travel, an individual can sit in a comfortable chair on a stormy night and learn as much as in an uncomfortable classroom. Educational technology can also provide learning experiences that are less dangerous than the reality might be. The use of trainer equipment with realistic film for the education of pilots is effective and does not endanger their lives or risk an expensive plane. A film or videotape of a complicated laboratory experiment may give students insights into all aspects of the experiment while avoiding the possibility of accidents or explosions or the waste of materials.

In the case of an elaborate laboratory experiment carried out over several weeks, the use of film also illustrates the possibility of providing superior educational experience at less cost. Film of the experiment can be shown many times in many different classrooms and institutions, and on television to an extended audience. Although expensive, the film, by eliminating space requirements, instructor supervision time, and the costs of raw materials and equipment for all the times and sites at which it might instead be used, may make for a far lower total cost and greater understanding than engaging all students in the actual laboratory experiment.

Some uses of educational technology permit the student to engage in more complicated tasks, and therefore in a larger number of similar tasks, than otherwise possible, with the probability of gaining new insights and competencies. The computer is one example. So long as all computations had to be carried out by hand, the time involvements and the possibility of error in any long sequence effectively forbade asking students to carry out complicated computing tasks. Even so, almost as much time was spent in developing shortcuts as in developing an understanding of the problem itself. For example, in the case of statistics, only a few years ago it took a long time to teach students how to compute by using deviations from some central item rather than the actual numbers in the frequency distribution. With modern computers, even with some of the pocket miniatures, individuals can perform in seconds computations that would have taken many hours. The engineer who for years depended on the slide rule for quick but approximate calculations now gets quicker, easier, and much more accurate results with the hand computer.

In addition, this ease of computation makes it possible for students to engage in a series of computation tasks using many different types of data and distribution. It also permits them to carry out multiple correlations and regressions and a variety of other complex analyses that only a few decades ago could be done only with a great expenditure of effort, time, and money. This technological improvement lets the student engage in a greater variety of analyses and have a more extensive range of contacts with various types of data and the problems of interpreting them.

Computer programs have been developed for use in equipment design courses so that students can, within a very short while, try out a number of different designs to meet certain requirements, and compute various coefficients that characterize the design. Students thereby achieve a sense of the role of various quantities, materials, and variables in developing effective designs. Thus today, the individual can compress into a few weeks or even hours experiences that past designers of equipment have had only over years. Moreover their learning was, in many cases, almost entirely empirical, simply because the complexity of the formulas forbade actual mathematical analyses. But this does pose certain problems in instruction. Just how much basic insight and understanding should be required of students before encouraging them to use devices that provide speedy, accurate results based upon complicated models that may or may not be suited to the task? It could be that students will acquire results without in the least understanding how they are achieved or what the implicit assumptions or consequent limitations may be. This is not new. Few drivers of motor cars have much understanding of how cars work, and few of the technicians using complicated scientific devices fully understand their origins or operations.

It should not be assumed that the major purpose of educational technology or of actual engagement with it is always that of providing a more realistic experience. It is true that the realistic integration of various separately discussed aspects of a complex experience is desirable. Field trips (expedited by cars, buses, or planes) and internships have been introduced into educational programs simply because they do provide an on-site experience in which the various facets of that experience are brought together in a realistic way not possible in a classroom. At other times, however, the purpose of educational technology is to simplify or to differentiate. One may look at a picture with considerable satisfaction and yet not fully sense, until someone points out the major curves and lines that characterize the composition, just why it creates the impression it does. A film depicting various stages in the painting of a picture may be highly effective in generating an understanding of the creative act. Someone seeing a steam engine running may have no notion how the steam engine works until a stripped-down model, a film, or a simplified diagram highlights the essential principles of its operation. A combination of enactive, iconic, and symbolic learning experiences will usually increase motivation, ease the learning task, and improve the quality of learning.

Another aspect of technology is that of simulation—perhaps using a computer. Usually a simulation is an attempt to set up an operating but simplified model of a complex situation or interaction. Market operations and university decision making (as well as many other things) have been simulated. Such complex situations must be simplified by establishing certain assumptions and interacting principles that may not be revealed to those engaging in the simulation. Even an overly simplified simulation may be realistic enough to make for insights and understandings that would not occur from a purely verbal treatment.

Simulation has obvious deficiencies and is distasteful to

some people. In counseling simulations, for example, in which one person assumes the role of a client and the other that of a counselor (possibly videotaped for repeated use), one person plays a role and the other attempts to act in a reasonably realistic way in a situation in which each knows that the other is pretending. Simulation requires a pretense of what is not and, hence, is not far removed from dissimulation or a concealment of what is. So, one must take care in using the process of simulation that its limitations are clear.

The simplification, analysis, and differentiation that are required for simulation are useful and necessary techniques in achieving an understanding of components of a complex situation or operation so long as the distinctions thereby created are treated with caution to avoid generating erroneous conceptions. Thus the distinctions made among drama, novels, biographies, autobiographies, history, and "real" experiences are subtle, unclear, and somewhat artificial, for many people are "acting" in real life. Individuals designated as administrators may simulate the role rather than execute it.

To some extent, the purposes of educational technology can be viewed through the range of experiences that may be provided. One purpose may be to integrate a number of separately identified and discussed stimuli. Thus, on the one hand, we have contiguity of stimuli as a purpose at one time and, on the other, separation or differentiation of stimuli at another. This may involve, in the former case, the development of a rich integrated sensory experience or, in the latter case, the identification and separation of distinct sensory experiences. In other words, we may use educational technology to achieve a greater reality of experience, or we may use it for the purpose of differentiation through simulation that inevitably involves simplification.

To some degree, then, we risk artificiality by using educational technology. But the structure of a college with departments and courses has already imposed upon external realities a certain artificiality that results in the difficulties students find in relating what they learn to their social environment or to their later careers. The artificiality of the college organization keeps the professor from understanding or even caring how what he does is related to the reality external to the campus.

One of the major accomplishments of effective use of educational technology is an increase in the active involvement of the students as against the passive receptivity observable in most classrooms, where the larger part of the activity, both mental and physical, is the professor's. Educational technology, whether used to provide an integrating or differentiating experience, provides for adaptability to the individual learner. Some people may have no difficulty in grasping part of a complex operation but great difficulty in putting it all together; others, intrigued with a complex operation, may not be able to single out the significant components.

In the usual classroom, a very high level of verbalization is employed. The rigidity of that pattern, although presumed to address the average students effectively and therefore not excessively to handicap deviation from the average, may, in fact, not convey full understanding to anyone. Whereas the heavily verbal approach tends to encourage memoriter learning, attended by little understanding and practice other than rote repetition, the effective use of educational technology can give the individual student practice. No one would argue that a prospective physician in training should be limited to observing other physicians operate. It seems perfectly obvious that each physician in training should have an opportunity to deal with human models (a form of educational technology), and then engage in simple manipulations and interactions with patients under close supervision, before taking full responsibility for the patient. Even an extremely limited and conservative conception of what constitutes a liberal education must accept the obligation to move the student from passive receptivity and verbal proficiency to self-initiated thought, valuing, and action.

To the extent that people vary in how easily they learn by various experiences (cognitive styles), the greater the range and variation of experiences provided, the greater the likelihood that a combination will be found that will motivate them. Furthermore, if the experience is provided with a feedback evaluation (as in programmed materials or computer-assisted instruction) that enables the individual to become self-critical about his or her performance, then insight and improvement become directly possible, without constant mediation by the teacher and without the risk of failure or ridicule. By contrast, in the traditional situation, the individual student's verbal response on a test or in class is generally taken as right or wrong and followed by overt or covert praise, sarcasm, or condemnation.

As already noted, educational technology can provide greater convenience in learning. Learning experiences may be carried to where an individual lives and, at times, be more suited to his or her schedule and moods than when everyone studying a particular topic is required to appear at a certain time and place. In fact, the typical approach to scheduling educational episodes is predicated upon the professor's and institution's convenience instead of the student's. In some cases (quite contrary to our too-ready assumptions), we provide a learning experience inferior to what might be readily available to an individual in his or her immediate environment.

At one time, learning in medicine and law was almost entirely a matter of serving an extended internship with a practicing professional. As we have moved to centralizing and closely controlling educational preparation of prospective professionals, we frequently subject them for long periods to the tutelage of professors (basic sciences in medicine, for example) who are not actively involved in the pursuit of the profession. The students must then engage in learning completely separated from the situation in which that learning will be applied. Recalling and using that information at a later date is surely not expedited by this separation. This discussion should not be construed as support for the idea that all learning should take place in practical situations. Rather, it is meant to reinforce our earlier assertion that the major purpose of educational technology is to provide, at a given time, an educational experience that enhances and enriches the learning of the student, and that this learning should be transferable to situations in which the individual will ultimately live and make decisions.

Need for a New Conception of the Teacher's Role

Educational technology has often been looked at as merely a set of aids to be used by teachers. Those taking this point of departure argue that the teacher is the ultimate manager of the classroom, and that every additional item or aid that is brought to the classroom must be determined and introduced according to a plan developed by the teacher. This is a limited and even erroneous view. *Teachers are mediators* between the best products of the human mind and those who cannot be directly in touch with these minds and their products because of barriers of time, distance, language, or incapacity to assimilate the ideas without help.

Teachers who ignore this mediating role and overestimate their potential for significant personal impact may interfere with learning. In fact, teachers who persist in inserting themselves and their views between great minds and great works do both the students and the authors, artists, and writers an injustice, for their intervention denies the possibility of direct communication and, especially, denies the students the opportunity to reach their own individual judgments. The student who sees a Shakespearean play as presented by an excellent cast may acquire from that experience insights that can never be transmitted by a teacher in the classroom. Or, a textbook may be an exposition of a segment of knowledge greatly superior to what the resources of an individual professor can provide. Hence it seems inappropriate to suggest that every aspect of direct student experience with outstanding personalities or their works should be dominated by a teacher, who offers only a second-hand critical scholarship applied to the creativity of others. We fully realize that teachers may add some insights for all students and provide essential guidance and direction for many; this is the mediating role we have emphasized here. Our contention is that, through technological advance, it may be possible to bring to the classroom or the individual's living room a teacher or learning experience superior to what a student typically experiences at school. In talking about technology and the best use of it, we refer to resources used by students in learning, not solely to aids used by teachers. And, in some cases, the best learning may be achieved through self-teaching that uses media offerings not generally available on a campus.

This possibility leads to the need for developing an evaluation system whereby the educational accomplishments of individuals can be recognized apart from the deficiencies, rigidities, and biases of individual departments and disciplines. In fact, it is entirely likely that enrichment of the learning experience of students by the fullest use of educational technology would force professors to engage in an expansion of their own learning and thus improve not only the quality of their teaching but also of their own insights and understandings of the discipline. Scholars tend to view their fields of specialization from a limited perspective and thus may have serious deficiencies in presentation of these materials to students. For example, one of the marked limitations of many professors of mathematics is that they know little about how the mathematical procedures or principles they present are used in other disciplines or in our current technology. The professors may avoid rather than welcome the use of materials that would reduce their deficiency. And, because of this, they cannot approach the teaching of their discipline in a way that either motivates or expedites student learning or expands students' capabilities of operating in other fields.

Educational technology is often thought of only as hardware, though what is, in fact, basically important is the software—that is, the materials and the procedures that determine the way the hardware is used and the ends to which it is directed. For many years, the undergraduate science laboratory (especially in the introductory courses) has been much criticized as being expensive and time consuming and as emphasizing manipulatory operations that yield little insight into the essential nature of science. This is a clear example of the commitment to hardware rather than the well-planned utilization of it to achieve understanding of the fundamental nature of scientific modes of thought. The use of textbooks as a backdrop for lectures is another example of misused hardware. Slide projectors, overhead projectors, and language laboratories have also been misused in this way. Teachers become enthusiastic about the availability of hardware without having thought through how it might best be used.

A teacher who is well grounded in the topics covered in a particular course may view the further range of learning experiences provided by educational technology as distracting and irrelevant. This narrow reaction may result from either of two circumstances. The professor who has been teaching Shakespeare's plays for some years may be uninterested in a performance predicated upon a different interpretation from his own. Another professor may be so well versed in the writings in her field that novel sensory experiences add nothing to what is already incorporated in personal associations and presentations. A teacher of drama may not realize that a purely verbal approach, however excellent, does not invoke the sensory experiences that result when a student both sees and hears a play and when the roles of the actors are reinforced by their motions, by their dress, and by the staging and scenery. In brief, a teacher who has preferred ways of approaching topics and knowledge may not be able to judge the effect of a variety of different experiences on the relatively naive student. Teachers may learn much more about computer-assisted instruction, programmed learning, or some other variety of technological presentation if their initial experiences with it are directed to a field not previously studied or to one that caused difficulty earlier. The potential of a particular experience for learning may be far better realized if that experience is in a field in which the individual is naive rather than proficient.

It is not unreasonable to expect that every teacher preparing to instruct in schools at any level have an awareness of a full range of learning experiences that can be provided to students, and some personal experience with at least a number of these in a classroom, either as a student or as a teacher. It is not enough to have read or heard a lecture on computer-assisted or individually programmed instruction. The prospective teacher should have been in a situation in which this was effectively used and, hence, had an opportunity individually to experience the impact of that approach as well as to assess its impact upon students. Basically, this requires the teacher to become acquainted with the available technological apparatus of teaching useful in motivating and facilitating student learning. This competency in use of methods and materials is not the same as competency in the discipline, although certainly the two are related and may reinforce each other. The effective use of learning materials is an essential accomplishment of the teacher. To deny this is, in effect, to assert that teaching is not a professional act and that it is only the delivery in perfect form of the knowledge to be acquired by students. The fact that this approach works with some students (and many teachers were once in that group) does not abolish the teacher's responsibility to attempt to reach all students.

So long as educational technology is housed in separate units in a college or university so that special effort and extra cost have to be expended to bring it into the instructional program of a department, it is unlikely that the prospective teacher will come to know, as student or neophyte teacher, the full range of teaching and learning experiences, or to recognize them as an essential component of instructional obligations. It took several centuries for printing to be fully used for educational purposes. It may require a few more years for teachers to take full advantage of modern technology.

Achieving Independence in Learning

The central purpose of education is to foster the development of an individual as a human being with an independent capability of making judgments and sustaining learning. Our educational system, at all levels, is weak in promoting this independence. Teachers, courses, schools, textbooks, and rigid schedules are regarded as essential to learning rather than as ways of encouraging it. Teachers look upon themselves and teaching as central to student learning rather than as mediating between learners and the materials and experiences that promote learning. The learner should develop facility in locating and using these materials without continuing intervention by teachers and without having to attend scheduled classes. However, much of the emphasis upon lifelong, continuing, and recurrent education indicates that we have cultivated a dependence on courses and class attendance. Like parents, teachers find it hard to foster or accept independence. Many students do not acquire the ability to read textbooks on their own (especially in mathematics and the sciences) because they have come to depend on clarification, simplification, and underlining of main points by the lecturer.

As we have seen, educational technology can greatly extend and enrich educational objectives by providing realistic experiences not otherwise readily available. But educational technology can be little more than drill on lower-level cognitive objectives that are largely aimed at *acquiring* knowledge. Overemphasis on textbooks, computer-assisted instruction, or any other highly structured approach to learning can also result in a dependence that hinders rather than forwards intellectual development. There is unlikely to be anyone available to write a computer-assisted learning program for everything the individual needs to learn *after* completing a degree. In contrast to some of the more expensive technological equipment, a programmable miniature computer, like a slide rule, can become a permanent part of the analytical and decision-making equipment of the individual. But even these tools can be deleterious if the individual has only learned to use them to make complex analyses without understanding the conditions under which the analyses are appropriate and the limitations that apply to interpreting the results.

Formal schooling, and much of the array of technology used in the process, is in something of the same category as the canes and crutches used by those with injuries or the furniture and adult fingers used by the baby just learning to walk. They serve their purpose best when they are looked at as temporary expedients that help the individual attain or maintain independence and self-direction. However, the use of educational technology to extend the range and increase the depth of learning has different implications. It is more analogous to an individual's progress—as when one who has been limited to walking or running moves on to the use of a bicycle, car, or airplane, enabling him to see more in less time and attain a new, broader, and relational perspective. This latter use of educational technology promises to improve the quality of education because it also introduces the individual to a pattern of learning that involves a richer array of sensory experiences, a greater sense of reality, and an awareness that purely verbal learning is not enough.

Suggestions for Further Reading

Briggs, L. J. *Handbook of Procedures for the Design of Instruction.* Monograph No. 4. Pittsburgh: American Institutes for Research, 1970.

Brown, J. W., Lewis, R. B., and Harcleroad, F. F. *Audiovisual Instruction: Media and Methods.* New York: McGraw-Hill, 1969.

Carnegie Commission on Higher Education. *The Fourth Revolution: Instructional Technology in Higher Education.* New York: McGraw-Hill, 1972.

Gibbs, G. I. *Handbook of Games and Simulation Exercises.* London: Spon, 1974.

Gropper, G. L., and Glasgow, Z. *Criteria for the Selection and Use of Visuals in Instruction: A Workbook.* Englewood Cliffs, N.J.: Educational Technology Publications, 1971.

Postlethwait, S. M., Novak, J., and Murray, H. T., Jr. *The Audio-Tutorial Approach to Learning.* Minneapolis: Burgess, 1970.

Skinner, B. F. *The Technology of Teaching.* New York: Meredith, 1968.

Spencer, R. E. *The Role of Measurement and Evaluation in Instructional Technology.* Urbana: University of Illinois, 1968.

Taylor, J. T., and Walford, R. *Simulation in the Classroom.* Harmondsworth, England: Penguin Books, 1972.

Wittich, W. A., and Schuller, C. F. *Instructional Technology, Its Nature and Use.* (5th ed.) New York: Harper & Row, 1973.

Zuckerman, D. W., and Horn, R. F. *The Guide to Simulation for Education and Training.* (2nd ed.) New York: Western, 1973.

5

Rethinking the Role of the Disciplines

Disciplines and the departments in which they are embedded have largely dominated college curriculum development and teaching. A serious problem of this domination lies in the limited understanding by teachers of the disciplines and of their role as humanizing influences. An understanding of the nature of the disciplines and of their relationship to education, life, and work is essential to contextual teaching. The teacher in any discipline or course should be able to direct learners to sources and experiences that help them comprehend the role of the discipline or course in the collective store of human knowledge. This chapter considers the discipline as a means of collecting, organizing, and using knowledge, and identifies distinctive characteristics of the several disciplines.

A discipline can be viewed in many different ways: a field of study, a mode of inquiry, an organized body of knowledge, an interrelated set of interests and value commitments, or a set of objects or phenomena that humans have tried to explain. Since a discipline is an artifact of man's thinking and has no existence or significance otherwise, it may also be thought of as a group of individuals sharing common concerns and interests in attempting to understand mankind, its world, its origins, its failures and successes, and its future.

Disciplines have generally arisen out of attention to aspects of the real world or of humans and their interactions with that world. These aspects and interactions constitute the original subject matter of the discipline. To move from the highly subjective observations of reality to a depth of objectivity and understanding, a set of concepts, interrelations, and operations is identified and defined. These definitions lead to a theoretical construct having many points in common with the reality that generated it. Once this structure is determined, a discipline may be developed with limited attention to that part of reality and its components that generated the discipline. But if the structure is reasonably well modeled after the nature of reality, the development of the discipline may suggest new concepts and principles useful in understanding the generating reality. The use of mathematical models in the natural and social sciences illustrates that process.

Figure 1 suggests (in part, by its symmetric character) the transfer through definitions, assumptions, concepts, and operations from identification of phenomena in the real world to a set of abstract concepts and ideas. These concepts and ideas can be manipulated in various ways to yield insights, propositions, and theories that may have relevance in understanding, predicting, and controlling events in the real world. *A discipline represents a systematic way of organizing and studying real phenomena by the use of abstractions.* As such, it has several identifiable components or structures. As Figure 1 indicates, this process involves the assimilation (learning process) by the learner of organized knowledge (learning). The really independent learner may learn to create learning as well as assimilate it.

Disciplinary Structures

In recent years, many writers have discussed the structure of a discipline as a basis for planning the curriculum. Phenix (1964) has made a strong case for such emphasis; King and

Figure 1. Conceptual Systems and Reality.

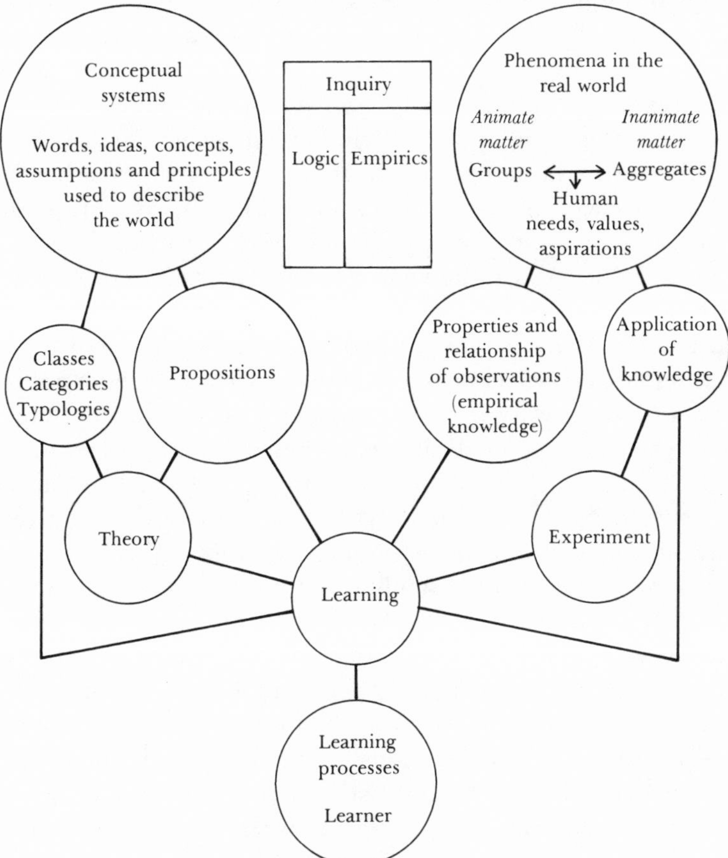

Brownell (1966) have also made a plea for considering the structures of the disciplines. Attractive as are these discussions, there are inevitably some difficulties with them. Primary is the fact that it is not altogether clear what a discipline is, and there are numerous indications that there is no agreement among members of the academic profession about what constitutes a discipline or what the specific disciplines are. To a considerable extent, scholarly specialization of interest, narrowness of focus, and idiosyncratic approaches to study and research have invalidated the concept of discipline for many scholars, and have limited teachers' understanding of the role of the discipline in education. Nevertheless, the concept is strongly evident in academic organizations, degree-program specifications, and statements of general or liberal education requirements. Particular difficulties attend the description and listing of those practical or applied courses that utilize materials from several disciplines.

Among the various disciplines of science, social science, mathematics, literature, art, history, and numerous other fields of knowledge, there is great variation in the nature of the problems attacked and the approaches used. Mathematics and the physical sciences can be viewed as highly structured. As soon as life is included in the domain of concern, the disciplinary structure becomes more complicated. Thus the structure of the various biological sciences is certainly less clear than that of the physical sciences. Whereas atoms are indistinguishable, life and love exist in people, all different. Few people are disturbed by eating chicken, but killing and eating a pet chicken can be a deep emotional experience. When specific attention is given to the human mind, as in psychology, further difficulties arise in deciding whether the discipline is a natural or a social science. On the decision hinges numerous other decisions with regard to the specific purposes of activities, the methods used, and the results desired. Art, dance, music, and literature, the esthetic areas, attend strongly to individual creative acts, and much of both creation and of reactions to it is nonverbal. The introduction of symbols, whether linguistic, mathematical, or ideographic, can raise something of a barrier between the esthetic ends that are the essence of these disciplines and the communication and understanding of these ends.

Self-understanding and effectiveness in human interactions are certainly affected by education, but in ways neither well understood nor fully programmable. Promotion of such changes is probably well beyond the formal obligations of colleges and universities and their faculties. Morals and ethics pose similar problems since, in a democratic society, individuals have the opportunity to choose a personal stance in such matters. The educated have a particular responsibility here as their level of understanding enables them to make judgments and influence others. History and philosophy are part of all knowledge and of each discipline. Thus, in a sense, they are both results of and contributory to understanding of the sciences, the social sciences, and the arts. Religion seeks to understand the here and now by recourse to the beyond.

Despite the great variation among the disciplines, there are certain commonalities operating in each that are worthy of identification and discussion. They are not only suggestive in organizing a curriculum but also provide teachers with ideas for engaging students in learning significant materials from these fields. We shall return to this discussion after identifying the components of disciplinary structure that make it possible to describe the various disciplines more fully.

Components of Disciplinary Structure

Structure may be an unfortunate word to use in describing the nature of a discipline in that the term suggests a rigidity that is not there. In fact, there are five different types of components present, to various degrees, in all disciplinary structures, as will be seen in the following discussion and in Table 3.

Table 3. Components of Disciplinary Structure.

1. Substantive, perceptual, and conceptual component.
   - 1.1 variables, problems, entities, and phenomena of interest (subject matter)
   - 1.2 assumptions, axioms, postulates specifying, describing, and, perhaps, limiting area of concern
   - 1.3 limitations, boundaries, restrictions that may be intrinsic and natural to the objects or problems of concern or extrinsic and artificial, imposed by the disciplinarians, by peers and preference or scholarly convenience
   - 1.4 basic or fundamental concepts (or constructs) and principles (relations between concepts)
   - 1.5 perceived processes, transformations, comparisons, relations, and interactions of interest
   - 1.6 body of previously acquired and organized knowledge (facts, concepts, principles, rules, theories, laws)
2. Linguistic, mathematical, nondiscursive symbols, and technical language component.
   - 2.1 an imposition on reality to facilitate mental manipulation, a limitation of attention in one sense and a source of ambiguity in another because the symbol is only a stand-in for the thing or the mental image

(continued on next page)

Table 3. Components of Disciplinary Structure, Cont'd.

- 2.2 modes of representation (language, mathematics, nondiscursive forms)
- 2.3 new specialized or unique symbols or assignment of specialized or unique meaning to existing symbols
- 2.4 part of the search for and identification of key ideas, concepts, or processes leading to further exploration of possible relations and explanations

3. Syntactical or organizing component.
   - 3.1 principles, procedures, and skills including:
     - definition of the field of inquiry
     - assumptions or limitations involved in defining mode of inquiry (see 1.3)
     - styles of human intellectual performance
     - relationship of inquiry procedure to perceived or hypothesized real relationships
   - 3.2 mode of inquiry (involving such thought processes as analysis, synthesis, evaluation, deduction, induction):
     - observation and criteria for collection of observations
     - data collection and organization
     - posing and testing assertions or hypotheses
     - relating assertions to broader generalities, theories, and explanatory schemes
   - 3.3 dependence of evidence on means of collecting and interpreting it (carbon dating, radio telescope, laser beam)
   - 3.4 reliability of evidence (precision, consistency, accuracy) increased by collecting more data of same type and under same conditions
   - 3.5 validity of evidence or explanatory hypothesis or theory (relevance, power, utility) increased by improving reliability, by clarifying definitions, or by shifting focus to other factors
4. Value component.
   - 4.1 individuals viewed as ends or as means (highly developed animal or special creation)
   - 4.2 truth (knowledge), beauty (form, function, matter, or combination thereof), justice (universal, sectarian, or personal)
   - 4.3 utility, practicality (action vs. contemplation)
   - 4.4 ethics, morals (absolutes, relative absolutes, or problem solution)
   - 4.5 esthetics (fun, challenge, satisfaction, pleasure, romance, elegance, coherence, profundity)
5. Conjunctive component (relation to other disciplines).
   - 5.1 emerging out of the preceding four
   - 5.2 substantive (assumptions, concepts, and objects of attention)
   - 5.3 symbolic (distinctive meanings of common words and symbols)
   - 5.4 syntactical (similarities and differences in methodologies and in type of knowledge sought)
   - 5.5 having values (common and contrasting)

Substantive Component. The substantive or conceptual component suggests how a discipline looks when we consider just what it is that the discipline relates to—its subject matter or problems. Physics, for example, deals with time, mass, and motion and with their interrelationships. Viewing matter or masses at rest or in motion over time, we may see various processes going on, select those that are of interest, and ignore others. In other words, the decision about the substantive and conceptual structure of a discipline may be focused as much upon specifying what the subject matter of the discipline is *not* as what it *is.*

Linguistic Component. As we define the phenomena of interest, we must develop a symbolism whereby particular elements can be identified and relationships defined and explored. This is partly definition, partly simple labeling, but, in general, it is a move from the real world to a set of abstractions that can be manipulated entirely in the mind or on paper by direction from the mind. These symbols are an imposition on reality. They are a limitation in the sense that they represent an attempt to extract those elements of the reality that are the focus of attention, while ignoring others. The symbols constitute an ambiguity, in another sense, since words and even nondiscursive symbols often take on implications or suggest meanings that go beyond what is intended. The sign used for multiplication, for example, is used to indicate numerous operations or relationships, including some that are far different from the use in arithmetic to which most people are accustomed.

Words and conjunctions of words also may suggest meanings and confuse the thought process because, unwittingly, meanings change in the process of thinking. This is why specialized and unique symbols with no other associations are often introduced. In mathematics and the sciences especially, but also in other disciplines, the assignment of unique meanings to already existing symbols is possible and, in some cases, highly desirable as suggesting parallelism in relationship across disciplines. The assignment may also be confusing and, hence this process of attaching symbols should be regarded as part of the search for and the identification of entities or ideas of significance. The search may lead to further exploration of possible relations and explanations. The language or symbolic structural component of a discipline facilitates thought, and it also directs it. Hence the definition and imposition of the symbolic component, followed by operation with it, must be a continuing concern in that the symbols or words may in themselves be confusing, or the particular phenomena of study may have been unwisely chosen.

Syntactical Component. The syntactical component is a set of search and organizing processes around which the discipline develops. It might be described as the grammar of the discipline. In a sense, the syntactical component is more fundamental than either the substantive or the symbolic components in that, once the syntactical processes of a discipline are reasonably clear, they may be applied to a set of problems different from those that generated the discipline. The words, mathematical expressions, and symbols selected are also subject to replacement or alteration for convenience or uniformity. Not infrequently, different scholars dealing with the same idea have used differing symbolic systems.

The syntactical component is concerned with disciplinary principles, procedures, and skills, and with the assumptions or limitations that define a field and mode of inquiry. This set of principles, procedures, and skills, along with its assumptions or limitations, may describe various methods or styles of human mental performance that continue to be employed because they have been found useful. They may lead to new modes of analysis. Technology (especially the computer) plays a significant role in these developments. However, the effectiveness of methods rests in their creative use by individuals. The practical success of any inquiry also depends on how well the variables and procedures are related to perceived or hypothesized real relationships. Flexibility and creativity are important in developing and using methods—or modes of inquiry.

A mode of inquiry is an essential element of a discipline, but the appropriate words for describing that inquiry vary with the discipline. The process includes collecting and organizing data, asserting and testing hypotheses, and relating these to broader generalities. Yet an artist painting a picture might find such a process more significant if it dealt with selecting various colors of paints and placing these on a canvas in some organized way to achieve a composite picture expressing the artist's intent and meaning. The way in which data are collected and interpreted depends upon the means available. The nature of the evidence collected and the procedures applied depend upon the technology used.

The concepts of reliability and validity are significant, although not always associated with the steps involved in moving from data or an idea to a conclusion or communication. If the data already available seem to be appropriate, the focus may be on increasing the amount of data—that is, collecting more of the same type in order to verify its consistency and achieve increased precision and accuracy. If, however, it appears that the definitions and hypotheses employed thus far are unproductive, there may be a shift in emphasis by changing the definitions or the variables or by introducing other concepts. In this case, validity, relevance, power, and utility redirect the focus of further data collection either toward increasing the reliability by more careful definition of the variables, or toward shifting to different hypotheses and sets of concepts.

These concepts of reliability and validity apply in all disciplines. The historian seeking to explain a particular period may find that the evidence sought is not available in sufficient quantity or is so inaccurate that he or she has to reconsider and redefine what is appropriate evidence. Conversely, early investigation may suggest or force abandonment of the initial hypothesis. One point is clear—in writing history, explanatory hypotheses do not automatically emerge out of collecting masses of evidence. In literature, the writer presumably desires to express and communicate something to himself and to others. Initially, the idea or emotion may not be entirely clear; but through writing, revision, and the use of personal and friendly reviews, the literary product goes through a number of modifications, striving toward reliability and validity. If the general form chosen seems appropriate, modifications in sentence structure and more careful selection of words may increase the reliability of the communication. But it may be that the entire approach, medium, or form used has to be rejected in the interest of achieving a valid statement.

Validity or reliability in the sciences may be, and usually is, entirely different from what it is in the esthetic disciplines. The scientist attempts to carry out an investigation in which the results are both reliable and valid, that is, where measurements prove to be stable and consistent and where the measures correspond to the characteristics under study. He also has the task of communicating these results to other scientists and to interested nonscientists. This poses a problem of reliability and validity in the choice and organization of symbols. In contrast, artists and writers are creating something and, besides the task of clarifying the specific nature of their own thoughts, they face the problem of how to express them to others. But part of the problem may be that the exact nature of the idea, concept, or value that the individual seeks to encapsulate in a form that can be enjoyed by others is the communication of ambiguity (accidental, irresolvable, or intentional) in the creator's mind. Part of the creative task may be personally to sense richness and depth of meaning, and to highlight confusions and conflicts in various interpretations of that meaning. The scientist attempts to communicate accurately a new finding with a high degree of certainty. In the esthetic realm, artists, writers, and musicians are perhaps more likely to be communicating uncertainties or arousing them.

However, for the human being, the projection, arousal, or clarification of uncertainty is an essential part of living. The disciplines of history, philosophy, and religion move beyond the coverage of presumed factual material to seek clarification and resolution of these uncertainties, although the effort may actually move them to a deeper or more complex, and yet still unresolved level. Indeed, it is the uncertainties of life that make people human and provide the opportunity for them to be individuals as well as members of the human race. Much of the gain in the search for knowledge over the centuries has been a gain in the reliability of our collection and exposition of knowledge. The increase in validity is less certain since the essential nature of matter is still unknown, as are the nature, source, and meaning of life. Knowledge and insight that pertain especially to understanding human beings suffer further with the continual change in the nature and primacy of values.

Value Component. Every discipline includes, implicitly or explicitly, some value commitments about what is worth studying and how it should be studied. These values change with changes in the real world. One such change is in the views held about individuals. Authoritarians, both in the past and present, seeking to impose personal goals or conceptions of a good society, may be convinced that the nation or particular cause itself is more important than individuals. Thus they regard individuals as means rather than ends. Some scientists view man as merely a highly developed animal and, hence, regard education as only a modified form of the training or conditioning that has been found to work with animals. In contrast, there are those who, through deep immersion in the works of mankind or conviction about the existence of a primal creative force, conclude that mankind is unique in having not only a high level of ability to think but also a sense of values and ability to make choices in reference to them. In this view, there can still be a unity of body and mind; but the religionists may prefer the duality implied in assuming that human beings have a soul.

From such fundamental differences as these emerge rather different views about basic knowledge. Truth, beauty, and justice, perhaps, represent the major values to which mankind has directed its attention. The university represents the social agency primarily designed to advance knowledge. In the present day, most educators believe that this advance of knowledge has to do with human existence in a finite universe, but there are those who believe that truth is ultimately a revelation from a transfinite source. Indeed, one can view the process of education in this finite existence as a process of revelation, with those who believe and act appropriately graduating into life eternal.

Those who emphasize the limitations of knowledge in a finite world also recognize that that world is far more complicated than traditionally regarded, and that the continuing search for truth rather than the actual acquisition of ultimate truth is the challenge. Ultimate truth, and the absolute certainty that might well be its corollary, would reduce life to a boring existence. Beauty and justice pose similar problems to that of truth. Does an object, an idea, or individual have beauty evident to all? In short, are there universal criteria, or is beauty indeed in the eye and mind of the beholder—a purely personal judgment? If everything were beautiful to everyone, where then would beauty be? Can justice be described in a set of universal conditions, or is justice to be dependent upon the actions of individuals? And, if the latter, who then makes the decisions about how justice varies in relation to behavior, intent, and admission of ineptitude?

Proponents of liberal education are prone to argue that an educational experience is significant in itself, and that it is destroyed by any demand or even expectation that it be immediately relevant to life or earning a living. Works of art, literature, or music are to be enjoyed for themselves. But if we regard a fundamental need of mankind as some sense of satisfaction and pleasure, then some purpose has already invaded liberal education or the arts. If, as is quite obvious, education is no longer directed solely to those who can live a life of leisure and contemplation, then utility and practicality become socially relevant. Even those who have urged this life of leisure as the ideal have been concerned about some responsible involvement in human affairs (Plato's "philosopher kings," for example).

All too much emphasis has been given to learning for its own sake, thereby encouraging educational institutions and their faculties to pass on finely ground tidbits of knowledge without concern whether these are understood by or are relevant to insights of the student. Perhaps this view of knowledge for its own sake has, more than any view, contributed to a concept of education in which the ideal is for the greatest authorities in any field to pass on to others that knowledge, without adequate attention to the ultimate purposes or objectives served by this diffusion. Authority tends to impose upon individuals what authority believes is appropriate, even in educational matters. If utility and practicality, as well as meaning and significance, are of importance, then the whole nature of the learning enterprise and its purposes requires rethinking, and not solely by those directly involved in it.

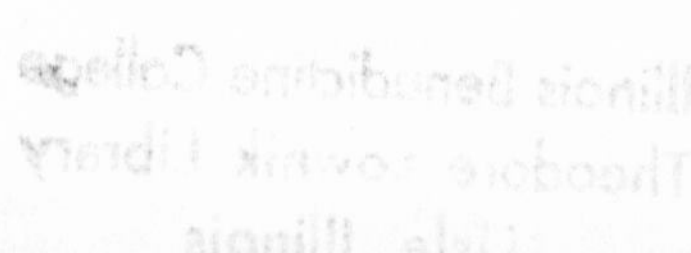

Another major area of values is embraced in the concepts of ethics and morals. Here again, the issues of absolute versus relative, individual versus society, or common man versus authority become prominent. Efforts to provide statements of ethics in the professions have often gone awry, since it is easier, after the fact, to determine whether a particular decision was unwise, inappropriate, or detrimental than at the particular moment a decision was made.

It also becomes a matter of considerable complexity to decide whether a judgment about morals or ethical behavior should be made on the basis of results or on some absolute basis. A moral judgment is relatively simple if, for example, we accept an absolute commandment barring sexual relationships between unmarried individuals. There are still those who hold such a view but, in our society, this rigid proscription generally no longer holds. It is still considered unethical for a professional person to have sexual intercourse with a client. If a psychiatrist, simply for pleasure, seduces a client, presumably there is a violation of ethics and, in the view of some, a violation of morality or law. If the psychiatrist has sexual intercourse with a client, having a well-considered and justified professional belief that in this case it is necessary or, at least, a promising step in the recovery of that patient, the decision about whether there has been a violation of professional ethics becomes more complex. If indeed the treatment works and the client fully recovers and testifies to the sexual experience as an essential stage of the recovery, blame is even harder to establish. If that therapy fails and the individual gets worse, do we say the psychiatrist is guilty because of the act itself or because of the failure of the treatment? And, as a final complication, if the treatment resulted in the psychiatrist and the client getting married, living happily ever after, and having a flock of well-behaved and successful children, very few people would find cause to reprove or punish the psychiatrist.

The esthetic realm involves satisfaction or pleasure induced by the qualities or results of contact with an object or person, interaction with others, or feelings induced by personal behavior. The words *fun, challenge, romance, elegance, coherence* also suggest feelings or reactions that constitute esthetics.

The learning process should encourage learners to seek for and have esthetic reactions through experiences that are not only within the domain of the esthetic. A surveyor using a transit to determine the exact location of a lot line in connection with a dispute between neighbors has a distinct esthetic reaction when the iron that he drives into the ground hits smack in the middle of the earlier survey stake placed years before. In some part, that reaction is simply from the coincidence, but it is also a reaction based upon the reinforcement and verification of the accuracy of his measurement. Much of the satisfaction of teaching lies in finding a way to impart effectively to students not just the words or substance but some depth of insight and gratification.

In brief, in every task well done there is, or should be, a deep esthetic reaction. An educational experience that does not help the learner develop this feeling is deficient, for significant learning is in itself an esthetic experience. Furthermore, all disciplines are strivings to establish order and understanding, and these two concepts are themselves values of high significance, particularly when further explicated by taste, style, simplicity, appropriateness, and universality.

Conjunctive Component (Relation to Other Disciplines). The conjunctive structure of a discipline is the way in which it is related to other disciplines. One very clear common element is a complementary one—the totality of disciplines represents the various ways in which the human mind has sought to explain the world and mankind's involvement in it. Disciplines are artifacts of human efforts at understanding and grasping meaning. Their artifactual nature becomes amply clear when one reviews over a span of years the way knowledge has been organized and notes, especially, the increase in the number of disciplines. On the one hand, in order to treat concepts and problems requiring concentrated and detailed attention, the disciplines have proliferated through the creation of new disciplines out of subfields of old ones. On the other hand, as disciplines have linked themselves to particular problems in the physical and biological world, these new relationships have become less well known and understood by those not working in the discipline. Human behavior has become a focus of concern in many disciplines with no one discipline capable of dealing fully or adequately with it. Thus many interdisciplinary educational programs and courses have arisen, but these have difficulty integrating essential knowledge from the number of disciplines required to understand and resolve particular social problems.

Other Relationships Among Disciplines

No teacher can fully understand or apply a discipline without some grasp of the five components (substantive, linguistic, syntactical, value, and conjunctive) that are embedded in each discipline and markedly influence its nature and further development. And awareness of the relationship of these disciplinary components to the context of teaching permits the teacher to locate his or her subject matter for the student within the curriculum, the disciplines, and the larger body of human knowledge.

The disciplines vary, however, in the extent to which these five structural components are present and rigorously utilized, and scholars within a discipline may differ in their views. The introduction of quantitative methods (mathematics, statistics, computer science) into a discipline can almost completely change the character of its subject matter, syntax, language, and values. By elaboration of these structural elements (and perhaps others), it might be possible to define a discipline rigorously, but it is uncertain that this would be a significant accomplishment. Is mathematics a discipline? Few would deny it, although it is also a tool useful in many other disciplines. Is history a discipline? If not, what is it? Is journalism a discipline or a profession? What can be said of engineering, law, medicine? At what point does a subfield of a discipline (biochemistry, for example) become a discipline? Is this achieved by the accumulation of knowledge, by new conceptions, by special methodologies, or by sheer numbers of people involved? Obviously, these are issues of some interest, but attempts to provide widely acceptable answers, other than pragmatic ones in particular circumstances, are not likely because of existing differences in the conception and practice of the disciplines.

Nevertheless, it is useful, especially to contextual teaching, to be aware of some of the associations made among disciplines. Thus the disciplines have been variously categorized by their major contributions to the development and expansion of human capability. These contributions are suggested by the following groupings:

- communication skills: language, literature, art, music, drama, logic, mathematics, statistics
- accurate inquiry: natural sciences, social sciences, mathematics, statistics
- valid reasoning: logic, science, mathematics, statistics
- synoptic understanding: history, philosophy, theology, metaphysics
- sensitivity to human values: art, music, literature, language
- wisdom in evaluation: ethics, esthetics, literature

Implicit in these groupings are judgments of the extent to which individual disciplines involve the characteristics or abilities named at the beginning of each item. These, in turn, are obviously interrelated with the five structural components of disciplines specified earlier. Note that these groupings differ significantly, and with good reason, from the curriculum distribution categories commonly listed as science and mathematics, humanities, social sciences, and fine arts.

Another conception of the disciplines emerges from their historical development and the insights into the intellectual and affective capabilities and sensitivities of the human mind that this development provides. It becomes clear that disciplines grew out of the efforts of human beings to understand themselves, the world about them, and the origin, role, and ultimate destiny of mankind. Thus the disciplines may all have been intensely practical in their initial stages—their structure and their modes of inquiry intertwined with the objects, phenomena, problems, and realities that people were trying to understand or to explain. As the disciplines have become more complex and esoteric in concepts, inquiry, modes, and use of abstractions, their relationships with specific objects, phenomena, problems, and actual behaviors have become less apparent. These connections between the abstract disciplines and complex realities have become unclear both to the practitioners of the disciplines and to the public that supports disciplinary study and research in the hope that they will achieve some progress toward human and social perfection.

Every discipline has a subject matter (a group of interrelated problems, ideas, and phenomena) of which some facets can be analyzed and better understood by use of the concepts and modes of inquiry of that discipline. It is likely that other disciplines might be equally applicable to the subject, although possibly directed to other components of the phenomenon. The fact that is so essential for teachers to grasp is that as disciplines have been better defined, their purview has been so narrowed that "real" problems of people and society can seldom be understood or resolved by recourse to a single discipline. Since study in depth of a number of disciplines is time consuming, courses drawing upon two or more disciplines have become popular. These courses, for reasons none too clearly defined and consistent, have variously been labeled interdisciplinary, intradisciplinary, transdisciplinary, and supradisciplinary.

A course developed to explore the broader meaning and significance of concepts, principles, or research techniques common to several disciplines is interdisciplinary and is useful in pursuing the study of a discipline as a mode of inquiry. Courses that deal with an identifiable subset of topics or ideas within a discipline chosen because of relevance to some subject matter of concern might, by analogy, be regarded as intradisciplinary, although that term is seldom used. Courses developed to examine a problem drawing upon many disciplines may well be described as transdisciplinary. Courses dealing with concepts, such as truth and beauty, that have some significance in all disciplines can be labeled as supradisciplinary (above the disciplines).

Courses that cross or ignore disciplinary fences may arise out of specific problems (minorities, regions), particular themes, or conjunctions of materials, concepts, and ideas regarded as interrelated and, therefore, justifying a course in which these interconnections can be studied. By this pattern of thought, black studies, area studies, women's studies, urban studies, and others have come into being. Separated from the disciplines that provide a measure of rigor and objectivity, and dealing with issues of great complexity and emotional involvement, such courses always run the risk of superficiality in coverage, limited requirements, and low standards. Whereas interdisciplinary core programs have often contained an excess of factual knowledge, this second approach to courses that draws on several disciplines has often been focused more on emotion and affect. Identification of a problem and a catchy course title does not ensure a substantive educational experience. In avoiding the courses, students often seem to have been wiser than the faculty and administrators who rushed to approve them. Nevertheless, courses that transcend traditional disciplinary boundaries are essential in that their existence arises out of a recognition that formal disciplines are complexly related to societal realities.

The fatal defect of the single disciplinary approach to phenomena is that the disparate facts and principles accumulated through the independent application of several disciplines to a problem or phenomenon cannot easily be conjoined into a coherent picture of the totality. This is particularly true as we move into the study of biological organisms and of the social groups they form. Thus with the expansion of the behavioral sciences in the use of scientific methods to study mankind and society, the interdisciplinary mode has become essential. Some of the initial interdisciplinary attempts in the colleges were to be seen in the broad-gauge general education courses, or what are now more commonly called core courses and core course programs. The trouble is that deciding to offer an interdisciplinary course is far easier than developing and maintaining one. There are numerous ways of cutting across disciplines. One way is to focus on a concrete physical object. For example, a diamond may be examined in terms of its beauty, its molecular structure, the problem of diamond cutting, the physical principles of light reflection, the business of producing diamonds and controlling the oversupply, or the reasons diamonds and other jewels have come to be valued so highly. The diamond conjures up all these issues. Each, to a considerable extent, could be studied separately, but the last question raised is one that could be answered only by some consideration of all of the preceding issues, and then only if those issues had been examined in the context of the broader question.

A second approach to an interdisciplinary perspective is through the concepts and methodologies used in a number of different disciplines. Thus a statistician might become interdisciplinary simply by pursuing the various uses and implications of statistics across all disciplines. Undoubtedly, in this process, the statistician would arrive at some generalizations about how probability operates in similar or contrasting ways with varying kinds of materials and phenomena. In some cases, interdisciplinary means nothing more than dealing with certain problems that cut across two disciplines. The long-existent course title of physical chemistry and the more recent one of chemical physics suggest this emphasis. Social psychology and psychology of social groups—the first offered in sociology departments, the second in psychology departments—indicate another common focus of two different disciplines.

From the viewpoint of the departments, interdisciplinarity comes most readily if they, as a group, simply designate those disciplinary courses that may be taken by students to satisfy the requirements of an interdepartmental or interdisciplinary major. Thus the integration, if any, of these courses is left to the student. The courses enroll all comers and devote little attention to interrelating the disciplines, either for their own sake or for understanding some externality. Such a program ought to be designated as interdepartmental rather than as interdisciplinary. The student may become interdisciplinary, but neither the department nor the instructors have done much more than make that possibility slightly more feasible.

Another possibility is that in which a course is organized around a theme or problem, and teachers from various disciplines are brought together to offer the course. Thus a course in history and civilization may draw upon professors from art, sociology, history, and science. By agreeing to join together to offer a course, they take on some obligation for interrelating, if not fully integrating, its diverse parts. The effectiveness of this approach obviously depends upon the participating teachers and their willingness to take on the obligations of learning what is taught in other parts of the course. It also depends, in great part, upon the way in which the course is offered. If the course is built around a significant era in history (such as Florence in 1500), and each member of the instructional team coordinates his or her phase of the course with that of others to enable the student to get a coherent, unified view of how Florence 1500 came about, the flowering of many disciplines at that time, and the impact of Florence 1500 on subsequent developments, then the course may indeed come to be integrated, both from the professorial and student perspectives. But the faculty depth in their respective fields may mean that they differ from each other as well as from the students in their individual integrations. The learner in such a course may direct attention to those areas of greatest personal relevance and achieve a coherence and unity of great personal significance. Whether or not this should be acceptable to the instructor could be a difficult issue to resolve. The initial form of such a course as Florence 1500 would probably be characterized as interdisciplinary or multidisciplinary (preferably the latter because of the sheer number of disciplines involved).

A course taught by a single professor may well become transdisciplinary over time because the professor will have reached the point of dealing with ideas and issues at a sophisticated scholarly level without recourse to particular disciplines to justify his or her terminology, analysis, or conclusions. It is also possible to rise to a supradisciplinary level by identifying concepts or principles useful in almost every discipline but having a depth of meaning that can be effectively dealt with only by seeking an ultimate unity and insight well above and beyond the disciplines. The disciplines, properly placed in a superstructure of disciplines, should make possible a unity that permits a look at ultimate questions (truth, beauty, equality) in the fullness of their meaning and implication, without the limitations imposed by a disciplinary structure. Ideally, every undergraduate should, sometime before receiving a degree, rise for a moment or two to the supradisciplinary level. Unless it is assumed that all students can and will do this on their own, acceptance of the ideal requires the presence of a few teachers who operate effectively at this level and successfully motivate students to do likewise.

Summary

Since teachers in higher education have such limited familiarity with the role of the disciplines in education, hampering their ability to teach in this context, we have considered, in this chapter, the nature of a discipline and the various components of disciplinary structure. The substantive structures of the disciplines include assumptions, variables, concepts, and principles and relationships among these at some relatively simple, perhaps observational or other verifiable levels. The conjunctive structure—that is, the relationship to other disciplines—is determined, in part, out of the substantive structure but, in part also, out of the syntactical structure. The disciplines grouped in the arts and humanities have substantive structures different from the sciences; but they also have different syntactical structures, and so the two groups tend to be clearly separated when they are placed in composite structures inclusive of all disciplines. Even when distinctly different disciplines are used to study the same entity, they tend to focus on distinctive aspects of that entity. Thus a human being can be viewed as a biological organism, an illustration of the principles of chemistry and physics, a creative individual, or a computer. The study of mankind falls into no one discipline, and the attempt at understanding humans calls for a composite integrated effort that must at least be interdisciplinary and may actually emerge as transdisciplinary in the sense that, although each discipline studies a part of mankind, the whole man is greater than the sum of these parts.

In the next chapter, the various disciplines are considered in sufficient detail that specific differences and commonalities among them become more evident. The disciplinary dimensions thus revealed provide the basis for further consideration of the recurring ideas, concepts, and themes that transcend or bridge the disciplines.

Suggestions for Further Reading

Anderson, O. R. *The Quantitative Analysis of Structure in Teaching.* New York: Teachers College Press, 1971.

Ford, G. W., and Pugno, L. (Eds.). *The Structure of Knowledge and the Curriculum.* Chicago: Rand McNally, 1964.

King, A. R., Jr., and Brownell, J. A. *The Curriculum and the Disciplines of Knowledge, A Theory of Curriculum Practice.* New York: Wiley, 1966.

Phenix, P. H. *Realms of Meaning: A Philosophy of the Curriculum for General Education.* New York: McGraw-Hill, 1964.

6

Defining Characteristics of the Disciplines

The various disciplines represent ways to investigate the totality of knowledge and the means used to acquire and organize it. The teacher and scholar should remember that disciplines are artifacts of mankind's search for meaning—they are means to attain and enlarge meaning. They reflect mankind's efforts toward becoming more human and its difficulties in developing and using symbols that permit reflection and communication. In this chapter, we present a capsule view of the disciplines, suggesting the manner in which mankind has developed the disciplines as a matrix imposed upon objective reality and subjective ideas. Our conception of teaching within a disciplinary context requires explication of the structure and characteristic features of the disciplines to guide the selection and organization of curricular and course content.

There are several major groups of disciplines, variously defined. Phenix (1964) has identified six "realms": symbolics, empirics, esthetics, synnoetics, ethics, and synoptics. Each of these realms includes several disciplines that share at least one common characteristic. Besides those six realms and the specific disciplines within them, there are many additional disciplines or fields of study that cut across these realms. The following discussion of disciplines draws heavily upon Phenix but departs from and elaborates his ideas for the immediate purposes of this volume.

Symbolics

Phenix identified the first of his six major groups of disciplines as *symbolics.* This grouping deals with humanly constructed symbols created to promote thinking and communication. The subject matter of these disciplines is concerned with how symbols are put together in a formal structure to express meaning. Since the symbols are developed by human beings working in a particular social structure, the symbols and their combinations are based upon arbitrary culture-bound social conventions, even though the symbols relate to the real world. Direct correspondence between symbols and meanings among languages is not to be expected, since a particular culture will focus on events as the needs and interests of that culture suggest.

The symbolic disciplines are essentially three. The first is language, which includes the basic elements of speech (stress, intonation, transition, terminal indicators, consonants, vowels) and visual elements such as semantemes (concrete concepts referring to objects, actions, and qualities) and morphemes (abstract relational concepts), as well as a range of concepts intermediate between these. Language also includes structural devices (syntax) for organizing meaningful elements into complex expressive patterns and procedures that make it possible to use symbols to communicate. It is especially important, however, to recognize that the use of language is largely practical, serving everyday needs of communication. Language is an essential part of every discipline and relates especially to those aspects of each discipline that have meaning and implications in daily living. The teaching of language in college is beset with the fallacy of assuming that language is best taught by an English department that is much more likely to be interested in literature, creative writing, or linguistics than in the day-by-day communication needs of individuals and society. To be meaningful in undergraduate education, language must be accepted not only as a means for study of all disciplines but also as an area of attention and contribution by each discipline.

The second discipline of the symbolics group is mathematics. Mathematics, as an autonomous discipline, is concerned with abstractions and deals with pure symbolic forms using a postulational and axiomatic approach to explore the logical implications of a set of assumptions. Mathematics, as a discipline, in this sense, seeks for rigorous reasoning and for the development of chains of logical reasoning that ensure consistency and precision in meaning. The subject matter of mathematics, then, consists of undefined terms and a number of operations and transformations. Symbols are transformed in accordance with rules that are part of the system definition. The aim is to develop formal, abstract symbolic systems within which all possible propositions are consistent with each other. Mathematics is concerned with demonstrating the existence (in the abstract) of certain concepts, with their relationships, and with invariance of properties. Since pure mathematics is not concerned with physical reality, it uses convenient artificial symbolic forms to represent such concepts as set, function, and operation. Nevertheless, mathematical systems can be devised or modified to model aspects of reality and lead to understanding of them. In fact, the actual use of mathematics, both by scientists and others, is largely practical, serving an everyday use as a form of communication and thought.

The third area of symbolic representation is what Phenix calls *nondiscursive symbolic forms.* As the designation suggests, these symbolic forms are figurative or ideographic imaginative expressions that directly convey (that is, without elaboration) feelings, values, commitments, or insights. The insights conveyed in themselves may become the subject of extensive discussion and thereby may come to be associated with and suggest many interrelated ideas and values. The Christian cross in its various manifestations is an example.

Nondiscursive symbolic forms include a wide variety of elements that carry meaning with varying degrees of intensity and ambiguity:

- signals—codes for communicating action cues, lights, bells, hand signals, dress codes, natural sounds and warnings
- bodily gestures—signals, symptoms that may be natural or artificial, spontaneous or premeditated, socialized or stylized (finger to lips for silence)
- facial expressions—smiles, frowns, sneers
- manners and customs—customs with the force of law, mores, social conventions, cultural patterns, folkways, fashions, habits
- rituals—religious, fraternal, patriotic (pledge of allegiance), personal, pathological, neurotic
- graphic or object symbols—flags, cross, zodiacal signs, swastika, colors (red), textures (pavement)
- dreams—visions, nightmares
- myths, allegories, parables, or fairy tales—figurative or metaphorical use of language

The three symbolic areas may be called disciplines; but, as already noted, the characterization of language and mathematics as disciplines leads to an approach to teaching them that has relatively little relationship to everyday needs of communication, reasoning, and problem solving. Nondiscursive symbolic forms have generally been viewed as an incidental part of various disciplines. They have not appeared in the curriculum as a separate discipline or course. These symbolic areas are not disciplines in the usual sense of being bodies of organized knowledge but, rather, are human constructs that promote thinking and communication and are, therefore, essential in all of the disciplines. Furthermore, study in any discipline should result in increased ability to use language, mathematics, and nondiscursive symbolic forms as means of thought and communication with others, and not solely for specialists in the discipline. Indeed, this ability should be regarded as the major outcome desired in a humanizing education.

Empirics

Systematic empirical inquiry seeks to understand and explain phenomena and to predict and control them. However, control implies application of knowledge beyond the direct purposes of pure inquiry as interpreted by some disciplinary scholars. Empirical inquiry is concerned with facts and truth, but it must have recourse to symbolics to define and assist in the search and to facilitate the communication and use of results. Essentially, empirical investigations seek to attain knowledge and understanding of certain aspects of the real world. The subject matter of the natural sciences includes all energy or matter systems, both physical and biological, and is concerned with the influence of forces acting on these systems over time to produce motion and change.

Physical Science. The physical sciences (physics especially) traditionally were concerned with phenomena involving inanimate matter. Physical science takes account only of those characteristics that can be measured or counted, and is thereby restricted to consideration of *matter* and *motion* or to the three concepts of *mass, length,* and *time.* The physical science disciplines (astronomy, chemistry, geology, physics) ideally progress by hypothesis, experimentation, and observation, with occasional and unusually creative breakthroughs. The physical sciences are also concerned with the interplay of constancy and change. The laws (for example, those dealing with conservation of energy, momentum, or parity) express relationships that remain invariant despite changes in the component variable factors.

As a result of the emphasis on measurement, the problems and implications of the measurement process are of central concern. The accuracy of any measurement depends upon the relationship between the size of the unit of measurement and the size of what is being measured. Accuracy also depends upon the nature of the measuring instrument used. Thus much of the advance in science is an interaction between the technology of making adequate measuring instruments and the problems involved in applying them to obtain better measurements at both the micro and macro levels. The accuracy of measurement further depends upon the control of variables that affect the size of either the object measured or the measuring device. Thus definition of standard conditions and the development of means of maintaining them become essential. Units of measurement also present problems. Inches and feet, for example, are thoroughly arbitrary units. Hence there has been developed, as in defining the metric system, a unit based upon the earth's circumference, although that dimension itself is not and cannot be precisely known. The velocity of light is a more fundamental measuring unit; it is assumed to be a constant but still presents problems in exact measurement. Weight varies with gravitational force, and forces of attraction between objects vary inversely with distance. Hence mass rather than weight is the primary variable in physical science. There is no absolute unit of time and, indeed, the passage of time depends upon comparative velocities.

The act of measurement affects the object being measured. For most human endeavors, this is not a significant factor. The addition of a speedometer to register the speed of an automobile has so little impact on the speed of the car that it is ignored. In contrast, actual measurement of the breaking strength of a beam destroys the beam itself. Attempts to measure precise position and velocity must be carried out independently since each affects the other, giving rise to the well-known Heisenberg Uncertainty Principle.

Most units of measure are arbitrary, but they can be defined operationally so that they are essentially fixed and, therefore, constant, so long as standard conditions are adhered to. Absolute units, such as absolute zero and the velocity of light, do not in themselves provide for units of measure, but they do provide fixed or constant figures against which comparisons can be made. Direct comparison constitutes the most fundamental way of measuring one thing against another. Whether one lays a foot ruler repeatedly across the top of a desk or stretches a tape from one edge to the other, the basic procedure involved is relating the desk top to markings on the tape or to the number of times that the ruler must be applied to reach across the desk top.

Biological Science. The subject matter of biological science includes all matter-energy systems that are alive or self-sustaining. The system uses matter and energy from external sources to conserve or preserve its own energy level and to reproduce its own kind. Living matter is ultimately composed of basic material particles. Thus the biological sciences are part of the physical sciences and depend more and more upon the physical sciences for organizing and interpreting the knowledge accruing in the biological science disciplines. The distinction between animate and inanimate matter is not entirely clear. Protoplasm seems to be the basic matter from which all living things are constructed, and the cell seems to be the basic unit of living matter. However, there are other particles—the virus, for example—that have some characteristics of living systems.

Biology was originally largely descriptive and depended heavily upon taxonomies. Terms such as *species, genera, orders, families, classes,* and *phyla* provided categories into which plants and animals were classified on the basis of similarities in their structure, function, or development. As biological science became more analytical, it began to focus on the causes and processes giving rise to special patterns of life. Evolution, based upon natural selection as a means of gradual change, with inheritable mutations and adaptations, has provided an integrating theory. And so the attention has shifted from classification to the patterns of organization of living things, with emphasis on nutrition, respiration, synthesis, and metabolism and self-perpetuation involving steady-state control, reproduction, and adaptation. The organism does this through organ systems composed of tissues, cells, and ultimately, protoplasm. The organisms themselves are further organized into larger groups such as families, societies, and communities.

Biology now seeks for general laws that help to understand and explain the origin and functioning of particular life forms and the observed similarities and differences in various types of organisms. A central concern in biological science is the relationship between change and constancy, a search for invariance—dynamic equilibrium. The biological organism seeks to maintain those standard conditions under which it can thrive.

Illness or destruction ensues when that stability can no longer be maintained by the organism itself or by suitable modification of the environment aiding the efforts of the organism.

Psychology—a Biological and Social Science. Psychology may be regarded as a branch of biology or as one of the social sciences; it is concerned with living entities and with the description and prediction of human behavior. The subject matter of psychology is the mind—that aspect of living things that processes information and determines behavior. The mind may be regarded as a separate reality from the body (something akin to soul), or merely as activity of the brain and other physical components of the individual that should ultimately be explainable by the physical sciences.

A shift in focus from the unseen workings of the mind to observable behavior permits psychology to be regarded as an experimental natural science. It employs hypotheses, experimental designs, and measurements characteristic of these sciences in the search for laws, principles, and concepts that may help to explain, predict, and control behavior. Findings based upon animals are assumed to have relevance in understanding human behavior. The key concepts of psychology, approached from the orientation of biological science, are: stimulus, response, reflex, learning (modification of behavior by experience), conditioning, reinforcement, transfer, learning set, and perception. Full commitment to this conception of psychology would relegate higher education to a low-level conditioning process, with attendant uncertainties about who is capable of planning the conditioning process.

Concepts such as memory, motivation, imagination, and purpose which, for the experimental psychologist, are merely inferences from behavior may be regarded by other psychologists as essential to the discussion and understanding of human behavior. For this social-science-oriented group, the paraphernalia of science (instruments, inferential statistics, measurement and operational definitions) are replaced by more personal and subjective approaches including qualitative, intuitional, and dialectical modes of thought. Emotions, instead of being purely behavioral manifestations measured by pulse rate, breathing, and glandular secretions, become part of personality, identity, and humanistic striving toward personal fulfillment.

Applied psychology is primarily focused on helping the individual toward self-understanding, self-direction, and attainment of personal satisfaction. In this mode, values, beliefs, anxieties, and personal responsibility become important. Whether one regards this as an attempt to *apply* the natural science of psychology to the problems of specific individuals, or as a highly humanistic approach, the subject matter, methods, and objectives (anticipated learnings) have been altered in this application.

For the purposes of stating individual objectives and outcomes of higher education, behavior may be defined as follows: Behavior is truly human only if it is (1) conscious, (2) purposeful, (3) oriented to other human beings, (4) motivated by feelings, attitudes, and values, and (5) *not* reflexive, instinctive, or automatic. This definition, to a considerable degree, negates precise behavioral analysis that seeks to explain conduct by reference to neurophysiological mechanisms. Reflexive behavior (immediate, direct, and unlearned) and conditioned behavior (formed by neoneural connections and controls or sets that facilitate or negate the behavior) are then replaced by ideated behavior, based on individual analysis of conditions rather than controlled (conditioned) by them. Concepts such as conscience, values, guilt, anxiety, freedom, responsibility, and religious beliefs become appropriate. Maintenance of stability and attainment of personal satisfaction in the face of uncertainty and rapidly changing circumstances become central to the individual and society. Psychology becomes a social rather than a biological science in humanizing education.

Social Science. Social science includes geography, sociology, economics, anthropology, and political science, as well as psychology as just defined. Social science is concerned with understanding, predicting, and perhaps, directing human behavior, individually and collectively, in various environments and circumstances.

Geography is a descriptive discipline devoted to collecting and organizing data on the earth as the habitat of mankind. Its subject matter is the interaction of humans and their environment, and its scholars seek, with geographical setting as the major organizing principle, to understand the interactions of people and places. Hence geography also plays a significant role in the disciplines of political science, history, and sociology. Emphasis on the purely physical aspects of geography moves the discipline into geology and the physical sciences.

The fundamental subject matter of *sociology* is the scientific study of human society. Sociology seeks meanings and explanations of human behavior by analyzing social processes and patterned interactions within and among groups. The focus is upon this interplay between individuals and groups and their social environments, not upon the individuals themselves. The fundamental unit of sociological analysis, then, is the group.

Sociology investigates the nature and causes of social relations and events by examining behavioral data from a special conceptual framework. Sociologists attempt to discover regularities and variations in social behavior, using the central concepts of social structure, stratification, social roles and status, social class, conformity, deviance, conflict, change, socialization, social norms, and values. Their methodology proceeds by defining, categorizing, and describing social phenomena, such as intergenerational mobility, demographic trends, family relations, rural-urban shifts, organizational behavior, sex roles, and occupations and work. Sociological researchers generate explanatory hypotheses derived from various theoretical frameworks to uncover social determinants of behavior. They employ statistical or mathematical models to establish causal and functional connections between social variables. No one coherent sociological perspective dominates the field; instead, sociologists may focus upon social processes, social psychology and group dynamics, demography and ecology, formal organizations, or theory and method building.

The subject matter of *economics* is the set of problems generated in managing the use of scarce resources to produce various commodities and to distribute them appropriately. Since there is no universally accepted standard for what or how much of various commodities are to be produced and how and to whom these commodities are to be distributed, the choice among the various alternatives must be made in reference to the values sought. These values include security, stability, freedom, and justice.

Economics in its infancy employed laissez-faire observation and analysis of the results of the operations of natural law and external forces. Increasingly, economics has become an interventional or policy science, as is implied by the definition of its subject matter. Economics embraces an extremely wide range of conceptions (labor, goods, services, consumer, producer, capital, market system, supply, demand, and so forth), with complex interrelationships that make prediction or intervention and control uncertain ventures. Since intervention in a democratic society necessarily operates through political systems that are more responsive to immediate demands than to long-term goals and values, such intervention is endangered by value conflicts and by the attempts of special interests to advantage themselves. This in turn endangers the intended results of the intervention, through carefully calculated misinterpretation.

Ideal models based upon well-elaborated theories may seem to relate policies and consequences, but the assumptions undergirding the ideal never fully apply, any more than does our functioning democracy fully adhere to the ideals sought by the founding fathers. Thus the methods of economics are largely confined to comparison of actual results achieved and those predicted by various economic systems. Quantification, measurement, and statistical analysis have caused economics to resemble the physical sciences, but the dependence of the interpretation and application of economic policies on human sciences and values places economics among the social science disciplines.

Anthropology seeks an understanding of mankind by comparative studies embracing both physical and sociocultural characteristics, without the limits of space and time. Anthropology comprises five subareas: archeology, linguistics, and physical, social, and cultural anthropology. Traditionally, what distinguishes anthropology from other social sciences is its concern with description and explanation of forms of social life among diverse human groups, both literate and preliterate. The discipline's comparative and ethnographic methods of study rely heavily on such qualitative techniques as participant observation and the ability to elicit and interpret oral histories, local interviews, and historical records. Recent expansions of the discipline take anthropologists into newly urban or emerging communities to study their internal human organization, population characteristics, social ecology, and dynamics for change.

Historically, *political science* was viewed as a discipline concerned with the purposes and procedures used by society to establish the state and government, its political institutions and functions. Through the years, this characterization of political science shifted to the study of power relationships among individuals, groups, and nations competing for control over social and economic resources. Today, the focus of study is on the making of public policy and political interactions in the society: the unit of analysis is often the political system itself.

In seeking to understand and predict human political behavior and the social structures by which political action is achieved, political research employs rigorous quantitative designs and empirical modes of analysis, techniques not unlike those applied in other social sciences. This research investigates the regulatory mechanisms used by society to control allocations and disputes over resources by studying legislation, law, public administration, political parties, interest groups, voting behavior, public opinion, and international relations.

Esthetics

The esthetic domain includes music, the visual arts, dance or movement, and literature. However, esthetic concerns are apparent in all disciplines, both in the logic and cogency of problem-solving processes and in the criteria for the acceptability of solutions. In a sense, all esthetic reactions are individual and subjective, but they are also learned through and can be modified by formal education and by association with and assimilation of the values and views of others.

Music. Music consists of patterned sound sequences. The

sounds are not conceptual symbols and they have no meaning. In one sense, the subject matter of music as a discipline is a musical composition that is heard as performed. The recording, editing, synthesizing, and reproduction of music overcomes some of the limitations of time and place but gives rise to questions about how faithful and valid the production is or must be. The production of a musical composition is presumably a matter of personal interest, choice, and commitment rather than ulterior or utilitarian ends. This is reflected in many musical patterns and variations (minuet, scherzo, rondo, theme, fugue, sonata) and in much of the creative work in music, producing brilliant compositions that fit the constraints or rules prescribed for particular patterns.

Musical sounds include only a portion of all wave motions similar to those that produce sounds, but there are infinite variations within the range of audible frequencies. Hence musical scales (diatonic, chromatic) and others are arbitrary divisions imposed upon the audible frequencies. A number of terms are introduced and defined to focus attention on various characteristics of sound. *Pitch* refers to the fundamental frequency of vibration. *Tone, color,* and *timbre* refer to the distribution of subsidiary frequencies or harmonic vibrations. *Loudness* has to do with the amplitude of vibration, *duration* with the length of time that the vibration continues, and *texture* with the nature of the construction, whether *harmonic* (that is, in chords), or *polyphonic* (a combination of melodies). The octave scale, with a succession of seven distinct tones of whole and half steps depending upon whether in major or minor mode, expands—by insertion of half steps—into a *chromatic* scale. The key tone or *tonic* indicates a point of reference around which a composition, or a phase of it, is developed. An elemental tonal pattern or *motif* constitutes the basic unit in the development of a composition. Thus there is something analogous to words, phrases, clauses, sentences, and paragraphs in the structure of a musical composition, and in the way in which these are organized to determine the characteristics of the larger musical patterns that emerge. The way in which a composer relates keys, themes, and motifs within that structure is part of the artistry of the task.

Music communicates, but its communication is dependent upon a listener who is not necessarily obligated to discern the specific intent of the composer, which may emerge only (if at all) when the composition is completed. Music also contains many symbolic, nondiscursive forms, including the lines and spaces on which the notes are displayed, variations in notes to indicate duration, and sharps, flats, clef signs, and numerous other signs and letter indications of how a particular note is to be rendered. These symbols are imposed upon sound sequences, but the individual who learns music through this imposed structure may find this symbolic language essentially inseparable from the music itself. This is perhaps why non-Western music is hard to understand and, indeed, almost unintelligble for Westerners who attempt to refer it back to their accustomed symbolic language.

In imposing our conceptions on sounds and setting up a symbolic system, we have provided for rich developments in music but have also limited the nature of those developments. Constancy or invariance is balanced against change and variation. In addition, communication about music has resulted in a highly specific technical terminology that someone who seeks to understand music, or hopes to teach it, must master (for example, distinguishing among terms, such as *pitch* and *timbre,* as discussed earlier). The sound itself is a source of delight to the practiced listener, but without some knowledge of the structure, the naive listener may be bored and is unlikely to become skilled or fully appreciative. The value in the conceptual study of musical forms is that it directs the listener's attention to esthetic characteristics and possibilities, whether intended or unintended, that might otherwise be ignored, imperfectly sensed, or completely misinterpreted.

The unit of attention from the viewpoint of the composer or performer of music is clearly the individual composition. Neither composer nor performer needs to talk about the composition, although both may do so. However, the listener (the consumer) who would wish to do more than express like or dislike of specific compositions must acquire a language involving certain rules and structural definitions. The listener can grasp the organic unity of a musical composition as a whole only if that whole is a recognizable form. Recognition of form provides a basis for a comprehensive view that permits the listener to relate successive parts and to reflect upon relationships between what has been performed, what is heard at the moment, and what is yet to come.

Much of the emphasis in musical composition, performance, and enjoyment is related to the principle of unity in variety. The composer makes music by imposing structures and definitions on sound, thereby providing certain common elements or unifying concepts that select from the chaos of sound something coherent and possibly pleasant. Yet within these structures and within any musical form, there is an infinitude of possibilities. Thus there is not only some unity in the variety, but a particular form or pattern also provides a challenge for exploring possible varieties within its limitations. Attaining harmony with a collection of musical instruments depends upon a coordinated group effort by the individuals who play them. Cooperation in a well-formed task, whether in an orchestra or on a football team, is an esthetic experience. Successful performances both breed and proceed out of esthetic experiences.

The Visual Arts. The visual arts include painting, drawing, the graphic arts, sculpture, and architecture. The major purpose of efforts in the visual arts is the shaping of tangible visible materials into esthetic objects. These objects have a permanence and can be envisaged in totality, as well as in part. In contrast, the re-creation of a musical composition at any point in time is a transitory phenomenon, and the relationship of parts is, to a large extent, a relating of mental images rather than simultaneous perception of parts and whole. Materials of the field of the visual arts are very extensive: paint, ink, pencil, wood, brick, stone, metal, clay, marble, paper, cloth. Indeed, almost any material, and means of imposing marks or structure upon that material, may be used by an artist. Films and videotapes provide the possibility of conjoining movement and sound with objects or images, and also of permitting variations over time in all of the materials used. Sculpture, architecture, and holographic reproductions permit the introduction of the third dimension, providing, in the visual arts, a realism and representation not readily attainable in painting, drawing, or graphic arts, except through the use of perspective.

In the visual arts, as in music, a case can be made that the unit of attention is the individual work. Yet no one can fully comprehend or express the meaning of art works unless sensitivity to the basic qualities, possibilities, and limitations of the materials comprising the art objects is cultivated. Just as the individual who attempts to perform a musical composition attains more insight into the nature of the music and the problems of re-creating it, so in art, actual manipulation, touch, or an attempt to produce an observed effect will heighten sensitivity to the complexity of the task and the quality of the results. In both art and music, the actual materials and the manipulation of them are part of the creative or re-creative task. This contrasts with science, in which no direct acquaintance with the instruments or with the construction of the instruments used in experimental inquiry is essential. One can use the electron microscope or the data received from it without having fully to understand the principles underlying its construction or the niceties of its manufacture. In art, the materials used very frequently have characteristics of their own that must be sensitively employed if the fullest artistic creativity is to be exhibited. For painting and drawing, the artist has such possibilities as oil, tempera (a colloidal medium), water colors, pen and ink, crayon, charcoal, sharp hard pencils or blunt soft ones, or even his or her own fingers. Woodcuts, engraving lithographs, stencils, etchings, carving, modeling, and casting represent other ways of producing art objects. Collages, mosaics, stained glass, ceramics, tapestry, and lace represent still other possibilities. Photography, by essentially removing the significance of most perfectly reproducing reality, is a relatively new conception to the visual arts but has itself turned into a flexible means of emphasizing aspects of reality.

Many of the terms used in other disciplines have relevance and meaning in visual arts. *Lines* can create a feeling of harmony or conflict, rigidity or flexibility; they can also indicate movement or closure. *Color,* in its variations (hue, relative vividness or saturation, value, relative lightness and darkness), permits creation of balance, contrast, continuity, and mass. The total composition itself is an exercise in creating balance and contrasts, symmetry, and pleasing departures from symmetry. The use of perspective creates a sense of depth; the intricacy of several perspectives may create a confusing, enlightening, or simply interesting composition.

Although, in one sense, the unit is the individual work, the desired outcome in the study of the visual arts is growth in the individual of a basis for appreciating or attaching meaning to a single work by comparing and contrasting it with others. This process of comparison derives from applying significant concepts and principles that have grown out of and taken on meaning by examining works of art, by studying the reactions of others, and by developing one's own structure for personal reflections and judgments. In particular, the study of art, as it has developed, permits some insight into the characteristics of art that are of enduring significance across the generations—a concern for constancy with variation and for invariance; this underlines and gives meaning to variance, and, in so doing, gives insights into the values and thoughts of various cultural periods.

To the artist, the artistic preoccupation of the moment is an attempt to solve a problem, to use the materials at hand, to express an esthetic idea; or, in other words, to achieve certain perceptual effects. The problem chosen may be that of accurate representation of an existing natural object, an imagined or idealistic representation of an at present inexistent object or individual, or the creation of something entirely new, such as nonrepresentational free forms that have esthetic appeal. The artist may simply engage in the task as a pleasurable experience or, more seriously, attempt to achieve perfection in the solution of a problem—that is, attempt to find just the right way of expressing certain actual or imagined perceptions.

It is doubtful that the art (or the music) of any particular period can be fully understood without relating it to preexisting societal conceptions and conditions. Primitive art is related to magic and to problems now the domain of both religion and science. Pictorial art provided an early basis for writing and language and, particularly in the medieval Christian church, art expressed the Christian message to those unable to read. Art has also dealt with mathematical or scientific problems. The development of paint with enduring qualities, originally a concern of artists, has become a major problem, with present-day air and water impurities destroying both the paints and the surfaces painted. The problems of perspective and foreshortening in an art work arose out of the task of creating or constructing a work so as to produce the desired effect on the observer. Also, imposed by the relationship of the observer to a particular composition and by the effort required of the observer, came the problem of seeing and then inferring what the artist intended to communicate. The individual reacting to art cannot do so with any assurance or satisfaction until his or her behavior is guided by a grasp of some general artistic concepts and principles that provide focus and suggest meaning.

Dance and the Arts of Movement. This sector of esthetics includes not only dance in its various forms (ballet, ballroom, ceremonial, religious, jog, tap, clog) but also magic, marching drills (including formation boating, diving, and flying), arts of combat, sports, games, and gymnastics. In colleges, the majority of such activities are grouped under some such rubric as health, recreation, and physical education. With some exceptions, these arts have no efficient and well-known systems of notation for recording or communication. The language developed for critiquing them often seems, to the layman, to be affected and unrelated to the actual performance.

The fundamental purposes and concepts vary with the art forms and their origins. Some movement arts have developed out of historical, religious, geographic, or racial facts, characteristics, or values and have yielded rigid and standardized styles. In contrast, expressional or free dance is an attempt to communicate on an impromptu basis a strong feeling or emotion. A performance may be aided by music, lighting, costume, setting, special structure, or architecture to express a mood, attitude, appeal, or purpose. A fundamental concept in these arts is the organic unity of the individual and the dynamic equilibrium that is an essential part of a performance. In group performances, as in music, there can be a prime movement and accompaniment or a melding of diverse movements into a unified whole. Effective performance in any of these movement arts requires grace, balance, and apparent ease in every movement and transition. Evidence of strain, imbalance, or breaks in rhythm detracts from the quality and unity of the performance. For particular motor skills or coordinated movements, there may be a code or set of rules prescribing a standard performance and facilitating comparisons, ratings, or judgments. Competition and emphasis on winning may seem to introduce an alien factor into the movement arts. Yet competition and physical combat are part of the human heritage, and it is not surprising that the martial arts (fencing, boxing, wrestling, karate), even when pursued to the defeat or death of an opponent, can also be regarded as art forms.

The variables in arts of movement are space, time, and weight (mass, if the performance is in gravity-free space). Much of the effort and artistry of performance is that of developing strength and nicety of timing so that movements, whether distinctive, unique, or common, are so performed that one or a combination of the variables of time, space, or weight attains unusual or possibly maximal or minimal values. Individuality and creativity are valued, but special and widespread appreciation usually attends, as it does in music, excellence in the performance of the traditional, standardized, or popular movements that observers recognize and relate to similar performances.

Literature. Literature uses language as a medium of esthetic expression. Literature puts content into a literary form regarded as functional in communicating some message. As in the other arts, there is much flexibility both in the selection of specific forms from the medium and in how these are put together. Some of the freedom is deliberately restricted by prior specification of literary forms, such as fiction, drama, and poetry. Each of these has been further broken down (for example, fiction into novels and short stories, and poetry into sonnets, ballads, epics, odes) with specific conventions regarding such characteristics as length, meter, and rhyme, constraining and, therefore, challenging the creativity of the writer. There are further distinctions such as genre, style, periods, and uses of language. Some of these are evident in the appearance or outer form—they can be seen in the structure of the work, the meter chosen, and the rhyme scheme. Others (allegory, fable, parable, legend) are found within the work and emerge from or are related to the purpose, mood, or setting.

Language plays a double role in literature. Implicit in its use is an effort to communicate ideas, but there is also an intent to arouse emotion. Myths, for example, convey significant cultural meanings by use of fictitious tales having no direct relationship to the immediate scene, yet they adopt concrete images that make the message timelessly relevant. Language is used figuratively to highlight its esthetic message and various social and personal meanings. Carefully selected words and phrases are manipulated to become symbols or create images. Metaphor, alliteration, analogy, and other figures of speech are used to express various meanings and levels of meaning. As with the other arts, someone who would fully appreciate a work must apply to it a measure of creativity that seeks at once for an intent, a meaning, and a conveyed emotion. When language is used for esthetic purposes, richness of experience and of repetition emerges from creativity and from intentional and inevitable ambiguity.

A literary work is meant to be enjoyed for its own sake, yet that enjoyment requires a prior experience with words and life. The depth and richness of any esthetic experience depends both upon what someone brings to a work and on what images, ideas, and associations the work communicates to that person. In some sense, the subject matter or the unit in all esthetic disciplines is the individual work, but one must also internalize definitions, procedures, and rules for enjoying and appraising classes of literary works as well as a single work. Otherwise, the study of literature as a collection of selected samples threatens to become nothing more than the characterizations given to individual works by critics, who draw upon the original stimulus and historical context influencing them to create learned critiques that have little meaning to the relatively naive art consumer. However, the individual who would deal both intellectually and emotionally with a literary (or other art) work must address it both on extrinsic (influencing factors) and intrinsic (internal structure) bases. This includes attention to the constants (adherence to conventions and standard forms) and variables (individual variations and creativity).

Synnoetics

Synnoetics is a word used by Phenix (1964) to suggest a realm of knowledge that encompasses an individual's interacting with and acquiring insight into individuals (including himself) who are interrelated in various ways. This knowledge (so called) is highly subjective, involving understanding of human relationships and dependence, personal knowledge, and existential awareness.

The subject matter is clearly the individual human being in personal interrelations with others. It has been extensively studied in the disciplines of religion, philosophy, psychology, and literature, and is also prominent in various therapeutic theories and practices. Such names as Buber, Adler, Jung, Freud, Rank, Horney, Kierkegaard, Heidegger, Sartre, Fromm, and Sullivan immediately come to mind. The nature and purpose of being and of becoming constitute the central problem. Questions like Who am I? Why am I here? Where am I going? trouble many people at various times in their lives. These questions are ego threatening and are often accompanied by deep anxiety and a sense of guilt. Nevertheless, there are no certain or satisfactory answers. Overconcern with such questions is destructive because it limits the individual's interactions with others and participation in encouraging tasks that may offer some sense of security and self-worth.

There is reasonable doubt that this area of knowledge constitutes a discipline, or that it is developed by direct instruction or cognitive learning. The knowledge, insights, and feelings involved are highly personal and relate to no well-defined body of knowledge or set of experiences. Therefore, it is doubtful that college credit courses in synnoetics are useful, justifiable, or even possible, if courses must facilitate definitive individual development. However, personal problems and human relations are touched upon by many disciplines, including the health sciences. Cognitive and affective outcomes from formal learning are relevant to personal development, but the extent to which these outcomes are internalized by an individual is more a result of contemplation than direct assimilation. Instead of personal solutions, a sense of certainty or security is achieved amid threatening changes. Individuals are more likely to resolve their problems through counseling, psychiatry, or psychoanalysis than through formal course work.

Ethics and Morality

Ethics and morality consider what an individual should do under specified circumstances. Their focus is on the identification of the right action in these circumstances and on deliberate and voluntary performance of it. The bases for determining "right" are varied and often interacting and conflicting. They include conscience, reason, and revelation, of which only reason is clearly affected by education. On a pragmatic level, the right action is the one that produces the right results, but adjudication of the right results may well be as hazardous as deciding upon the right action.

Ethics and morality relate to many facets of human behavior. They embrace basic human rights such as freedom, justice, integrity, equity, and dignity. They also have to do with sex and family relations, social classes, ethnicity, religion, citizenship, professions, economic and political life, and property rights. Law provides tentative answers to many questions about such human behavioral issues but, frequently, leans on what is reasonable, feasible, or acceptable, rather than on what is right. The distinction between first- and second-degree murder is one of intent and, perhaps, of deliberate planning; but who can determine intent with certainty—especially after the fact? Frequently, the decisions involved in ethical and moral issues, in turn, include other ethical considerations and highly fallible human judgment. If abortion is justified only when the prospective mother's life is threatened, on what evidence is the decision based? In this, as in other areas, human beings seek for certainties that would ease the anxiety of decision making and ensure that the right decision be made. Yet certainty rules out options and opportunities and, carried to extremes, makes man either a martyr or an automaton. Formal education should dissipate myths and magic and replace them by knowledge, and that knowledge and its implications open up alternatives that make each decision more complex than before. Education makes man more human and, in rejecting pat answers of others, and accepting more responsibility for his own, man comes to recognize that to err is human—and to fail to recognize or to admit error is even more human.

Personal morality and ethics are hardly subject to direct formation by academic experiences. Ethics and morals can be introduced into the subject matter of courses, but then the courses become social science offerings, studying the societal context of moral and ethical issues. Ethical issues are best dealt with in the context of problems in the various disciplines. Even then, judgments about the ethics and morals involved are treacherous, for the intent underlying behavior is often more revelatory of ethical positions than is the observed behavior and its results.

Synoptics

The synoptic disciplines include history, philosophy, and religion. They are labeled synoptic because they attempt to provide a synthesis, synopsis, or integration of knowledge. Each approaches this integrative task in a somewhat distinctive way, as indicated in these brief characterizations.

History. History undertakes to report concretely or imaginatively the human events of the past. The unit of study is a particular event, a happening or sequence of events, or an identifiable episode occurring in a particular time and place. The writing of history may be reasonably characterized as imaginative because, starting with some set of factual material, the historian has the task of reporting the particular event in its entirety. In effect, he paints a word picture of just what happened. Too, he appropriately raises the question of why it happened, thereby tracing factors preceding and associated with, if not providing, the direct causes of the event. Finding the facts themselves and validating them is not always an easy task, since records disappear, are prone to error, and may have been purposely destroyed or altered. Necessarily, then, history includes ways of checking upon or validating both primary and secondary materials and, in that process, may draw upon an extensive range of knowledge from other disciplines. Piecing together evidence to provide a description of an event in its entirety, and of the factors leading to and perhaps causing that event, is clearly an imaginative task and, as such, may lead to different interpretations by historians. Additional evidence accruing at subsequent periods may cause a particular interpretation to be modified or completely replaced. The importance attached to particular items of evidence may also change, perhaps necessitating total reinterpretation.

In focusing on human events of the past, history undertakes to look at these from the inside. A mere chronological list of events over a span of time is not history. A collection of particular and verified facts constitutes the final objects of knowledge in history from which the historian may undertake to generalize about or characterize particular periods. The substance of history is always fragmental, and the basis upon which the fragments are tied together grows out of some insight or hypothesis put forward by the historian. The historian then undertakes to relate the evidence in such a way that the event seems to be explained by the hypothesis posed.

Philosophy. Philosophy, like history, is concerned with all types of human experiences—past, present, and future. The purpose is to elicit principles and laws of great generality, relating widely diverse fields of experience by some meaningful conceptual scheme. Every discipline represents an effort by human beings to interpret or give meaning to one or more realms of knowledge and the human experiences within them. Philosophy attempts to evaluate, validate, and interpret these meanings. Philosophy is concerned with transcendent meanings (metameanings) and metaphysics. The ultimate aim of philosophy is synthesis—the organization of meanings into a single comprehensive, composite pattern of meaning.

The questions asked by philosophy include: What does it mean to know? What does a certain expression really mean? What is real? What is the ultimate nature of things? These questions arise, in part, because our means of communication are never adequate to convey the full character of reality in form, depth, or complexity. Moreover, the words chosen, and how they are organized, inevitably reflect differing personal interests, commitments, and meaning.

Philosophical investigations proceed by what is called a dialectical method. This involves posing questions, proposing answers, and seeking their implications. This procedure brings out various meanings of concepts and ways in which these meanings can be more clearly specified. To avoid the ambiguities of common words and symbols, an affect-free means of characterization and manipulation of fundamental concepts may be sought. Symbolic logic (see Alfred North Whitehead and Bertrand Russell, 1915) represents one such effort, closely akin to mathematics.

Philosophy, like history, is a component of all disciplines. There are one or more philosophies of language, science, mathematics, esthetics, art, music, history, ethics, and religion. There are also personal philosophies within synnoetics. These disciplinary philosophical orientations relate to: (1) the nature of universals (real or nominal); (2) the structure and function of hypotheses, principles, generalizations, laws, theories, and models; (3) the nature of inquiry and analysis (experimental, deductive, inductive, imaginative, comparative); (4) methods of observation, discovery, and verification; and (5) methods of synopsis, synthesis, and integration. The philosophy implicit in a discipline and the composite structure of that discipline are hardly distinguishable. One can argue either that the structure emerges from the philosophy or that the philosophy emerges from the structure. In fact, a philosophical examination is an essential element of defining and clarifying structure in any discipline.

Religion. Religion is an attempt to integrate all realms of meaning by a venture into the supernatural. The uncertainties of human existence, the complexities of efforts to organize and unify knowledge, and continuing experiences with the unexplainable encourage mankind to seek beyond the finite for ultimacy, the absolute, and the eternal. Everything can be explained by evoking or creating gods and vesting them with supernatural powers. When revelation is invoked as a communication of truth from supernatural beings, these explanations come to be regarded, through faith, as statements of fact. Faith is not understanding, but can, for the devout, replace it.

Understanding of and by religion is sought through prayer, meditation, ritual practice, active commitment, and vesting authority in priests, presumably selected by and operating under divine direction. Silence is a significant aspect of religion, in part because it can be interpreted as unearthly communication. Silence signifies a depth and quality of communication not expressible in words. By attributing commandments, attitudes, and behavioral injunctions to ultimate authority, mankind can replace complete uncertainty by a divine assurance that obedience will be rewarded. Religion in this sense, requiring faith and obedience, has nothing to do with the educational task of applying knowledge and understanding to personal decisions and judgments. To believe otherwise is, in effect, to argue that the individual who really thinks critically will accept a preferred set of beliefs. Study of religion as indicative of what mankind has achieved and insight into human nature is not actually religion but a part of the social sciences and the humanities. If God is personal, as some views suggest, then religion is part of synnoetics, which is also outside the realm of human heritage and common knowledge.

Some professors treat their disciplines as religions and regard research as revealing truth. If love of truth in a discipline is the religion of such professors, it should come as no surprise that they regard their lectures as revelations. Whether scholarly lectures ensure salvation or indicate that it has already been acquired is uncertain.

Interrelations Among Disciplines

In Figure 2, the various disciplines are exhibited in a way that points up certain interrelationships. These relationships are

Figure 2. An Organization of the Disciplines.

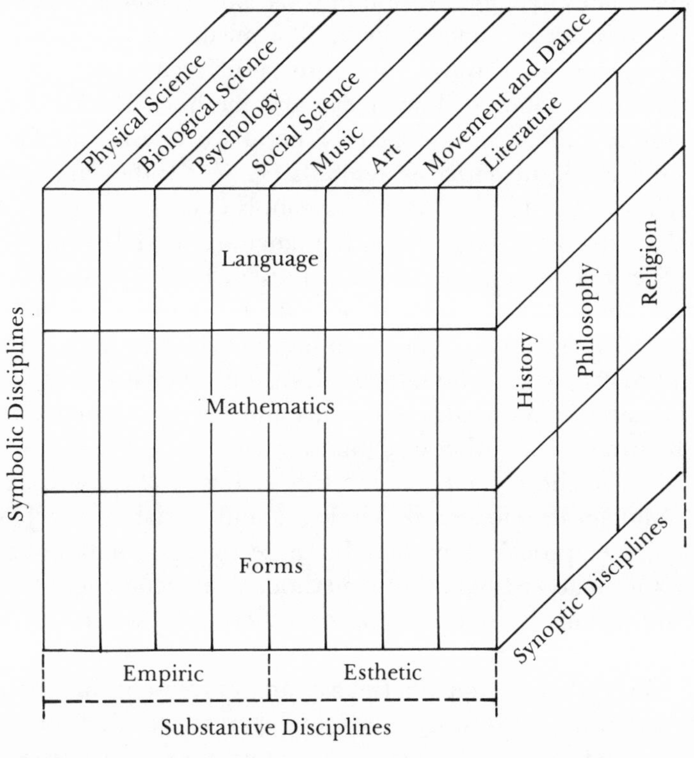

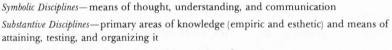

Symbolic Disciplines—means of thought, understanding, and communication

Substantive Disciplines—primary areas of knowledge (empiric and esthetic) and means of attaining, testing, and organizing it

Synoptic Disciplines—interpretation and integration of meaning

reasonably obvious but are largely ignored when attention is focused on discussion of teaching or on the curriculum. On the left, the symbolic disciplines are arrayed; these include language, mathematics, and nondiscursive symbolic forms. Language, as here used, indicates the assignment of words as ways of referring to and talking about objects or ideas. These words are conjoined in various ways with connectors and modifiers into sentences, paragraphs, and longer statements and, by various manipulations, provide means of thinking and communicating about ideas over all areas of knowledge. Mathematics, on this same vertical dimension, indicates the use of numbers and symbols elaborated into various forms and modes of analysis. Mathematics, as considered here, is a means of thinking and communication that draws upon, but is different from, mathematics as a discipline of knowledge and method. The third element on this dimension is that of nondiscursive forms. These are found in mathematics as symbols (+, –, ×); they are found in religion in the form of various symbols (a cross, †) signifying rites that are performed. Even the language used in some religious rites becomes essentially a nondiscursive form, since it is repeated by rote time after time, with no immediate sense of meaning. This symbolic dimension indicates clearly that the disciplines of language and mathematics should be viewed as areas of fundamental knowledge and skills and taught in such a way as to be useful in all other disciplines.

The sciences named at the top of Figure 2 (physical science, biological science, psychology, and social science) are essentially empirical in nature. In these sciences, data are collected and analyzed by various methods. The general concepts, laws, and principles that emerge from these analyses are the discipline's primary concerns.

The esthetics domain (music, art, movement, and literature) is approached through study of separate works. From the purely esthetic point of view, the importance of a particular work is to be found in that work. In music, art, and in movement, language, mathematics, or nondiscursive forms are not actually necessary to the creation of knowledge. However, without the addition of symbolics, analysis within these esthetic disciplines is impossible. Literature differs from the other esthetic areas because language is used to create it. Words, phrases, and sentences, then, are somewhat equivalent to sounds in music, to colors and media used in art, and to separate movements of dance. Viewed as a structure created out of words, language for the discussion of esthetic literature might appear unnecessary; but, again, until a language is created for assessing a piece of literature, there is no possibility of scholarly criticism or appreciation. The empirics and esthetics combine to make up the primary disciplines. Empirics move from undifferentiable or essentially identical entities to generalizations that apply to all.

Hence the laws or principles that emerge can be applied to solve specific problems. Esthetics moves from unique entities to generalizations that can be applied to critique these entities.

History, philosophy, and religion attempt to provide a different kind of understanding of knowledge in the various disciplines. They are wholly dependent upon symbolics for thought and communication. Each of the primary disciplines has a history and has made a major contribution to the development of history. Thus, to understand a discipline, knowledge of its historical development is crucial. And, in viewing the history of mankind and its interaction with the physical world, one must draw upon not only the separate disciplines but also their interrelationships. One must review the development of knowledge in all areas and seek general insights that transcend particular bodies of knowledge. It must be kept in mind that the several primary disciplines are artifacts of human endeavors and, although there is, to some extent, a philosophy implicit in each of the disciplines, the broader approach to philosophy transcends the disciplines. Religion depends upon language, and sometimes (for example, with the Trinity) on mathematical concepts and symbolic forms, but it also relies upon the force of relationships, organization, form, and matter that constitutes the subjects of the primary disciplines. Religion attempts to reach out beyond the immediate world and to find ultimate answers, both about the origins of mankind and the physical world and the ultimate fates and purposes served.

Morals, ethics, and synnoetics are not included in the Figure 2 diagram. As subject matter for study, they appear in the social sciences, psychology, literature, history, philosophy, and religion. Personal development and commitment are influenced by learning, but they are not separable parts of the formal processes of education.

Summary

In this chapter, we have presented the major characteristics of the disciplines within the six realms of meaning identified by Philip Phenix. Teachers must have knowledge of these characteristics not only for curricular planning but also for effective teaching within the context of the disciplines. The various disciplines are viewed as mankind's effort to organize knowledge and to attain and enlarge meaning. For teachers, the patterns of meaning exemplified in the various disciplines should guide their selection and organization of course content. For their students, teachers must foster a general understanding of the disciplines—not as ends but as means of maximizing growth in meaning and full educational development. By learning about the structures of and interrelations among the disciplines, students will come to recognize the connections between their education and the larger patterns within the disciplines and will learn to search for interdisciplinary solutions to complex academic and societal issues. Humanizing education encourages comprehension of the disciplines as a means for attaining meaning and deepening understanding. Within this disciplinary context, teachers will embody Phenix's characterization of their educational role as "humanizers of knowledge."

In the next chapter, the implications of this conception of teaching within the disciplines will be considered.

Suggestions for Further Reading

Ford, G. W., and Pugno, L. (Eds.). *The Structure of Knowledge and the Curriculum.* Chicago: Rand McNally, 1964.

Hong, H. (Ed.). *Integration in the Christian Liberal Arts College.* Northfield, Minn.: St. Olaf College Press, 1955.

King, A. R., Jr., and Brownell, J. A. *The Curriculum and the Disciplines of Knowledge, A Theory of Curriculum Practice.* New York: Wiley, 1966.

Phenix, P. H. *Realms of Meaning: A Philosophy of the Curriculum for General Education.* New York: McGraw-Hill, 1964.

Whitehead, A. N., and Russell, B. *Principia Mathematica.* New York: Cambridge University Press, 1915.

7

Teaching Within the Disciplines

Teaching within a discipline is fragmentary and antithetical to a liberal education unless the learner acquires insights into the origins, essential nature, and development of the discipline. Both its distinctiveness and its interrelations with other disciplines must be grasped. A discipline is both a mode and an area of inquiry possessing a set of interrelated concepts and principles accumulated, validated, and continually expanded by use of those techniques that characterize its mode of inquiry. A discipline has usually emerged from the study of practical problems, but its continuing investigations and theoretical development do not depend directly on these original problems, although theory development often helps clarify them. Many of the areas of inquiry of a discipline arise from inconsistencies or contradictions implicit in its basic concepts and assumptions and, hence, in its findings. The discipline itself may be changed by attempts to resolve those difficulties, as, for example, in the transition from classical physics to relativity. Likewise, attempts to extend the discipline to a new set of problems may lead to modification of the discipline, or to conjoining it with other disciplines to define a new interdisciplinary or transdisciplinary field of study. Education, medicine, law, and engineering are examples. Neither a discipline nor a field of study can be equated to existing courses or to a definite body of subject matter. The possible substantive content of a discipline is unlimited because its mode of inquiry can be applied to diverse content, subject matter, or problems. A discipline is not committed to extrinsic ends but solely to the expansion of knowledge.

There are a number of ways of approaching the task of disciplinary-based teaching in a course or field. One is content coverage, which emphasizes the teacher's obligation to acquaint students with those facts, concepts, and principles that define the basic content of the discipline as viewed at that period in its development. A second emphasis is on the mode of inquiry of the discipline (as of that moment), including both the means of inquiry and the logic and organizational structure. A third emphasis is on the applications of the discipline and frequently sacrifices fundamental disciplinary understandings to the use of specific concepts in the analysis and resolution of problems. This emphasis moves toward a transdisciplinary orientation. A fourth emphasis stresses the values and biases implicit or explicit in a discipline and in its application to individuals and society. Ethics and morals may enter the discussion. A fifth emphasis stresses selection of content and educational experiences for immediate and long-term personal development and social needs. Indeed, each of the first four emphases can be regarded as particular manifestations of this fifth emphasis, although teachers selecting one of the first four may allow their disciplinary commitments to override humanistic and social orientations. The fifth emphasis can and has led to "educational" programs that are mere "housebreaking." If the primary emphasis in higher education is put upon development of learner cognition, balanced with affective sensitivity and value commitments and supported by psychomotor skills, then the call for relevance in the fifth emphasis will lead to instructional practices to promote integrative learning, incorporating all five emphases. Teachers who attempt this will find that, although disciplinary boundaries may continue to provide convenient ways of structuring learning experiences, the learnings that are retained and used are largely those that are incorporated into a transdisciplinary view of the world—the problems, opportunities, and satisfactions of living in it and ultimately leaving it.

This chapter will consider the views of scholars in various disciplines that support a disciplinary or transdisciplinary approach to teaching and learning. Three of the realms of knowledge discussed in Chapter Six—symbolics, empirics, and esthetics—will be used to organize these views.

Symbolics

Language, mathematics, and nondiscursive symbolic forms are closely related to thinking. Indeed, thinking is a process of intercommunication and interaction with oneself. Symbolics are essential also for collaborating in thought with others and for communicating to others the results of one's thoughts, whether in empirics, ethics, or synoptics. Moreover, ability to communicate in some measure in all of these realms is important for full personal development. Communication is fundamental; the effectiveness of all other aspects of education depends upon it (Wynne, 1952, p. 60). This conception of symbolics indicates that the subject matter of this realm is much broader than composition, grammar, reading, and speech, vested in English and speech departments. It includes foreign languages, journalism, cinema, television, logic, linguistics, and semantics, as well as all of the substantive disciplines.

Communication must always be about something, and the nature of the communication process and the symbols utilized depend upon the subject matter. There is, therefore, no such thing as teaching someone how to communicate generally. Communication always takes place in the context of an interest and a desire for knowledge. Over twenty years ago, Rice (1960) advocated abolishing freshman English and forcing all departments and teachers to accept responsibility for student communication skills. This view simply recognizes that learning is itself a communication process, in that acquiring, organizing, and applying knowledge require both the reception and the expression of knowledge.

Grittner (1969, pp. 24-25) points out that one's native language puts limitations on one's world view that are not even perceived so long as the individual remains wholly monolingual. All languages distort meanings by the structures imposed. Even limited incursions into the complexities of phrasing an idea in two or more languages, or into comparing summaries of the same event in different languages (how, for example, British, American, and French historians have dealt with the events at Yorktown in 1781), makes the point. The distinction between a concept and the words used to express it is almost impossible until the concept is considered in two or more languages. The English *flat* (a form of apartment housing) goes into Spanish (at least in Venezuela) as *la propriedad horizontal*!

To some extent, mathematics in the modern day is independent of time, place, language, and culture, because much of mathematical symbolization has become international. Moreover, some mathematical expressions or forms are almost as closely related to the idea or operation indicated as is an arrow to the direction in which it points. The arrow, as an example of a nondiscursive symbolic form, would appear to be an unambiguous indicator of direction. However, even such forms may be culture or place bound. An arrow pointing up means one thing on a highway sign and another on an elevator button. Is a wind from the west blowing east an east or west wind? The symbol – can mean subtraction (minus) or can indicate a following elaboration (dash) of what preceded.

The following learning experiences can be used to help learners grasp the nature of the symbolic disciplines:

1. Express a concept (number, for example) without using symbolic forms.
2. Express a concept orally or in writing, using symbols or words different from those used in the textbook or by the teacher.
3. Find the equivalent expression (word, phrase, or symbol) for a concept, idea, or adage in one or more other languages.
4. Express in ordinary language the definition of a concept, symbol, object, or geometrical curve. Examples: + (plus),

† (cross), X (multiplication), ÷ (division), circle, inertia, beauty.

5. Write the mathematical equation of a curve using various axes of reference. Indicate those reference axes that provide the simplest formula. What happens to the curve as the axes are changed?
6. Communicate a new concept or idea to someone with little or no background in the field where the concept is commonly used.
7. Select a number of common words and look up the various possible meanings, especially those relating to use in different disciplines. Examples: *color, value, force, constant, principle, law.*

Empirics

Physical Science. Science training is useful if it enables a person to understand a scientific phenomenon or to learn by observing it. This requires a background of information acquired in such manner that the learner can assimilate additional information and apply it to novel scientific problems. The learner must understand that science is both experimental and philosophical. As Nedelsky (1965, p. 51) has noted:

> He [the student] should be shown that physics is not isolated, independent, and autonomous assertions and methods; that these, on the contrary, are interrelated; and that physics has coherence, unity, and its own kind of beauty. He should also be aware of its difference from and relation to other disciplines. Without integrative content it is unlikely that a student will reach an enduring understanding even of the separate parts into which, for teaching purposes, physics must be divided. The integration may proceed in several ways. For instance, the teacher may emphasize historical development or the analysis of situations that involve principles of several disciplines; or he may compare and contrast the goals, methods, and basic assumptions of physicists and scholars of other disciplines. Whatever organizing principle the teacher chooses, he should make clear to the students what it is and how he proposes to use it. Explicit peda-

gogy may itself be considered a type of integrative content, for it may help the student form a more coherent image of the course.

To acquire insight into the structure and changing nature of scientific knowledge, the learner needs to have some grasp of:

- the history of science and technology and their impact on human culture and history
- the continuing confrontation of science with religion and the humanities
- the contributions of science to other disciplines (history) and fields of study (medicine), and the resulting changes in them
- the difficulties of exact formulation and communication in the sciences
- the limitations of scientific inquiry to those aspects of a problem or phenomenon that are susceptible to scientific analysis, and the resulting difficulties in attaining a unified and complete conception of the world and of man
- the increasing concern of science with the moral and ethical issues raised by its findings, accompanied by recognition that science cannot provide answers to the fundamental issues of rightness, good, equity, or beauty
- the fact that science provides insights within the limits of certain assumptions and commitments, and that the answers it provides lead usually to more profound and complex questions

As Taylor (1952, p. 222) has pointed out:

> This is not to say that science is sterile in dealing with problems of human conduct. It does provide a sanative influence in behavior problems. Its end is knowledge, *scientia,* and it can testify to the qualities that are conducive to those ends. In the attainment of those ends the scientist will employ a whole spectrum of virtues. Industry, fidelity, detachment, objectivity, patience, perseverance, cooperation, these are among the qualities which he will bring to the solution of a scientific problem—

and he learns that by their employment he can then more effectively gain his objective, new scientific knowledge. Science and the works of the scientist call attention to the primacy of truth and reason, can reveal the virtues of a life dedicated to rational values and emphasize the dangers of any attack upon truth. But these virtues and dangers are not exhibited only in the scientific disciplines. Philosophy, history, art, theology, all emphasize the virtues of reason and the pursuit of truth, the dangers that stem from the assault, from whatever quarter, on such activities.

The findings of science should be viewed as approximations to truth rather than as ultimate truth. Moreover, much of science rests on faith in unproven and unprovable principles. Scientists cannot *prove* that the first and second laws of thermodynamics are true. They *can assert* that no one has yet succeeded in creating perpetual motion machines. The determinism of science is simply an assumption of order and of the operation of definite laws that the scientist seeks to uncover by observation of physical phenomena. These laws of nature are laws of probability, statistical conclusions based generally on a large number of participating undifferentiable units or events. The scientist studies the statistical behavior of crowds, not of identifiable individuals within them. Scientific inquiry leads to symbolic knowledge. The real nature of what science studies and tries to explain continually eludes the measuring procedures.

The items of scientific understanding needed by the learner, as listed earlier, suggest a range of desirable learning experiences. The history of any scientific development over a span of years reflects both the ingenuity of the human mind and the difficulties of probing into the nature and cause of events in the physical and biological world. The experiences of Galileo and others with the church demonstrate the confrontation of science and religion, extending even today into debate about the place of evolution and creationism in public education. The impact of scientific findings and technology on art, paper making and printing, dating of archeological discoveries, and medicine and health care provides ample opportunity for reading and study materials that reflect the pervasive role of science in human culture. Discussion of recent explorations into space, on the one hand, and into the ultimate particles of matter, on the other, furnishes insights into both microscopic and macroscopic frontiers of scientific research.

Perhaps every student should have the experience of hearing or reading the critiques and interactions of scientists' reports of new developments. The letters section of *Science* (the publication of the American Association for the Advancement of Science), for example, clearly indicates that scientists are not always objective.

The costs of "big science" in the modern world (atom smashers, telescopes, and space explorers) should be brought to the attention of every student, along with the awareness that these costs often entail the postponement or abandonment of desirable social programs, on the one hand, and the loss of competitive and combative power, on the other. The survival of nations may ultimately have to be weighed against the survival of mankind.

Social Science. Knopf and Stauss (1960, p. 82), in discussing the teaching of elementary economics, provide an analysis applicable to all of the social sciences. They consider that the fundamental objective of a college education is to develop the student's ability to think and thereby to continue learning. They propose that a course develop a learner's ability to engage in self-directed learning by requiring papers and discussions, with emphasis on the clarity of communication. They propose the *case method* as a unique approach because it requires preparation of new materials describing real life problems that call for solution. These materials may include descriptions of the application of various economic tools, as well as historical examples of use or misuse of economic concepts or principles. The cases can be chosen to sample a wide range of problems and to encourage the student to use various sources of economic information. The case method provides both for creative individual practice and for discussions or quizzes. Carefully selected cases can be sequential and cumulative. Individuals or small groups may become motivated to find or develop cases for study and analysis. In analyzing cases, learners must act in some ways like economists; they practice economics rather than simply acquire economic knowledge. Students become aware of the value commitments of the economic system (growth, stability, security, freedom, and justice) and the conflicts generated by policies adopted to promote these values. The case method also provides experience in the problem-solving approach and inherent communication difficulties in using it. Students learn that the choice of a solution is influenced by many factors, including the magnitude of the problem, the conflicting beliefs and traditions of pressure groups, the politics of decision making, and costs in both dollars and benefits forgone. The use of cases permits individualization and encourages curiosity about the effects of economic issues on society, which may lead to an abiding interest in economics.

The case method (or problem) approach has advantages in providing a focus for student activity distinctly different from that of reading a text or listening to lectures and momentarily memorizing the content covered. However, this approach requires a continual flow of new cases or problems in order to remain current and to ensure that students do not simply shirk effort by acquiring the notes of cases used in previous classes. Furthermore, this approach requires the teacher to exercise great restraint while observing, listening, and making suggestions to students as they review the cases. The reading of student papers assigned to encourage analytic thought is quickly found to be more arduous than assignment of grades.

For some teachers, the use of the case or problem method accompanied by in-class analysis by students means forgoing the preferred and academically prestigious professor-scholar-lecturer role. However, economics presented as a set of concepts and theories devoid of the difficulties that arise when attempting to apply it to social and fiscal problems, especially in recent years, provides little understanding of the role of the discipline in society. Indeed, the discipline is widely regarded—even by those operating within it—as confused, chaotic, and sterile. Even if this state of affairs in regard to the discipline is accepted, some grasp of its nature and of the problems of applying it is desirable for all educated citizens.

Political Science. Connery (1965) provides a number of

sage observations on the teaching of political science. He notes that most beginning courses are based upon American government, comparative government, political theory, or a combination of these. Far Eastern governments or those of underdeveloped countries might be more appropriate starting points, he argues, since they would be both new and different to students. He suggests that carefully selected readings should accompany regular courses, that instruction in reading such materials might be helpful, and that special efforts should be made to arouse students' interest in them. He further raises the unanswerable question of whether politics can best be studied by examining the history of the past or by reading great works of literature.

Hyneman (1965, p. 225) emphasizes the analytic essay as a means of promoting student learning. After presentation and discussion of a model, each student is required to select an act (law) for close analysis and for the evaluation of the restraints imposed to protect a widely recognized value. Loyalty oaths and obscenity statutes exemplify the nature of the analysis task. Hyneman points out that care must be exercised in selecting statutes appropriate to the learners' maturity, that a set of instructions must be provided by the teacher, and that any act reviewed by a high court for constitutionality is best avoided because of the great volume of material and the prejudicial impact on the student of the court decision. This type of assignment is similar to the case study approach used in economics and shares with it the advantages and disadvantages of student involvement and professorial restraint.

Brookes (1965, p. 81) points out that "a university teacher's job is not so much to teach political science or economics or history as to teach the ultimate wisdom of life, the accumulated treasures of the ages through the medium of political science or economics or history." However, the ultimate wisdom has not been found and is not likely to be. Better understanding or insight is about all we can hope for in the social sciences. Krug (1967, p. 83) states:

> It is important and potentially helpful to remember that while each of the social sciences has developed its own particular terms and even its "jargon," most social science concepts are

truly interdisciplinary. "Class," "status," and "elite," for instance, are concepts freely used by sociologists, anthropologists, political scientists, and economists. However, in each science the concept is used in a different way and context, and each has produced a useful body of research results explaining the meaning of these concepts for a better understanding of human behavior and society.

The preceding suggestions about instruction in economics and in political science can readily be adapted to sociology, geography, psychology, or other social sciences. Many historians would include history. The phrases "ultimate wisdom of life" and "better understanding of human behavior and society" from the quotations also indicate that these disciplines can be so treated as to contribute to broad educational goals and to personal development rather than as ends in themselves.

Esthetics

Literature. The recognition of literature as a discipline is threatened by the tendency of many literature professors to see their major goal of study as an extensive knowledge of major works and writers. If to English and American literature, one adds the literature of the non-English sector of the Western world and that of the non-Western world, the total number of significant writers and works becomes encyclopedic and overwhelming, even for very large departments with many courses and professors. Rote recall and association of names and titles, accompanied by a few well-polished descriptive phrases, can become the accepted indicators of literary competency. Such a misconception readily lends itself to (or perhaps is derived from) broad surveys of literature that, at best, provide a veneer of knowledge. These courses afford no real understanding of literature as an art form, grounded in language and history, shaped by current religious beliefs, and reflecting the culture from which it arises. However, if general education survey courses are discredited on these or other grounds, and single courses devoted to particular genres, authors, or works placed on the intellectual bill of fare, this subordinates literature and its essential developmental aspects to the appreciation of each work as complete and intrinsically satisfying in itself. Caught in the impossible choice between expansiveness in coverage and concentration on a few selections, learners may fail to develop ability to analyze specific works in terms of the interplay of the message with mode of delivery, the environmental background, and the literary skill of the artist.

Courses in literature often fail to develop in learners a recognition of literature as a discipline and an art form. Accordingly, they also fail to develop those capacities that might encourage individuals to expand their exploration of literature as a means both of pleasure and of the realization of the interconnectedness of knowledge—especially of the relationships among perceptions, thought, language, emotion, and logic.

If a literature course is to provide these broader, deeper, and more pervasive habits and abilities, the following learning experiences may be productive.

1. Develop an outline or set of questions to guide student assessment of any literary work. (Table 4 is an example). Ask all students to use this form in appraising some work not discussed in class. Review in class the range of responses to each question and consider the cogency and applicability of the responses. Continue with a second work using a selection differing in some respects, such as author, period, or genre. For further efforts, ask students to work by themselves on a work they select, or in small groups on a work the group selects.
2. Present students with elaborations of the same issue or idea in several different genres in order that the students perceive something of the relation between ideas and modes of expressing them. Alternatively, students may be asked to seek their own examples.
3. Expand the experiences described in the preceding suggestion to include works of art, music, and movement that seem to treat the same issues.
4. Call upon those students in class with some language facility. Ask them to consider the problem of expressing an idea in a language, in contrast to word-for-word translation of an idea from one language to another.

Table 4. A List of Abilities in Critical Judgments in the Humanities.

Part One: Informal Notes

Immediate (Pre-Analytical) Subjective Reactions.

1. The subject matter and idea of the work and its expressive, communicative and evocative roles.
   a. Recognition of the subject matter or explicit recognition of the fact that there is no subject matter in the representational, imitative, or referential sense.
   b. Statement of personal thoughts and feelings of the student evoked by the work.
   c. Explicit recognition by the student of the subjectivity of personal thoughts and feelings evoked in him or her by the work.
   d. Comment on the probable ability of the work to arouse subjective reactions in people other than the student.
   e. Description of ideas and feelings of the maker that seem to be expressed in the work.

Analysis.

2. *Function and Context:* The action and roles of the work of art in relationship to the various combinations of circumstances (contexts) within which it has had or does have meaning.
   a. Recognition of any political, religious, sociological, or economic functions of the work, or of the fact that it has none.
   b. Recognition of the esthetic function of the work, its role in bringing pleasure through perfection of form.
   c. Demonstration of the influence of various external factors, such as social context and environment, on the nature of the work.
   d. Speculation on the influence that the work might have upon society.
3. *Medium:* The nature, use, and importance of medium in the work. In this section, medium is used to mean language in literature and instruments or voice in music, as well as medium in paintings.
   a. Recognition and description of the medium used in the work.
   b. Recognition and description of the general methods of expression used in the work.
   c. Recognition of the conventionality or unconventionality of the medium, use of language, use of instruments, or method of expression.
   d. Comment on the way that the limitations and possibilities of the medium influence the nature of the work.
   e. Comment on the way in which his esthetic problem influenced the maker in his choice of a particular medium.
   f. Ability to distinguish between performer and work performed, reproduction and original.
4. *Formal Elements and Organization:* Consideration of separate major parts whose relationships to one another create the significance of the

(continued on next page)

Table 4. A List of Abilities in Critical Judgments in the Humanities, Cont'd.

form of the work, and of things done to give unity, order, consistency, and intrinsic significance.

a. Discovery and isolation of major or predominant elements ("devices" in literature) in the work.
b. Objective description and characterization of the major elements ("devices" in literature).
c Comment on the expressive quality of separate elements ("devices" in literature).
d. Comment on the independent function that separate elements ("devices" in literature) have in the total work, or recognition that there is no independent function.
e. Recognition of symbols or symbolic usages *together with* descriptions of their use and meaning in the work.
f. Recognition of the conventionality or unconventionality of the use of elements ("devices" in literature).
g. Recognition and description of a plan, scheme, or structure on which the work is based—a principle of organization governing the relationship of formal elements to each other in the total work.
h. Recognition of qualities or aspects of organization (without necessarily naming them as such): dominance, subordination, unity, variety, balance, symmetry, proportion, continuity, consistency, emphasis, tension, rhythm, movement, repetition, distortion, and so forth.
i. Exemplification of qualities or aspects of organization found in the work by concrete references to the work.
j. Speculation as to whether external factors have influenced the nature of the organization of the work.
k. Comment on the use of organizational devices or overall organization for expressive purposes.

5. *Style:* Qualities of the work that are characteristic of the various forces that have affected its production.
   a. Description of style characteristics generally typical of the historical period or era.
   b. Description of style characteristics typical of the particular school, trend, or movement within a historical period.
   c. Description of style characteristics typical of the maker of the work.

Part Two: Critical Judgment

6. Part Two offers students an opportunity to express a total reaction to or judgment of the work. Presumably they will make use of ideas or facts perceived during the analytic process of Part One, but they are free to select, reject, and add as they wish. Their statement should sum up their concept of the general meaning or significance of the

Table 4. A List of Abilities in Critical Judgments in the Humanities, Cont'd.

work. While this statement should be an overall reaction, including the factors concerning the work that they think are most pertinent, it cannot be expected to cover and include all of the various kinds of significance that the work has within its total field.

a. Demonstration of a total, overall coherent perception of the significance of the work.
b. Perception of the interrelations of form and content in the work.
c. Evidence that the student has attempted to respond to the work at its primary level of significance—verbal, visual, sonic, tactile, and so forth.
d. Effective use of factors noted in Part One, and evidence of care in both inclusion and exclusion.
e. Evidence of an attempt to express reactions other than logical or rational.
f. Demonstration of the ability to separate personal, subjective judgments from judgments based on qualities intrinsic in the work.
g. Recognition of the various contexts within which value judgments can be assigned (comparison of this work with other works by the same artist, with works of art of all kinds and in all times, with important human endeavors in any field).
h. Recognition of the unique quality of the particular work and the unique nature of the student's experience in perceiving this particular work.

Evaluation of Student Responses

The preceding outline is used by the student as a set of suggestions for observation and comment in reference to a particular work in art, literature, or music. Following are some suggestions for evaluating student response.

1. The instructor must become familiar with the abilities listed and with the categories in which they fall. Perhaps the best way of doing this is for the instructor to respond to the same work as the student, write out answers, and review them critically. If several instructors are jointly involved, an open discussion of the range and nature of the responses will be excellent preparation for the evaluation of student responses. However, the instructors engaging in evaluation of student responses must not expect that students will give the same response that the instructor has provided but, indeed, must expect that student responses will, in toto, expand the range of possible responses.
2. The instructor must read through the student responses carefully and seek for demonstration of the abilities. The abilities implied by the points of the outline will not always be in one-to-one correspondence with the actual ability revealed by the student in a particular com-

(continued on next page)

Table 4. A List of Abilities in Critical Judgments in the Humanities, Cont'd.

ment. Thus it is important to note, when particular abilities are evidenced, whether or not they appear in response to a particular outline point. Comments evidencing a particular ability may vary greatly in insight and language sophistication. It should be sufficient to the immediate purpose if a count is made of the demonstration of an ability regardless of the quality or sophistication. Feedback to the student and discussion among students will help embed the various criteria involved in the list; and instructor comment will, in time, increase the insight and sophistication.

3. The instructor may be interested in counting the number of abilities demonstrated by student responses in order to determine the range in initial student responses and set a base line for determining, over time, how much the number of significant reactions increases. A similar, though somewhat more complicated, evaluation procedure can be developed to cover increase in critical insight and sophistication in use of words and phrases.

Source: P. L. Dressel and L. B. Mayhew, *Critical Analysis and Judgment in the Humanities* (Dubuque, Iowa: Brown, 1956), pp. 74-76.

Although these suggestions may require a flexibility that forbids coverage of a predetermined set of works or authors, it is likely that this type of structure will encourage such explorations more than a completely open-ended plan.

History. The first thing that anyone should learn about history as a discipline is that the past does not become history until someone attempts to determine exactly what happened in a certain time and place and explain how and why it happened. History is an imaginative reconstruction of an apparently interrelated set of events, accompanied by an effort to explain them. The explanation is largely philosophical, involving judgments based upon both scholarly values and commitments modified by unrecognized biases. Foremost among the latter are nationalism and ideologies, including religion.

In a very real sense, every generation writes its own history. New evidence is found, new interpretations of old evidence are made, and the hypotheses of previous writers are reexamined. The lapse of time puts events into a fuller perspective in relation to other events of the same or later periods.

The following criteria for selecting experiences that will

assist students in attaining these insights are a paraphrase of those presented by Krug (1967, pp. 8-36, especially):

1. Promote realization that history is not the actual past but the ever-changing attempts of historians to reconstruct segments of the past. Comparative study of various interpretations helps to bring this realization about. Students may even conduct their own investigations and question established historical interpretations.
2. As a useful and absorbing learning experience for students, develop an understanding of how a particular historian approached his writing of history.
3. Allow students to become aware of worthy and unworthy acts, of basic strengths and occasional blunders of statesmen, and generally of the accomplishments and failures and unfinished tasks of nations.
4. Have students follow up on the later modification or discrediting of certain historical generalizations, such as Beard's (1935) economic interpretations of history or Turner's (1920) hypothesis on the influence of the frontier on the course of American history.
5. Expose students to the use of primary historical documents, such as letters.
6. Enable students to participate in the controversy over Toynbee's (1959) conception of history.
7. Help students understand how an organized and coherent knowledge of history can permit better insight into contemporary and controversial issues. Thus the history and past decisions of the Supreme Court increase understanding of recent Court decisions on publication of obscene materials. Some basic knowledge about the history of China is essential for understanding current Chinese foreign policy.
8. Have students read historical works such as those of Thucydides, Plutarch, Macaulay, Gibbon, Trevelyan, Parkman, and Prescott.

Krug (1967) further comments on the relation of history to the social sciences and technology:

History differs from the social sciences in other important aspects. While social scientists concentrate their efforts on the formulation of general concepts and on the discovery of widely applicable patterns, generalizations, and laws, historians (while not ignoring "laws" and "higher" generalizations) are at least equally interested in the *singular,* the *concrete,* and the *unique.* For instance, classical sociology, as defined by Max Weber, is interested in the constant and repetitive element in human society, past and present, in what social facts have in common, and ignores the unique aspects of events and treats them as social types. History, on the other hand, focuses its attention much more on the *special* event, the *outstanding* personality, and the *unique* trend of developments in a *particular* situation [p. 47].

A number of historians have recently testified to the debt they owed to psychology and psychiatry for a better understanding of the subjects of their inquiries. David Donald (1960) acknowledged the great benefit he derived from frequent consultations with psychiatrists in the course of writing his biography of Charles Sumner. He was especially grateful for the psychological insights which provided a better understanding of Sumner's complex character and especially his puzzling reactions to the assault on him by Congressman Brooks (p. 63).

Historians as a rule have neglected, and still neglect, the impact of science and technology on history. Scientist and novelist C. P. Snow, who complained about the culture gap between scientists and humanists, remarked that the steam engine helped shape the modern world at least as much as Napoleon and Adam Smith, but only rarely do historians admit the fact. The statement is obviously an exaggeration, but historians have until recently paid little attention to art, science, and technology [p. 103].

The volume by Stone (1981) is especially useful in pointing up the changing views of what history is and how it should be approached.

Philosophy. Philosophy differs from other disciplines largely because it employs a comprehensive, synoptic, and integrative approach to problems of nature and man. All disciplines start with the same observations and experiences based in reality, but each discipline, other than philosophy, history, and religion, limits its perspective to phenomena that appear interrelated yet are separable from the phenomena left to other disciplines. Although disciplines fragment and proliferate, they also overlap and interpenetrate, so that a full understanding of the character and focus of any discipline requires an intimate knowledge of its history and philosophical preconceptions. This emphasis, in turn, leads to greater cognizance of those concepts and methods of inquiry that emphasize the interrelations among disciplinary study and the interconnectedness of the disciplines in integrated human experiences.

Wynne (1952, pp. 63-64), in speaking of the place of philosophy in general education, says:

> Philosophy, like science, has its method as well as its subject matter. It consists in philosophizing as well as in the results of philosophizing that has been done by others. Like science, too, philosophy corresponds to the psychological aspect of human experience that is usually known as intellect. Both science and philosophy are functions of thought. Whereas the subject matter of science consists of organized facts and principles derived from an empirical study of limited fields, the subject matter of philosophy represents a synthesis of generalizations in regard to certain aspects of the whole world of nature and of man. Whereas the method of science consists in the empirical study of specific problems with respect to the nature of specific phenomena, the method of philosophy consists in the criticism of the assumptions of the sciences, the fine arts, and the practical arts as well as of other aspects of experience. The subject matter supplied by the other subjects as well as by philosophy itself is all grist for the philosopher's mill. The sciences have their fundamental assumptions, the fine arts have their theories and principles, including those of literary criticism, and the vocational and the recreational arts have their principles and standards. The subject matter of philosophy includes all and any subject matter of all other fields, both the principles that provide them with intellectual support and the practices in which such principles are exemplified. It also includes the great world of unclassified experience. *Philosophy is a process of criticism perhaps best conceived as the criticism of criticisms.*

Consistent with this view:

1. Students should be encouraged to analyze and criticize their texts and readings in all disciplines.
2. Lectures by the professor may contain, by deficiency or de-

sign, weaknesses of which students should be made aware. Opportunity for comment (perhaps anonymous initially) should be provided.

3. Students should become self-critical and engage regularly in evaluation of their individual and collective efforts. It is essential that the criticism be conducted in an objective rational fashion with the purpose of promoting learning, rather than becoming ego-annihilating or descending to mere competition for grades.

These philosophical approaches will inevitably bring ethical, moral, and other value issues into discussion and also engender cross-disciplinary references.

As Greene (1952, p. 101) has remarked:

> This characterization of philosophy in terms of its greater scope is useful despite the fact that the "horizontal" boundaries of the specialized disciplines are by no means rigidly established, each discipline tending increasingly as it advances to overlap certain other disciplines. The growing interpenetration of physics and chemistry, chemistry and biology, biology and psychology, psychology and sociology indicates that these disciplines are concerned not with radically different realities but rather with different aspects of the same all-embracing reality, and that the chief generic types of experience are in fact interrelated phases of a single all-embracing human experience.

Summary

This chapter has put strong emphasis upon how teaching within a disciplinary context must stress the way the subject of study in any discipline is interwoven with those of other disciplines, despite the current demarcations of single disciplines. Students must learn both the interrelations and the distinctive features of the disciplines to obtain a comprehensive and integrated understanding of educational experiences. Chapter Eight will pursue further these interrelationships by identifying transdisciplinary concepts and ideas.

Suggestions for Further Reading

Albert, E. M. (Ed.). *The Teaching of Anthropology.* Berkeley: University of California Press, 1963.

Anderson, O. R. "The Effects of Varying Structure in Science Content on the Acquisition of Science Knowledge." *Journal of Research in Science Teaching,* 1968, *5,* 361-364.

Applebee, A. N. *Tradition and Reform in the Teaching of English: A History.* Urbana, Ill.: National Council of Teachers of English, 1974.

Beard, C. A. *An Economic Interpretation of the Constitution of the United States.* New York: Macmillan, 1935.

Boulding, K. B. "The Task of the Teacher in the Social Sciences." In W. H. Morris (Ed.), *Effective College Teaching.* Washington, D.C.: American Association for Higher Education, 1970.

Brookes, E. H. "Through British Eyes." In R. H. Connery (Ed.), *Teaching Political Science: A Challenge to Higher Education.* Durham, N.C.: Duke University Press, 1965.

Carpenter, P. *History Teaching: The Era Approach.* Cambridge, England: Cambridge University Press, 1964.

Commager, H. S. *The Nature and Study of History.* Columbus, Ohio: Merrill, 1965.

Conant, J. B. (Ed.). *Harvard Case Histories in Experimental Science.* Cambridge, Mass.: Harvard University Press, 1957.

Connery, R. H. (Ed.). *Teaching Political Science: A Challenge to Higher Education.* Durham, N.C.: Duke University Press, 1965.

Council on Education in Geological Sciences. *Audio-Tutorial Instruction: A Strategy for Teaching Introductory College Geology.* Washington, D.C.: Council on Education in Geological Sciences, 1970.

Dean, D. S. *Preservice Preparation of College Biology Teachers: A Search For a Better Way.* Washington, D.C.: Commission on Undergraduate Education in the Biological Sciences, American Institute of Biological Sciences, 1970.

Donald, D. *Charles Sumner and the Coming of the Civil War.* New York: Knopf, 1960.

Dressel, P. L., and Mayhew, L. B. *Critical Analysis and Judgment in the Humanities.* Dubuque, Iowa: Brown, 1956.

Einstein, A., and Infeld, L. *The Evolution of Physics.* New York: Simon & Schuster, 1938.

Eiss, A. F., and Harbeck, M. B. *Behavioral Objectives in the Af-*

fective Domain. Washington, D.C.: National Education Association, 1969.

Elton, G. R. *The Practice of History.* New York: Crowell, 1967.

Eulau, H., and March, J. G. (Eds.). *Political Science.* Englewood Cliffs, N.J.: Prentice-Hall, 1969.

Gerber, J. C. (Ed.). *The College Teaching of English.* New York: Appleton-Century-Crofts, 1965.

Greene, T. M. "Philosophy." In H. N. Fairchild and Associates, *Religious Perspectives in College Teaching.* New York: Ronald Press, 1952.

Grittner, F. M. *Teaching Foreign Languages.* New York: Harper & Row, 1969.

Hyneman, C. S. "Some Crucial Learning Experiences." In R. H. Connery (Ed.), *Teaching Political Science: A Challenge to Higher Education.* Durham, N.C.: Duke University Press, 1965.

Joint Council on Economic Education. *College Preparation for Teaching Economics.* New York: Joint Council on Economic Education, 1969.

Knopf, K. A., and Stauss, J. H. (Eds.). *The Teaching of Elementary Economics.* New York: Holt, Rinehart and Winston, 1960.

Krislov, S. *A Laboratories Approach to Teaching Political Science.* Minneapolis: Department of Political Science, University of Minnesota, 1970.

Krug, M. M. *History and the Social Studies: New Approaches to the Teaching of Social Sciences.* Waltham, Mass.: Blaisdell, 1967.

Lado, R. *Language Teaching, A Scientific Approach.* New York: McGraw-Hill, 1964.

Lumsden, K. (Ed.). *New Developments in the Teaching of Economics.* Englewood Cliffs, N.J.: Prentice-Hall, 1972.

Nedelsky, L. *Science Teaching and Testing.* New York: Harcourt Brace Jovanovich, 1965.

Rice, W. "A Proposal for the Abolition of Freshman English As It Is Now Commonly Taught from the College Curriculum." *College English,* 1960, *21,* 361-367.

Rorecek, J. S. (Ed.). *The Teaching of History.* New York: Philosophical Library, 1967.

Smith, A. H., and Fischer, J. L. (Eds.). *Anthropology.* Englewood Cliffs, N.J.: Prentice-Hall, 1970.

Stober, R. *The Nature of Historical Thinking.* Chapel Hill: University of North Carolina Press, 1967.

Stone, L. *The Past and the Present.* Boston: Routledge & Kegan Paul, 1981.

Taffe, E. J. *Geography.* Englewood Cliffs, N.J.: Prentice-Hall, 1970.

Taylor, H. S. "Physical Sciences." In H. N. Fairchild and Associates, *Religious Perspectives in College Teaching.* New York: Ronald Press, 1952.

Toynbee, A. J. *A Study of History.* (6 vols.) London: Oxford University Press, 1959.

Tricart, J. *The Teaching of Geography at University Level.* London: Harrap, 1969.

Turner, F. J. *The Frontier in American History.* New York: Holt, Rinehart and Winston, 1920.

Wynne, J. P. *General Education in Theory and Practice.* New York: Bookman, 1952.

8

Learning Through Transdisciplinary Teaching

A transdisciplinary structure provides a contextual framework for the learner. In the present college pattern in which instructional units are largely defined by disciplines, even the most thoughtful learner has some difficulty in understanding the nature of any single discipline studied and has relatively little chance to contrast and compare disciplinary approaches and the basis and utility of them. Attempts to develop courses that provide a transdisciplinary integrative experience have not been highly successful. For example, the typical general education social science course often becomes merely congeries of ideas and concepts selected from a group of disciplines identified as social sciences, in which the meaning of the disciplines is lost in terminology. Likewise, instructors of a course in a single discipline become so preoccupied with covering an unwieldy body of disciplinary content that often too little time is left to focus on the discipline itself. Moreover, individual teachers often lack the necessary knowledge and experience to explore the differences between the immediate discipline and other disciplines that use the same concepts or deal with the same problems.

Hence the linkages between the discipline and the real world, and the attention to definitions, values, units of measure, and procedures for ordering and validating relationships, are ignored in a formal educational process. This process assumes that individual students will learn to act like professors in particular disciplines. Therefore it is not surprising that teaching, which usually occurs as an administratively assigned function or as a teacher-assumed role, shows little relationship to the model of learning sought by the learner. Under the present pattern of undergraduate education, the teacher too frequently presents relatively unattractive packages of largely irrelevant material to students, who have paid in advance but with little knowledge of and no choice about the product they purchased. *Disciplines have come to have intrinsic value to the specialists in them, whereas the learner seeks for their extrinsic values.* This accounts for much of the inadequate teaching and learning found in college.

Role of Transdisciplinary Concepts in Learning

Integrative, transdisciplinary concepts are important in learning because they permit the individual to organize learning and to apply it intelligently to new situations. Concepts permit or encourage:

1. appreciation (illumination, motivation, inspiration, liberation)
2. direction (endorsement, exhortation, habituation, requirement, environment)
3. economy in and facilitation of communication (discussion, cooperation)
4. mediation (introduction, foundation, key ideas or tools)
5. imagination (creativity, discovery, inquiry, hypothesization)
6. identification (observation, description, specification, definition, measurement)

7. prediction (estimation, calculation, explanation)
8. differentiation (classification, analysis, discrimination, separation, comparison, contrast, qualification, delimitation)
9. integration (organization, unification, synthesis, summarization, generalization, relation, harmony, order)

Such functions occur in all disciplines and are fundamental to understanding disciplines and their composite meanings.

In addition to the cognitive and esthetic functions just listed, there are many other types of concepts. The following list, with at least one parenthetical example, suggests those types now emphasized:

1. ideas (balance, function)
2. rules (use of punctuation)
3. generalizations (all mankind is interdependent)
4. principles or laws (gas laws, laws of thermodynamics)
5. theories (evolution)
6. problems (conservation of natural resources)
7. aspects of life and life processes (metabolism)

Of these, the first is perhaps the concept in the pure form, whereas the second through the sixth require a statement of relationships among concepts. The seventh, and perhaps also the sixth, require derivation of relationships among concepts in order to deal effectively with issues or problems.

Three illustrative and distinctive analyses illuminate the origin of concepts and steps in their development. The first, from Russell (1956, p. 121), simply indicates the initial experiences that give rise to a concept. In most cases, several such experiences, observation, memory, and sense of relationship (perhaps iconic) to other concepts combine to make or to reinforce a new concept.

The second analysis, from Wesley and Adams (1952, pp. 290-311), attempts to order social concepts from the very simplest to the most complex, thereby suggesting the sequence of educational experiences that need to be planned for progression through these levels:

1. things, places, persons, actions, and qualities
2. occurrences and events in place
3. relationships among individuals
4. relationships between man and nature
5. time and space
6. relationships between individuals and groups
7. personal and social codes, standards, and ideals
8. relationships among groups
9. relationships between society and groups

The third analysis, that of the concept of music, also represents a concrete attempt to produce such levels of conceptualization:

1. Concepts of highness, lowness, loudness, and softness are as concrete as concepts can become.
2. Higher abstractions are chords or phrases.
3. Consonance, cadence, and harmonic rhythm are at another level of abstraction.
4. Still higher are concepts such as counterpoint, cyclical form, and modulation.
5. These can be followed by still more abstract concepts such as types and form of music.
6. It is possible to merge musicological concepts with sociological concepts.

Various discussions on the nature of concepts place great emphasis on the emergence of their meanings from functional relationships. For example, with a child, an early concept of milk may be of white fluid to drink. This concept, however, is certainly not consciously generated or recognized in those words; rather, it is *operational* in the sense that the child notices the milk and associates it with drinking. Later, the concept of milk is extended to include something held by a glass, something provided by a cow, processed by a dairy, procured in a carton, and used by the body. At more sophisticated levels, after study of science and nutrition, numerous other relationships will be associated with the concept.

In contrast with the operational approach to a concept, one may attempt to make *abstract* definitions that are nonfunctional or nonoperational, but these reduce the environment to a world of things rather than a relationship of processes. For example, if milk were initially defined in terms of its chemical nature, this would have little meaning to a child because it would not relate in any way to immediate experience. Concepts, in order to be meaningful, must be made up of elements of past experience brought into some form of functional relationship.

A final consideration in selecting concepts is that of developing criteria for selection. The following seem appropriate:

1. important, central, key, fundamental
2. transmittable through planned educational experiences
3. based on or related to research
4. stimulate search for meaning and encourage further investigation
5. interrelate facts and lower level concepts
6. useful in decision making
7. directive, cumulative, and integrative

For effective learning, a student needs a framework made up of an appropriate set of clear, stable concepts, principles, or ideas at various levels of generality or inclusiveness (Ausubel, 1975, pp. 93-101). This a priori structure provides the optimal possibility for correlating, anchoring, bridging, or grouping new ideas in relation to those already known by inserting (subsuming or superordinating) them in the existing framework.

This framework serves as an organizing vehicle both for the assimilation of ideas and for their recall, transfer, and application in relevant circumstances. Organizing concepts and principles also helps bridge the gap between what is already known and what is to be learned from the task at hand. The types of concepts required for such a structure are those that relate to the five components of disciplinary structure:

1. subject matter concepts of great inclusiveness

2. concepts having to do with sequence, logic, organization, or practice
3. conjunctive or linguistic concepts that help to relate disciplines
4. concepts that relate to mode of inquiry
5. value concepts

The disciplinary approach has readily identifiable values. A discipline is an organization of accumulated knowledge and also a way of acquiring knowledge. A discipline includes, because of its origins in reality or in human concerns extending beyond reality, enactive (manipulation, performance), iconic (pictorial, graphic, representational), and symbolic (words or signs) aspects that can be used to expedite understanding. There is economy in learning through disciplines because knowledge is organized and constantly reinforced by addition and modification. Disciplines have power in promoting understanding and communication and provide control and predictability.

Nevertheless, recognition of the power and worth of the disciplines must not obscure the fact that disciplinary boundaries are arbitrary and unclear, and that *the primary role of education is as a humanizing process rather than as a process of disciplinary mastery.* In the remainder of this chapter, this humanizing role is used as a background for considering, in greater depth, the nature, relationships, and contributions of the various disciplines. This is accomplished by identifying pervasive concepts and several themes that affect the development and application of all disciplines. We suggest a type of approach rather than espouse a particular one. The good teacher must be, in some measure, transdisciplinary, but there is no formula for accomplishing this; if there were, transdisciplinary teaching could become as routine and dull as is much of disciplinary instruction.

The concept of a discipline is an artifact of man's search for understanding of himself and the world around him. Each discipline can be viewed in terms of the aspects of man and world that it treats, or the forms of thought and expression it uses. Either man or physical objects can be studied in terms of physical characteristics, chemical composition, beauty, or utility. Each discipline is limited in its focus, but there are certain ideas that are recurrently used across disciplines. In the biological sciences, taxonomies (phylum, class, order, family, genus, species) imposed upon fauna and flora have proved useful in study, understanding, and characterization of the many varieties of plants and animals. Social science uses the terms status, class, stratification, caste, tribe, clan, sept, and race to recognize group distinctions. Chemistry has in its periodic table a complex categorization of elements that has proved useful, not only in identifying and understanding chemical reactions but also in predicting new elements and interactions. Mathematics uses classes, sets, groups, and fields. Language itself uses many categories, including parts of speech, verb tenses, sentence types, and figures of speech. The development of a useful set of categories and the criteria for classifying within these categories the entities under inquiry are major components of every discipline. The multiplicity of terms—classification, categorization, stratification, separation, taxonomy, typology—indicates the tendency to differentiate large groups into homogeneous smaller ones.

Units of measure and principles for counting, ordering, or sequencing across the disciplines are important; these vary from counting and use of various types of measurement based on some unit to other unique measuring devices predicated upon particular qualities of the phenomena. The word *measure* as used in music refers to a unit. The attempts in the social and behavioral sciences to develop measures of attitudes and beliefs transfer to those disciplines some of the methodology found so essential in the physical sciences.

An idea that recurs in many disciplines is the clarification of the relationship between real and ideal. Physical laws based upon ideal gases are an example. In many cases, inability to agree on an ideal results in a compromise. Obvious real characteristics on which there is high agreement are specified while others are ignored or left to the ingenuity of following generations. Form or appearance may be exalted over function, especially when the latter is uncertain. There is, for example, no ideal classroom, instructional facility, teaching method, or pattern of learning experience for all instructors, students, and disciplines. We often settle for space, light, air, movable chairs, and an instructor's podium—an environment not necessarily conducive to learning or teaching.

The differentiation between real and ideal introduces the concept of value. Values prevail in some form in every discipline but vary in meaning and nature from discipline to discipline. Beauty has meaning to a mathematician, but it is hardly the same concept of beauty as conceived by the artist. Economy and efficiency are values of significance in business and engineering, whereas humanists may regard them as disastrous demands that endanger human values. The scientist prizes continuity and complementarity in the development of scientific knowledge and generally favors the simplest hypothesis that will explain all of the facts about a particular phenomenon at present known. Truth is a common concern in all disciplines, but it takes on distinctive meanings in the various disciplines and uses quite different procedures for validation or proof. Truth, too, is continually sought rather than finally found. Integrity (soundness, wholeness, completeness, honesty, propriety) is also a desideratum, as are simplicity (taste, elegance) and purity (perfection, virtue).

Each discipline is concerned with a range of relationships among the entities defined within its boundaries. Sociology studies groups and the collective behavior of individuals as they operate in groups. Psychology focuses upon individuals and the interrelationship of a number of identifiable characteristics of individuals. Study of these relationships helps to clarify and explain social entities, but such study also produces hypotheses that, in turn, permit investigations extending the range of disciplinary principles. Consistency in its various meanings (agreement, conformity, uniformity, accord, harmony, consonance, and complementarity) is prized in the sciences and the arts, and in history, religion, and philosophy. But complete uniformity is viewed as unlikely and even inimical to equity and recognition of individuality.

Constancy and Change

Much of mankind's efforts over the centuries has been directed to understanding and, through understanding, to achieving some sense of the meaning of life. These efforts can be characterized as a search for balance between variance or change, on the one hand, and invariance or constancy, on the other. If everything is fixed, there is little opportunity for individuality or creativity—man is condemned to an animal existence. We do not have to posit a devil to explain original sin. Simple boredom with security in a Garden of Eden could have been the stimulus for seeking a new experience with uncertain consequences. However, if nothing is fixed or predictable, we live from moment to moment and with no opportunity for thought or planning—again, an animal existence. The evolution of man is one of biological development, on the one hand, and application of the powers of thought to broaden certainty or constancy, on the other. This application of thought provides a basis for coping with change by understanding the reasons for it, by modifying it, or even by provoking it. The statement attributed to Archimedes that, given a place to stand, he could move the world, nicely captured the idea of a fixed position from which to provoke change. Man seeks for some unity in variety, for symmetry and order in confusion, and for opportunity with limited risk.

Change and Variation

The interplay between change or variation and constancy or invariance is apparent in all of the disciplines. It appears in language where many different factors, such as development of a written language, interactions between different language groups, the enforced change of language of a conquered people, and the accumulation of knowledge, have forced an introduction of new concepts and modifications. Likewise, new insights have led to changes in assumptions and the introduction of new concepts into mathematical thought—both theoretical and applied. Social needs and problems lead to the development of laws; and laws, in turn, by their interpretation and enforcement, modify behavior and generate new needs. It is useful to compare and contrast change and variation, on the one hand, and constancy and invariance, on the other. Further, it is important to consider those circumstances in between in which dynamic stability or steady-state control is sought, so that variation is permitted but is also controlled. The characteristics that are subject to change include the form, shape, or appearance of any object, individual, or group. Naturalistic or stylized representations in art are examples of variations in form or appearance. Changes in costume from one age to another constitute another example. Such changes may be based on esthetic considerations or the whims of authority, or may be responses to utilitarian needs. The history of the automobile exemplifies the interplay of both esthetic and utilitarian factors, and its use has major impacts (not all of which are beneficial) on society. Size, whether of objects or of people, also is subject to change—consider, for example, the vital impact of nutrition on the height and weight of human beings.

Structure—that is, the organization, composition, arrangement, or interrelationship of parts—is another factor in which there has been change. Changes here may be responses to changing esthetic values, to attempts to strengthen some physical object, or even to patterns arising out of new or modified religious dogma. Economy in the use of materials also produces changes. For example, the frame house, with more-or-less standardized components, represented a more economical use of wood as well as greater flexibility and adaptability to need or preference. The function, purpose, or use of any particular object or building is also subject to change by necessity or by insight, as is the substance or material used, whether stone, wood, steel, or concrete. The hoe or spade of the peasant of the Middle Ages easily converted into a weapon, the sharp edge being equally efficacious upon field and flesh. The location, environment, and consequent accessibility of objects and facilities represent additional characteristics that change over time.

As a composite, the condition or quality of individuals and objects and the relationships among these various characteristics subject to change are also variables subject to further change. The *substance* or material used is related to *structure* and form, and the composite can be based upon or determine function and purpose. Maintenance and standards of efficiency, effectiveness, and esthetic appearance are also involved in the present condition and quality of any object, performance, or individual. One of the long-time developments in civilization was the move from a fixed status for each individual based upon birth to a changeable status, depending upon opportunity and perseverance.

There are many different ways in which change can take place in these variables. One continuum of change is that of growth and shrinkage, as in the life of the individual. In general, growth has come to be accepted as a significant value, and one of the criteria of a thriving society has been expansion in all directions. Yet shrinkage is also a value, as in technology, where initial developments produced oversized computers but later modifications in materials and in structure and form gave rise to microcomputers. Without this miniaturized technology, space exploration would have remained impossible. A second continuum of change is that of improvement and impairment. This continuum is closely related to that of growth and shrinkage, but growth is not necessarily improvement and, indeed, may lead to impairment, as exemplified in the growth of cities and mounting crime rates in the 1960s. A third continuum of change is that of systematic, controlled or directed change, on the one hand, and fluctuation or random change, on the other. Societies and their governments have generally moved in the direction of systematic, directed change to eliminate the fluctuations and unregularized events that recurrently victimize individuals and nations. Indeed, the whole development of civilization could be viewed as an attempt to replace random change by directed change. Some success has been experienced, but societal variables are so complexly related that attempts to bring about desired changes in some areas cause unanticipated and disastrous effects in others.

The means of change may be either passive or active. Inanimate objects, because of flexibility, ductility, or elasticity, may respond passively to forces impinging upon them; human beings may respond in like fashion. Individual adaptability over time and biological evolution also represent passive gradual change. However, living beings often engage in active purposeful change by making adaptations, or by devising new social organizations, materials, or equipment. Change has come faster and faster as mankind has been able to take a more direct, active, and purposeful role in bringing it about. Change, and particularly rapid change, requires the use of resources and hence leads to economic fiascos, as numerous examples in the past and present illustrate.

Constancy or Invariance

Comparing the concept of variation or change to its opposite of constancy or invariance, one finds a considerable parallel at various points. First of all, the characteristics that have been mentioned as subject to change are obviously also characteristics that may be maintained as constants. We have only to point to a few characteristics to indicate the significance of constancy or invariance in the development of technology and culture. Constancy in size, for example, has been one of the great developments of technology that has permitted interchangeability and assembly-line construction. Constancy in substance or material has been essential to developments in the fields of chemistry and pharmaceuticals.

The continua of invariance are, in some respects, of a nature different from the continua of change. There are absolute constants, such as π, which is the ratio of the circumference to the diameter of a circle. There are arbitrary constants, such as a meter, which was intended to be one ten-millionth part of the distance measured on the meridian of the earth from the equator to the pole. That length, or an approximation to it, has been captured in a platinum bar which then became the standard. But the length of that bar is, in itself, subject to change and so, clearly, the meter is an arbitrary constant and becomes fixed only by international agreement or legislation. Stability also represents a continuum of invariance as represented in weighty objects with a large base. Such objects are not easily disturbed, although the objects themselves do change and are movable if sufficient force is applied. Stability, in this sense, is reflected in social customs and mores. Finally, there is a kind of invariance exemplified by the rigidity enforced by the temperature absolute zero at which all action is suspended.

Among these preceding examples may be perceived several different bases for constancy. The constancy of the velocity of light may be regarded as a natural law. The value π, as an absolute constant, represents a fixed relationship implicit in the definition of an entity called the circle. A meter is a constant that is an example of agreement or specification of an arbitrary length, although attempts have been made to give physical meaning to the unit. Stability or invariance based upon inertia is incorporated into numerous physical laws dealing with conservation of energy and mass.

Dynamic Stability or Steady-State Control

Steady-state control is the maintenance of stability in the face of changing internal and external conditions. In many situations in which change is the expected course of development, it is possible that by natural or artificial means, balance, a steady state, or dynamic stability can be achieved. The prestidigitator, juggler, or acrobat who successfully balances himself and others in precarious positions or maintains a number of objects in motion achieves a state of stability or balance in which the tendency toward deviation is countered by timely and precise application of correcting forces. The driver of an automobile is constantly making small corrections with the steering wheel. Safety valves for relieving pressure are controlled by the centrifugal forces operating on the valve control. Quality-control measures applied to the manufacture of many different objects maintain quality within fixed limits by rejecting variance beyond those limits. Rails impose very narrow limits of movement on the trains proceeding along them.

Among these various types of stability, there are laws that regulate permanent relationships and permit direction, control, and prediction in motion or performance. Principles specify regular, uniform, continuous, or symmetrical types of behavior; and theories constitute an attempt to describe and to explain complicated sets of interactions. The concern for maintenance of dynamic stability, or recognition of it, is exemplified by numerous concepts. *Metabolism* refers to the maintenance of individual life, *evolution* to the maintenance of species through growth and differentiation, reproduction, and adaptation. *Transformation* refers to change in appearance, form, or structure, and is used in ordinary language as well as with specific meanings in mathematics, mechanics, and other disciplines. *Transmutation,* a change in substance, implies rather more marked change approaching that of metamorphosis, or a change into something entirely different. And, even in the last case, the essential material is present, although form, structure, and function change.

Much of the history of each of the disciplines can be interpreted in terms of the interplay of change and constancy, particularly in the maintenance of a dynamic stability that permits a reasonably steady state in small intervals of time but also permits gradual systematic, adaptative, and constructive change over longer intervals. The extent to which measurement and principles for ordering and sequencing are to be found in all disciplines becomes more apparent when this word *measurement,* which implies fixed units and a quantitative approach, is augmented by words that admit qualitative characteristics. Such words include *comparison, discrimination, ranking, evaluation,* and *judgment.* The word *evaluation* specifically involves placing a value on something and implies, in that process, a subjective judgment. These attempts at measurement or ordering are reflected in numerous other words that suggest relationships among the several variables of study. These words include *dependence, correlation, contingency, cause-effect, connection, association, interrelationship, linkage, proportion, inversion,* and *reciprocality.* The last three specify definite relationships, whereas the others imply only connection or association. Both correlation and contingency have been tied to the computation of particular coefficients that provide measures of the relationship of two or more entities. Thus many of these terms refer to statistical probability associations, whereas others refer to specific mathematical formulas. What is significant is that there is no area of knowledge in which inquiry can be carried very far without use of one or more of these terms. In addition, the investigator's attention is given to such matters as precision, accuracy, correctness, rightness, exactness, validity, and reliability—in other words, not only to meaning in relationships, but to how far relationships can be specified in quantitative or qualitative terms.

Laws and Principles Involving Invariance

In the broadest sense, there may be nothing that is fixed or permanent. The invariance of any object or idea holds only under stated conditions and within specific limits. Everything in the universe in which mankind is located appears to undergo change, but this change proceeds at different rates for different phenomena and is related to the time frames of those who make the judgments. In the time frame of living individuals, rocks or mountains (excepting such phenomena as volcanic activity) seem to be essentially constant or invariant. In the longer term, mountains appear and disappear and, indeed, the entire surface of the earth and the character of the universe in which it is embedded undergo marked change. Mankind seeks for laws or fixed relations that hold under stated conditions and within specific limits, including time. There are many examples of such laws.

1. The quantity of mass is invariant in amount and independent of physical state, environment, or motion. This law clearly comes from physics. In effect, it says that mass can neither be created nor destroyed. And mass and energy are essentially one and the same. This law is also a statement of symmetry over time.
2. Sociocultural evolution, especially in its material aspects, becomes more and more rapid. The source of this statement is sociology and, although it resembles the law just

stated from physics, it is much less unequivocal. The modifying adjective, *sociocultural,* forces us to define evolution carefully; *material aspects* present a similar problem. The phrase, "becomes more and more rapid," could be paraphrased in physical terms as "continually accelerates." This statement thus appears more as a generalization than as a law. It speaks more to change than it does to invariance by stating that cultural evolution is an accelerating process, but it is also a statement of certainty about change.

3. Every change in nature is produced by some cause. Taken at its face value, this law suggests that constancy of any natural phenomenon is to be expected, unless one or more causes bringing about change can be found operating upon it. The law is very much like Newton's first law of motion—that, left to itself, a body will maintain its state of rest or motion. Newton's second law follows closely upon this—that motion indicates application of a force, and that change due to a specific force is the same regardless of other acting forces. The third law of motion is that to every force there is an equal and opposite reaction. In short, these laws imply that change may be a natural state and constant factor but emphasize that, whether a body remains in a fixed position or changes its motion, some balancing of forces occurs.
4. In economics, the law of diminishing returns recognizes that, in most circumstances, there comes a point at which the increased use of resources or expenditure of effort does not achieve as much improvement as it had previously. This law leads to a necessary concern with optimizing the relationship between use of resources and output rather than simply maximizing output. Optimizing requires a value judgment.
5. In chemistry, there are numerous laws that have grown out of observation. There is, for example, the law of definite proportions: when elements combine in more than one proportion to form two or more compounds, the successive proportions are related. Likewise, the law of mass action indicates that the chemical action of any reacting substance is

proportional at any moment to its reacting mass. Laws based upon observation are generalizations that may require qualification or elaboration in the light of further observation.

6. The first law of thermodynamics speaks to the interchangeability of heat and energy; the second holds that entropy differences tend to disappear. Entropy refers to the amount of energy available for use, and the law itself implies that hotter entities tend to lose energy and colder ones to gain it. The third law of thermodynamics specifies an invariant relationship as a limit—the change in entropy approaches 0 as the temperature approaches 0. All thermal motion ceases at absolute 0. At that point, the universe has run down.
7. Leibnitz has been credited with formulating a law of continuity that holds there is no break or discontinuity in nature. Nothing passes from one stage to another without going through intervening stages. There are no miracles. The length of time in which the change takes place is variable.

These laws from various disciplines speak, in each case, to the existence of some fixed or continuing relationship, involving a number of separate independent factors. Some combination or function of them is equal to a constant and, therefore, invariant.

Another aspect of invariance is found in the existence of constants or fixed magnitudes. One such constant, already noted, is determined by the relationship (denoted by π) between the circumference of a circle and its diameter. The base of the natural logarithms, e, is another such constant. Both are transcendental numbers—that is, numbers incapable of being defined by any combination of a finite number of equations with rational integral coefficients. To five decimal places, π is 3.14159, and e is 2.71828.

The velocity of light, denoted by c, is another constant; it is roughly 286,000 miles per second. The velocity of light is *assumed* to be the maximum velocity attainable. Thus it establishes a definite limit. Another constant is the gravitation constant of acceleration, produced by a unit of mass at unit distance. Physicists have also found that an absolute standard length is built into the composition of elementary particles. Another aspect of constancy is found in the specifications of constant circumstances, such as temperature and pressure, that provide the conditions or limitations under which a law, principle, or other relationship holds.

A theory is a set of related statements accounting for elements of prior theories and for available data. The statements are so arranged as to give functional meaning to the phenomena to which the statements apply. The theory may contain many factors, including descriptive, stipulative, or fundamental definitions, assumptions, postulates, hypotheses, laws, and generalizations. Theories represent an attempt to tie together a number of variables to explain a series of events and, perhaps, also to permit prediction and control. They create a state of readiness for impending changes. Thus theories can be viewed as expressions of constant relationships. Recognition of protoplasm as the basis for life injects a constant element into attempts to define life.

Social customs, including tastes, folkways, mores, amenities, religious rites, etiquette, and laws (even those regarding highway speed, stop signs, right of way) all inject an element of constancy or uniformity into situations in which infinite variation is possible. These customs are embedded to various depths and may be supported strongly by rigid sanctions and forms of punishment or simply by informal social disapproval. Power, force, influence, authority, tradition, and habit suggest the varieties of support and punishment.

To establish invariant conditions, constancy in meaning among those using definitions is essential. Invariance may pertain to location, size, shape, area, appearance, taste, or sound. By imposing a quality check, wine or coffee tasters attempt to maintain a standard (invariance) in taste and aroma. Quality-control procedures in industry place sufficient restraints on the manufacture of certain objects that those not falling within a specific range of quality are rejected. Recalls, for example, in the automotive industry, indicate that rigorous quality control is not easily achieved. Governmental review of reliability or truth in advertising is a similar example. The achievement of constancy frequently requires adjustment of contributory variables. The amount of baking powder and other ingredients specified by a recipe for baking bread may be varied with altitude and other factors, with the intent that appearance, taste, and size of the product be invariant. Human preoccupation with invariance is reflected in many commonly used terms: regularity, uniformity, consistency, conformity, continuity, symmetry, homogeneity. All of these imply the desire for predictability. We seek unity in variety and, if we find no natural laws that assure it, we may impose our own.

This concern for constancy or fixity leads to the concept of maximization or optimization, in which we seek controls to maximize or optimize the desired output. If the output itself involves a number of independent inputs, then we may define a relationship among them that represents an optimum combination. We may choose to maximize output, minimize costs, or achieve a desirable (optimal) balance among a number of desired outputs and the necessary inputs.

Change and the Maintenance of Dynamic Equilibrium

The preceding paragraphs have discussed the achievement of a degree of certainty, fixity, constancy, or invariance by identifying constants or absolutes and by indicating fixed relationships and imposing certain conditions that assure constant results. The latter approach implies dynamic equilibrium, steady-state control, or homeostasis. The implication of these phrases is simply that, in a continually changing environment, constancy or invariance can be achieved only by continuous adaptation. The problem is one of maintaining stability in an organism in the face of changing internal and external conditions. This maintenance requires continuous transformation and adaptation, an exchange of matter and energy with surroundings to maintain within the organism a comfortable, satisfactory state. Metabolism is such a process carried on by the body for self-perpetuation. Evolution, involving gradual change and adaptation, permits perpetuation of species through new trait combinations and the gradual development of new species better adapted to change through natural selection. Society's recent concerns for conservation of energy and other resources lead it to seek a steady-state control so that future generations will have access to these or equivalent resources. There are numerous synonyms that suggest the changes involved in dynamic equilibrium or steady-state control. These include adaptability, flexibility, elasticity, variation, evolution, ductility, modifiability, and adjustment. The existence of these words again reflects the extent to which maintenance of a steady state amid change is an ever-present individual and societal concern.

Change provides both threat and challenge. A society in which no change is taking place is a static society. Change becomes threatening when it requires people to adapt more rapidly than is comfortable, or when it jeopardizes other needs. Change also becomes threatening when it may deprive individuals of accustomed rights or belongings, or may force them into patterns of behavior that contradict their beliefs. For example, the possibility of a lowered standard of living is extremely threatening and will be strongly resisted, even in the face of dangerous inflationary trends.

People regard change as desirable, but only if it moves them in a desirable direction. In the Middle Ages, alchemists attempted to transmute baser metals into gold. This effort was regarded as acceptable and desirable by kings and nobles who supported alchemists in their efforts, with full expectation of personal benefit and control of any process discovered. Had some alchemist found a way to transmute gold into lead, the venture would not have been welcomed, and the alchemist would have been viewed as a dire threat by those possessing gold. We tend to equate change with growth, progress, development, and improvement. The regular patterns of change that occur in all aspects of material bodies, particles, and force fields include various types of interactions and decay. These interactions among atomic nuclei, gravity, and electromagnetic interactions are the immediate concerns of physicists, but the understanding of them has potent implications for all facets of human existence.

We give much attention in science to rates of change (velocities) and rates of change of rates of change (acceleration). We recognize some variations as inevitable and have developed statistical methods and theories to describe these variations, particularly to screen out random fluctuations that are sources of error or ambiguity. We seek to bring about controlled change in society but have trouble agreeing on what changes are desirable and what incentives and controls are appropriate. Moreover, any planned alteration becomes, in the eyes of those who must change, one that is forced upon them by others. For these reasons, directed or planned change is difficult. Any significant change takes on the characteristics of a metamorphosis, requiring complete alteration in form and structure rather than modest adaptation. Social evolution is, for most people, preferable to revolution. The concept of inertia applies not only in the physical world but also in the social and individual world. Resistance to change among people is just as tangible as, and rather more audible than, that encountered in an attempt to change the direction of the axis of a spinning gyroscope.

Symmetry

The concept of symmetry has long been a central consideration in art, mathematics, music, language, and literature. The physical world exhibits many of the thirty-two forms of symmetry, and the structure of the human body demonstrates symmetry with sufficient variation to assert individuality and arouse interest.

During the past fifty years, symmetry has become of central importance in particle physics. As one of the essential features of nature, symmetry principles have become means of formulating unified field theories. Ultimately, there may be a single unified field theory covering all the forces of nature, based upon an underlying symmetry common to all fundamental particles. At the moment, there exists a particle in which symmetry is apparently violated, but this may indicate only that the list of particles is incomplete or that the symmetry concept requires modification.

A symmetry operation, as viewed by physicists, is an operation, whether real or imagined, that leaves the physical world unchanged. Time is regarded as a symmetry operation because the same physical laws hold now as at an earlier date. Symmetry also exists with regard to displacement by a fixed amount of everything in the universe. This translation in space, so it is believed, would have no observable consequences. These two symmetry operations in regard to time and space are fundamentally involved in conservation of energy and momentum. Another symmetry operation is that of change in the charge of each particle. Most atoms do not exhibit charge conjugation symmetry. The symmetry operation called *parity* involves a change in the sign of all spatial coordinates. This transformation involves a mirrored reflection followed by a rotation of 180 degrees. Ordinarily, the parity transformation changes a right hand into a left hand, and the significant feature of parity as a symmetry operator is that there would be no such handedness.

The immediately preceding comments are based upon an article by Hinds (1981), who elaborates upon the significance of these symmetry operations and upon the expectation that the immediate problem with parity is likely to be resolved in some way that preserves symmetry. The various forms of symmetry, including bilateral, rotational, reflective, spherical, spiral, dilational, translational, and mirror image, present sufficient possibilities that the search will certainly continue and the expectation is likely to be realized.

As Weyl (1952) has put it, relativity deals with the inherent symmetry of the four-dimensional continuum of time and space. Some comments on symmetry by Shubnikov and Koptsik (1974) are also of interest: "Symmetry, considered as a law of regular composition of structural objects, is similar to harmony. More precisely, symmetry is one of its components, while the other component is dissymmetry. In our opinion, the whole esthetics of scientific and artistic creativity lies in the ability to feel this where others fail to perceive it" (p. 9). "Artists have a horror of the words law, order, symmetry, geometry; they prefer harmony, beauty, style, rhythm, unity, although the true meaning of these words differs little from that of the former"

(p. 366). "In the theory of knowledge, symmetry enters as a method of observing and describing invariant laws (laws of conservation) arising in the form of specific modifications of the principle that matter can neither be created nor destroyed" (p. 368).

Symmetry is so fundamental in the universe that the concept can scarcely be regarded as an imposition on the universe by mankind. Rather, it must be regarded as a concept arising out of human perception of the various forms of order and harmony in the universe. Such a concept both transcends the disciplines and provides a key idea for differentiating among them by reference to its specific meanings and implications or its equivalents in particular disciplines. Yet departure from symmetry is inevitable, and lack of symmetry is both remarkable and interesting.

Values

In discussions of constancy and change, value involvement is a recurrent theme. This value involvement reflects people's hopes and fears. Unless it is presumed that there are transcendental beings who take an active interest in what goes on in the universe, whatever happens in a world devoid of human beings simply happens. Explanation, meaning, and goodness or badness are of no concern without conscious and conscientious beings. Perhaps the most immediate value human beings put on the events of the world is continued existence. As was pointed out earlier, neither complete constancy nor inconstancy is conducive to a satisfying and meaningful life. Even our attempts at the preservation of human culture lead us into conflict. Nuclear fission and fusion developed to maintain our way of life may destroy it.

Humans continually seek certainty and do not always realize that uncertainty makes life challenging and, therefore, worthwhile. Uncertainty provides opportunity for change; certainty denies it. Yet exploitation of opportunity requires a degree of certainty; it also requires risk, and few will risk all for uncertain gain. For example, attempts to achieve social control of production and distribution are in accordance with public policies to attain and maintain security, stability, freedom, and justice. Security includes basic needs such as food, clothing, shelter, health, group affiliation, and affection. Stability implies a degree of continuity and the presence of constant, fixed, or enduring practices and policies. Freedom suggests the presence of individual choice and the absence of disabling cares, worries, or restraints. Justice indicates that rights are determined impartially by law or equity. Aristotle regarded justice as the practice or application of virtue to others, differentiating between distributive justice based on merit and corrective justice directed toward rectification of injustice. Justice is neither fixed nor absolute; rather, it is an abstraction indicating respect for the rights of ideal members of an ideal society. The justice due to an individual demands impartial judgment of his or her behavior and intent. Justice does not necessarily excite pleasure or satisfaction in those to whom it is rendered. Just retribution may be either reward or punishment, depending upon those who render judgment.

At the *immediate* level, continued existence involves such basic needs as food, clothing, lodging, health, comfort, convenience, and respect. To be human is to have aspirations for achieving values at *intermediate* and *ultimate* levels. To deny all human aspirations is to doom mankind to unchanging circumstances. Ultimate concerns and values involve understanding of the source, nature, and purpose of life and expectations about the existence of life after the earthly one. Intertwined with these values are doubts and uncertainties whether, for mankind, the maximal development of each individual or an optimal development for all is the desired goal.

Summary

This chapter has outlined the components of an integrative approach by identifying significant transdisciplinary concepts and by noting some of the values underlying developments in all disciplines. We have enlarged upon some of the human aspirations and problems involved in mankind's continuous search for meaning, balancing demands for constancy and certainty, on the one hand, and change and improvement, on the other. In Part III, we explore the value for teachers of a disciplinary context in designing college courses and programs; we also propose principles to guide curricular organization, and identify characteristics and commitments essential to those entering the teaching profession.

Suggestions for Further Reading

Ausubel, D. P. "Cognitive Structure and Transfer." In N. Entwistle and D. Hounsell (Eds.), *How Students Learn.* Readings in Higher Education, 1. Lancaster, England: Institute for Research and Development in Post-Compulsory Education, University of Lancaster, 1975.

Bell, D. *The Reforming of General Education.* New York: Columbia University Press, 1966.

Denemark, G. W. "Concept Learning: Some Implications for Teaching." *Liberal Education,* 1965, *51,* 54-69.

Fairchild, H. N., and Associates. *Religious Perspectives in College Teaching.* New York: Ronald Press, 1952.

Hawkes, J. *The Teaching of Writing to College Freshmen.* Stanford, Calif.: Graduate School, Stanford University, 1968.

Hinds, E. A. "Parity and Time-Reversal Invariance in Atoms." *American Scientist,* 1981, *69* (4), 430-436.

Kaysen, C. (Ed.). *Content and Context: Essays on College Education.* New York: McGraw-Hill, 1973.

Kitzhaber, A. R. *Themes, Theories, and Therapy: The Teaching of Writing in College.* New York: McGraw-Hill, 1961.

Kruskal, W. *Mathematical Sciences and Social Sciences.* Englewood Cliffs, N.J.: Prentice-Hall, 1970.

Mayville, W. V. *Interdisciplinarity: The Mutable Paradigm.* AAHE-ERIC/Higher Education Research Report No. 9. Washington, D.C.: American Association for Higher Education, 1978.

Morris, D. *The Naked Ape.* New York: Dell, 1967.

Phenix, P. H. *Realms of Meaning: A Philosophy of the Curriculum for General Education.* New York: McGraw-Hill, 1964.

Russell, D. H. *Children's Thinking.* New York: Ginn, 1956.

Shubnikov, A. V., and Koptsik, V. A. *Symmetry in Science and Art.* New York: Plenum Press, 1974. (Translated from Russian by G. D. Archard; edited by D. Harker.)

University of Chicago, Members of the Faculty. *The Idea and Practice of General Education.* Chicago: University of Chicago Press, 1950.

Wesley, E. G., and Adams, M. A. *Teaching Social Studies in Elementary Schools.* (rev. ed.) Boston: Heath, 1952.

Weyl, H. *Symmetry.* Princeton, N.J.: Princeton University Press, 1952.

9

Adapting Courses and Programs to a Transdisciplinary Context

The major purpose of the college or university as a social institution is to help people make sense out of their life experiences. Knowledge is surely not something to be rotely accumulated for its own sake, even if so organized and interrelated that it can be readily recalled. Learning is more than acquiring knowledge, and the purposes of learning have not been fully achieved until knowledge influences thinking and behavior. Institutions of higher education have separated the acquisition of knowledge from life by emphasizing formally organized knowledge as collected and structured into traditional disciplines, departments, and courses. These courses reflect a conception of knowledge as static rather than as part of a dynamically changing set of interrelationships among objects and ideas. The courses generally fail to reveal the continuing attempts to expand, organize, interrelate, and apply knowledge as reflected in the disciplines.

Although the educated person in our culture must have some grasp of the disciplines and their interrelationships, the disciplines are only artifacts of the way scholars happen to focus upon and interrelate problems. Each discipline deals only with parts of the phenomena relevant to that discipline, and its efforts may be increasingly unrelated to the actual need of human beings to make sense of their environments and to act effectively within them. Focus on the disciplines tends to ignore the broader dimensions of knowledge, skills, and concepts that show up in all forms of human activity. Values embedded in ethical and moral behavior are ignored or treated only peripherally because they transcend rather than fall within the artificial disciplinary boundaries that have become the basis for curriculum structure and teaching. Almost invariably, the emphasis in discipline-based courses has come to be on acquiring specific items of knowledge. It is assumed that gaining sufficient knowledge of essential principles, the ways of ascertaining them, and the means for judging their validity requires such a high level of proficiency that only after a lengthy series of experiences in a discipline can one understand and utilize its basic conceptions, modes of inquiry, syntactic structure, and value commitments. Soltis (1979, pp. 14-15) has noted this point.

As a result of this approach to education, both teaching and learning come to be regarded as grim, somber experiences. The professor engaged actively and perhaps pleasurably in research may be somewhat irked at the interruptions caused by teaching responsibilities that come to be viewed as irrelevant and unrewarding. There is no ready way to relate frontier research activities to undergraduate instruction. Other professors who would rather teach find that the time available for preparation and for interaction with students is diminished to the point that teaching is reduced to a series of lectures. As a result, many critical observers of colleges have found a great deal of boredom in both teachers and students, a feeling that classroom activity is pointless and irrelevant to the world at large. Students are required to read many pages in one or more books, carry out pointless laboratory exercises, or work particular problems according to a specified routine with no sense of the meaning of either the methodology or results. Patterns of behavior originally intended to convey understanding become so routinized that the thinking student may be reprimanded for departing from the routine.

Those who would insist that education rise above this emphasis on the accumulation of knowledge may go too far the other way. Some professors interested in the discipline as a mode of inquiry insist that students learn the methods of collecting and interpreting evidence and develop the ability to judge for themselves whether certain generalizations are justified. In the extreme, this pattern would require every learner to achieve some limited capacity to function like a researcher in each discipline. The assumption here is that the educated person who would apply knowledge must also be able to determine the validity of all the knowledge acquired. This raises numerous questions. Do we assume that the knowledge provided through scholars in colleges and universities has already been adequately validated and can be accepted on faith? Or do we assume that every item of knowledge dealt with in any course must be accompanied by adequate data so that each learner can judge its validity? Or must every statement and proposition be *re*-searched by each learner? Teaching should take into account that individuals will be acquiring additional information all of their lives and the principal purpose of any course is to provide those critical tools that enable learners to assess the meaning, significance, and applicability of knowledge as they acquire it. From this point of view, there is an obvious middle ground between a program of education that assumes that everyone should become a competent researcher or an expert critic and one that presumes to stuff each student with some body of common knowledge. Surely, too, it must be expected that not every student will have the interest, capability, or time to probe every discipline. Indeed, disciplinary scholars increasingly find it difficult to maintain contact with research in their respective fields.

Criteria for judgment of the competency and purpose of an authority as a prelude to accepting that authority will, in many cases, be closer to the needs of the educated. For some, the authority of the scholar may be less relevant than the influence of the popularizer who, in the interest of simplicity, departs from scholarly rigor and focuses on practical implications. Undue rigor, especially at the undergraduate level, tends to made education somber, threatening, and irrelevant. If overdone in the undergraduate classroom, rigor can readily degenerate into rigidity.

Work and Play

Too much of the educational process, both for teachers and learners, involves boring activities and requirements that take up time and have no obvious relevance—chores that are performed with minimal effort. What should be recreation or play is made into work. Learning, when regarded as work with no constructive ends, appears justifiably avoided in pursuit of more pleasurable experiences, even to the most docile learner. Learning, if it is to be a continuing and satisfying behavior, must become something of a leisure-time activity. Work can be play, but only if it provides opportunities for thought, feeling, and overt action to motivate the individual to continue the activity, either because it is pleasurable in itself or because it is obviously related to desirable ends.

The drills and practice that gymnasts, dancers, and athletes continue over days and even years are both boring and painful, but they can also be pleasurable if there is apparent progress and the ultimate goal and steps toward it are clear. In any physical or motor activity, there usually is some initial stage of conditioning. In perfecting any complex behavior, major and separable aspects of the composite activity are defined as skills. Many of these are practiced separately until a reasonable stage of proficiency is developed. These various skills are then brought together into the composite activity, and training continues at that level until it becomes sufficiently automatic that athletes or dancers can maintain a high level of proficiency in the activity while also remaining aware of conditions around them. This sensitivity in observation becomes the basis for adapting the physical performance to the existing conditions.

Although these remarks seem to pertain entirely to physical or motor activity, the necessary modification of physical activity on the basis of cognition injects an intellect component. Learning in any context is likely to be more productive and more pleasurable when it includes a composite of cognitive, affective, and psychomotor behavior than when it is approached through only one of these forms of behavior. This truism provides the justification for directed observation as well as controlled laboratory or other practical experience in most disciplines. Continued personal attempts to create or perform are likely to be unsuccessful unless both goals and criteria for reaching them provide direction to practice.

Realistic and relevant learning may be demanding and still be enjoyable and resemble play. Phenix (1968, p. 301), in an excellent essay on the play element in education, described the characteristics of play. Based on this essay, with some additions, the essential characteristics of play are the following:

- Play is voluntary; it is neither an obligation nor a requirement.
- Play can be highly imaginative.
- Play is for fun rather than for some utilitarian purpose.
- Despite its fun and voluntary characteristics, play frequently involves a degree of competition.
- Play is limited in time and space and thereby provides some containment of tensions which, if allowed to continue and expand, might become disastrous. Play that continues indefinitely tends to be compulsive and obsessive; it ceases to be play.
- As patterns of play become established, the necessity for rules soon becomes evident, even with small children.
- Play is a social or communal activity. Much play activity involves cooperation with others and a commitment to a joint endeavor.
- Play clearly has cognitive, psychomotor, and affective behaviors woven in complex ways into its fabric. Also it tends to have mathematical and nondiscursive symbols as part of its language, rules, and records.
- Play exhibits cognitive behavior both in its strategy and tactics, as exemplified by the game plans developed by coaches or imputed by sports writers.

- An element in many of the preceding characteristics of play is that of chance. One chance element is that of the fortuitous, unanticipated event that may be turned to an advantage by an alert, adept performer. Another comes when individuals are faced with choices among several actions, each of which has known records of successes based upon the past; chance here provides the opportunity for judgment and the use of unusual talents or of carefully laid plans to achieve success.
- Though work and play appear in general usage to be antonyms, there are numerous circumstances in which they come close to being synonyms. Both work and play involve action. Work one enjoys can be play. Play can be just as tiring as work, and the nature of the results often determines whether a particular act is regarded as work or play.

Since the words *work* and *play* overlap so much in meaning, it may be more appropriate to draw a contrast between stereotyped and exploratory behavior. Behavior that is stereotyped is constrained either by external forces or by socially or self-imposed limitations. In either case, persons engaging in *stereotyped behavior* perform certain acts in a routine way, with no apparent interest and with no possibility of individual input into varying those tasks or altering their outputs. In contrast, persons engaging in *exploratory behavior,* as described by Morris (1967, pp. 113-114), are sensitive to the novel or unfamiliar and assess its potential for continuing interest and for other values. In those cases where further attention seems justified, they investigate (play around with) the unfamiliar until it becomes familiar. This is clearly an enactive stage. In the process of becoming familiar with the novel, they engage in repetitive exploration of a number of possible actions or manipulations and may impose a form of rhythmic repetition, as with a sequence of words or of physical actions repeated in cadence. Having explored variations, they select the most satisfying and develop them to the exclusion of others. These variations are combined and recombined in various ways to explore their composite meanings. All this they do just because it is fun, for its own sake, and as an end in itself. Exploratory activity in this form is essentially creative play and is frequently engaged in by individuals for their own satisfaction without any intent to share with others, although what emerges may turn out to be a source of pleasure for them also. The ultimate behavior may be rote, but they arrive at it by a route they determine themselves.

In summary, much of what goes on in science, business, and the world in general is (or should be) a kind of extension into adult life of the play patterns of childhood. Many educational experiences can embody the spontaneity, joy, and satisfaction conventionally assigned to playful activities. Scientific research in its purest sense becomes a form of play and is probably most thrilling when the researcher's imaginative hypothesis or hunch is verified. Significant research findings that result from sensitive observation or curiosity also reflect a playful approach to science. In a sense, scientific detachment itself is an aspect of a play approach. Pure scientists take great pleasure in research, and they may derive as much satisfaction from demonstrating that something cannot be done as by demonstrating that it can.

Desirable Qualities of Educational Experiences

If a student's program of courses is to hold interest, have obvious relevance to living now and in the future, and be a pleasurable experience, more thought must be given to the nature of the educational experiences and the qualities that seem essential to promote the desired benefits. The curriculum itself usually emerges out of departmental discipline-related decisions that have little to do with student interests and needs and degree-program unity and integrity. Course titles, content coverage, and specific requirements are much less important than we are inclined to think. Much more significant are the learning activities, the actual learning, and student reactions to that learning.

Wynne (1952, p. 32) lists six qualities of experience: (1) contingency, (2) interest, (3) originality, (4) thinking, (5) group membership and interaction in learning and resolving problems, and (6) integration, balance, and unity. These qualities of experience are very close to the continuums described in Chapter

Eight. The qualities can, with some modification, form the basis for extending the continuums into a set of criteria for appraising the probable quality of any projected educational experience. As a step in that direction, the following comments reflect upon Wynne's statements, modify them somewhat, and move them toward the concepts within our continuums.

The *first* desired quality of educational experience is relevancy or contingency. Relevancy implies that the teacher sees the experience as being directly relevant to the achievement of certain specified educational goals. In another sense, the teacher is expected to consider whether the educational experience will be seen by students as relevant to the real world in which they live. The contingent implication, to some extent, specifies the conditions or limitations under which relevancy is apparent to both teacher and student. A particular concept or problem is not always or universally relevant but, under some conditions, it may be very definitely so.

The *second* desirable quality of experience is that it hold interest for students and have elements that arouse intrinsic motivation. This is not the same as relevancy. Puzzles that have no relevance to anything are intrinsically interesting to many. Conversely, issues that are highly relevant locally, nationally, or worldwide at a given moment may be so complex or so far removed from students that they do not interest or motivate.

The *third* desirable quality of experience is that it permit and even encourage originality and creativity. All too many tests and classroom recitations revolve around a set of highly specific questions to which every student is expected to give an essentially identical answer. These conditions emphasize memorization and recall and thoroughly discourage unusual responses that indicate originality or creativity.

The *fourth* desirable quality of experience is that it permit or require thought and the exercise of reasoning. The fact that an experience does require thought does not necessarily mean that it permits or encourages originality or creativity. The thought process involved may be at any of several levels. It may require defining a problem or deciding upon the mode of analysis that should be employed. In some courses, it seems to be expected (at least hoped) that all students will recognize a problem as one of a particular type, select the same process and, barring error, arrive at identical answers. In contrast, arriving at alternative interpretations of a problem, applying various methods of resolution, and devising different solutions indicate creativity and the exercise of reasoning powers.

The *fifth* quality of experience is that it make for cooperation or collaboration with others. This quality may appear at a number of different levels. There are relatively few problems in our society that individuals can solve without recourse to laws, mores, and other societal constraints. It is worthy of note that the preceding sentence could equally well have ended at "solve." The student studying mathematics problems never solves a problem solely by his or her own efforts. He or she already has some knowledge of mathematical procedures attained by taking courses, reading books, or otherwise. Thus in solving a given problem, the student is dependent upon what others have already done. By extension, this may be regarded as cooperation or collaboration. Most problems in society can be solved only if numerous people collaborate in the process and if the majority affected by a solution find it an acceptable one. Thus it is important that there be significant educational experiences requiring students to collaborate or cooperate with each other in defining the problem, collecting information, considering possible solutions, and devising an acceptable one. Teachers and textbooks may be part of this cooperation and collaboration but must not control it.

The *sixth* desirable quality of experience is that of integration, balance, and unity. This quality becomes important because, as one moves from generalized objectives of education to specific experiences, there is a tendency to see each experience in isolation from every other one. In planning, the teacher may be aware of interrelationships that are missed by students who move through educational experiences in sequential fashion. Thus, at any point, they may have forgotten earlier experiences and not realized desired connections between those prior experiences and present ones. In general, they will not be aware of experiences that will come later, and so they will not be able to view the immediate experience in a long-term perspective. In particular, ultimate objectives often must be broken into a number of components, each of which may be pursued independently for a time until enough skill is developed. Then, and only then, combining and integrating several hitherto independent skills becomes possible.

If, in planning courses, teachers select educational experiences according to any of these six qualities, there is still no assurance that each student will recognize or experience that quality. The teacher may still need to present a particular experience in a context that makes clear to students under what circumstances and how it is relevant to learning in that field and outside it. The goal is that each course provide an interesting and productive experience in learning, in application of what is learned, and in increased insight into the meaning and implications of life beyond the classroom. However, unless courses reinforce each other and are organized in some sequential manner that forwards the development of cumulative, integrated learning, education remains fragmented and integration a matter of chance. Incidentally, overemphasis on highly structured teaching methods in particular courses may contribute to fragmentation.

Criteria for Course and Program Sequencing

If programs are to be composed of an organized sequence of courses, then a number of criteria must be applied, both in program planning and in the specific courses offered in the program. The first set of criteria for sequencing grows out of recognition of *individual abilities,* interests, aspirations, and environmental backgrounds. The materials used, assignments made, and expectations of student performance may all be varied according to the general level of a group of students. But, at the same time, differences within a student group may demand, for effective learning, considerable variation in the assignments to and the expectations about individual students. Besides, some teachers will be more effective with certain types of students than with others.

The second set of criteria for sequencing relates to various aspects of the *learning process.* Obviously, these interrelate with the set of criteria for individual differences. Particular factors to be noted under the process of learning are:

- speed of learning
- ease or difficulty of learning, including, for example, such factors as the number of dimensions involved in or the level of abstraction of an idea
- retention or memory
- power for further learning
- relevance and transferability or utility of what is learned
- convenience of the learning process or experience to the learner
- the motivation or pleasure that the learner derives out of the process of learning

Each of these can be consulted in determining whether certain types of learning experiences should be offered early in a program or course or deferred until some later point. Some things that can be learned quite speedily may well be offered early in a program to give students confidence that they are making progress. If the experiences are conveniently available, and particularly if they provide some power for further learning, the importance of early placement would be reinforced. However, information that will not be retained long and will not be immediately useful probably should be deferred or omitted.

The third set of criteria for sequencing involves the *content of learning* (the material, ideas, and skills that are to be learned). Complexity, the representational mode, and utility represent three major elements in determining the point in a course or program at which certain specific content should be introduced. Some highly complex ideas (symmetry, for example) may well be introduced early in a simple form, involving enactive and iconic learning. As the discussion of symmetry in Chapter Eight indicates, this is a concept applicable at very complex levels, and its significance can be expanded in time by relating it to new objects and ideas and introducing more complex conceptions of symmetry. Furthermore, the utility of the concept in examining, understanding, and appreciating ideas and objects in all of the disciplines is quite clear.

The fourth set of criteria for sequencing involves the *desirable characteristics of the process of learning.* These include continuity, which is achieved by providing threads or connections that bridge the content discussed from day to day in a course and from course to course in a program. A common tendency in many courses, especially at the level of fundamentals, is to introduce what are considered to be the basic ideas in successive chapters or lectures but not to show the clear relationship among them. The intent seems to be that at some later date these ideas will all be related in some manner; but students meanwhile get confused, lose interest, or perceive the material as irrelevant. Thus they may not continue into advanced courses in which some sense of unity is finally introduced. The assurance that these ideas will be related at some later point is not enough to establish continuity, and certainly not enough to provide a coherent experience in which what is already known is related to and reinforced by further learning. When a course regularly seems to be covering numerous isolated and unrelated ideas, it becomes necessary to reconsider not only the course but also the entire program. A reorganization of knowledge in some distinctive order of courses might be more logical, interesting, and relevant for the learner. This leads immediately to a consideration of various types of structures that provide coherence and sequence. These include:

- simple to complex
- specific to general
- chronological
- dependence or cause-effect relationship
- contiguity or proximity
- conceptual relationships
- contrast and similarity

The fifth set of criteria for sequencing involves the *element of cost* in instructor time, equipment, and space. Although many science teachers have insisted upon the need for laboratory work even in a first course in general education, there is really no evidence that fully justifies this. Live demonstrations or videotapes can bring to large groups of students an insight into the nature of scientific experimentation that they are unlikely to achieve in the "cookbook" type of laboratory performance common to beginning science courses. Hence costs, equipment, and space considerations are appropriate and should be weighed carefully in developing a sequential set of courses, especially when early courses serve a much larger group of students than later ones. Each of the other sets of criteria also may be considered in determining whether an idea should be introduced at an early stage and later expanded or abandoned. There is no single principle for determining whether learning should be sequenced from the specific to the general, or the general introduced and the specifics then reviewed as examples. For sound learning, students probably should experience both approaches, and teachers will do well to vary them from time to time to maintain their own enthusiasm and to assure themselves that their approach is based upon some set of rational criteria.

These sequencing criteria and the underlying principles of continuity, cumulative experience, coherence, and integration highlight the importance of developing a course and teaching it with some understanding of the range of prior, concurrent, and future experiences of students. When students with a wide range of backgrounds and interests take a course, it can be hard for the teacher; but the very presence of this wide background underlines the need to develop the course so as to provide some points of relevance for each student. When the students in a course are part of a larger program, having all or most courses in common, the individual course should play a well-determined role in that total, a role that should be clear to the students in the course as well as to students and instructors in other courses. Good teaching is not possible unless that teaching is in context, and that context requires some familiarity with students and their programs as well as with the institution in which the teaching is done. In particular, teaching is not simply a matter of classroom performance and content coverage. Good teaching takes, first of all, a good education and, second, a sense of obligation that students not only learn but also learn how to continue their learning in whatever context they find themselves.

Suggestions for Further Reading

Belknap, R. L., and Kuhns, R. *Tradition and Innovation: General Education and the Reintegration of the University*. New York: Columbia University Press, 1977.

Blackburn, R., and others. *Changing Practices in Undergraduate Education.* Berkeley, Calif.: Carnegie Council on Policy Studies in Higher Education, 1976.

Briggs, L. J. *Sequencing of Instruction in Relation to Hierarchies of Competence.* Pittsburgh: American Institutes for Research, 1968.

The Carnegie Foundation for the Advancement of Teaching. *Missions of the College Curriculum: A Contemporary Review with Suggestions.* San Francisco: Jossey-Bass, 1977.

Dressel, P. L. *Improving Degree Programs: A Guide to Curriculum Development, Administration, and Review.* San Francisco: Jossey-Bass, 1980.

Gibbs, G. I. *Handbook of Games and Simulation Exercises.* London: Spon, 1974.

Harvard Committee. *General Education in a Free Society*. Report of the Harvard Committee. Cambridge, Mass.: Harvard University Press, 1945.

King, A. R., Jr., and Brownell, J. A. *The Curriculum and the Disciplines of Knowledge, A Theory of Curriculum Practice.* New York: Wiley, 1966.

Levine, A. *Handbook on Undergraduate Curriculum.* San Francisco: Jossey-Bass, 1978.

Mattfield, J. A. "Toward a New Synthesis in Curricular Patterns of Undergraduate Education." *Liberal Education,* 1975, *61* (4), 531-547.

Morris, D. *The Naked Ape.* New York: Dell, 1967.

Phenix, P. H. "The Play Element in Education." In R. T. Hyman (Ed.), *Teaching: Vantage Points for Study*. Philadelphia: Lippincott, 1968.

Posner, G. J., and Strike, K. A. "A Categorization Scheme for Principles of Sequencing Content." *Review of Educational Research,* 1976, *46* (4), 665-690.

Rudolph, F. *Curriculum: A History of the American Undergraduate Course of Study Since 1636.* San Francisco: Jossey-Bass, 1977.

Soltis, J. F. "Education and the Concept of Knowledge." Inaugural Lecture as William Heard Kilpatrick Professor of Philosophy and Education, Teachers College, Columbia University, February 7, 1979.

Wynne, J. P. *General Education in Theory and Practice.* New York: Bookman, 1952.

10

Rethinking the Role of Teachers

This final chapter draws upon the ideas and structures of preceding chapters as well as upon some additional personal views on the nature of learning as a process and an accomplishment. We identify those characteristics and commitments essential to good teaching, indicate the preparation of teachers that will foster the development of such characteristics and commitments, and provide suggestions for evaluation of teaching and learning that will enhance teaching practices productive of learning. Both learning and teaching must be enjoyable if they are to have both immediate and long-term impact on those who learn and on those who stimulate that learning. Finally, we suggest that acceptance of the role of teaching involves commitment to a set of responsibilities and a code of ethics that emanate from the concept of teaching as a profession and a social service.

This conception of teaching is at odds with that of teachers who consider themselves primarily experts in a discipline and regard their main obligation to be the expansion of the discipline. In this book, teaching is viewed as more than knowing and dispensing a discipline. We have taken the contrary view that the sole purpose of teaching is to inspire and assist learning that enables students to deal more effectively with personal and societal problems and that lends meaning to their world. In this view, teaching invokes diagnosis, prognosis, prescription, and evaluation of the resultant learning. The goal of teaching and learning is to make each learner as independent as possible. This includes helping the learner recognize the need for learning, for making a commitment to learn, and for mapping out a process whereby that learning is acquired. Even though teaching can facilitate learning, it can never ensure it.

There is an unfortunate tendency in formally organized education to regard the teacher as an authority who dispenses knowledge of a discipline to students hungry and grateful for it. This conception of education is the basic reason for most poor teaching. It follows that, if the way to learn is by attending classes where scholars dispense knowledge, then continuing to learn requires a lifelong *formal* experience. Colleges and universities, through their continuing education centers, are thus performing a significant social service by providing lifelong education experiences for adult students "until death do us part." One of the obvious indicators of success in this conception of lifelong education would be a marked increase over time in the number of students dying in class. Inattention and sleeping are forerunners of that ultimate fate.

If, on the contrary, the purpose of learning is to produce independent learners, then the teacher must be regarded, not as a dispenser of knowledge, but as one who dispenses with knowledge as the major outcome of education. Even the college or university teacher acts, at best, as a mediator between the ideas of highly intelligent scholars and potential learners who eventually should rise above the limitations of these intervening teachers to attain their own distinctive ideas and meanings.

The attachment of the graduate school to the undergraduate college, and the conviction that the qualification for college teaching is an advanced disciplinary degree, have brought into the undergraduate program some people designated as teachers who have no real understanding of the process and uses of learning. Colleges aggravate this situation by selecting as teachers those with terminal degrees based upon mastery of a discipline and original research in it—research often irrelevant to the teaching task assigned. If the vast expenditures of colleges and universities are to be justified, a different view must be sponsored.

When students consider going into teaching, several factors have influenced them. First, there is usually a pleasurable personal experience, accompanied by high grades in some series of disciplinary courses. Recognition as an outstanding student in any department is almost invariably accompanied by encouragement into graduate school for advanced degrees. However, someone considering a college teaching career has limited and, to some extent, erroneous information on which to make a decision, usually lacking information about the nature of good teaching, the personal qualities needed for good teaching, and the responsibilities and conflicting demands imposed by it. The teaching component of a professional career is simply not the most highly regarded function among faculty members in our colleges and universities. Beyond that, administrators, boards of trustees, and alumni conspire to achieve national and international renown for their institutions in research, Nobel prizes, athletic supremacy, or other areas that have little positive effect, and sometimes a negative one, on the quality of undergraduate education and teaching.

Under present circumstances, it is difficult for a student urged to enter higher education to make any wise judgment of his or her own competency for and interest in college teaching. With some exceptions, the student's perception is likely to be that the highest paid and highest ranked faculty are those who engage in research and publication. Few students have completed a four-year college program without learning of at least one incident in which a highly regarded teacher is seemingly discriminated against in salary, status, or the granting of tenure. Colleges and universities not only promote personnel policies that prize research (at times, regardless of quality), but they also give cursory recognition to the showcase teacher and then largely ignore all those who continue to promote student learning on sound principles requiring time commitments that restrict engagement in research.

Desirable Characteristics of Teachers

What qualities are desirable in a prospective teacher? What commitments are necessary? Perhaps the first composite characteristic is that of *interest in and respect for individuals, their aspirations, and their potentials.* Without this, the teacher becomes a purveyor of information. However, when respect goes beyond concern for the individual as a competent, self-directed learner and intrudes into his or her personal life, the teacher assumes responsibility and attendant risk for interfering with the learner's values and behavior. A certain teacher may well be a model for some learners, but the choice of model and appropriate behavior should be made by the learner, not imposed by the teacher.

A second desirable teacher characteristic and commitment is a *pervasive, yet directed curiosity.* Some wise observer once noted that a distinguished scholar is one who avoids involvement in irrelevancies. Much of scholarship is devoted to what appears to be unimportant detail, but which, in fact, can only be judged so once the scholarly investigation has been completed. The characteristic of pervasive, yet directed curiosity requires a grasp of essential meanings, variations in meaning, and the implications of applying concepts in different disciplinary contexts. The teacher who encourages his or her students to seek extended meanings demonstrates that each learner can discover, create, express, and use ideas in an original and stimulating way. Reflection upon experience, both previous and subsequent, elaboration upon these reflections, and application of principles and generalizations derived from prior experiences can be both modeled and stimulated by the teacher as a continuous learning process. The teacher who consistently attempts this will also strive carefully to present to learners all relevant data and assumptions underlying a particular viewpoint. The criteria (even if only personal biases) for deciding the relative significance of various data, and both the affective and logical chain of generalizations leading to a conclusion, will dramatize for the learners the process of disciplinary inquiry and analysis.

A third essential teacher characteristic and commitment is that of *continuing self-appraisal* as the motivator and facilitator of learning related to student, self, and course content. The teacher who does not extend the meaning of content and personal learning is unlikely to be a teacher in the fullest sense. Learning is not something transferred from one mind to another but is, rather, a process in which the inexperienced learner profits from interaction with the experienced learner, both by modeling behavior and using materials designed to encourage learning.

A fourth desirable characteristic requires both *able communication and demonstration of ideas.* It encompasses an understanding of the role of language, mathematics, and nondiscursive symbols in creating and organizing ideas, and in communicating to others not only the essence of a discipline but also its origins, structure, methods, presuppositions, and possible range of application. Words, symbols, and formulas are not enough to stimulate learning. Demonstrations, sometimes wordless, and the participation of learners are essential to learning and significant teaching.

Finally, essential to the role of teaching are several affective characteristics that influence the quality and continuing impact of the teaching-learning relationship. Many teachers prefer lectures because, somewhat like a published paper, they lend a sense of fluency in presentation of mastery of ideas, and of efficient coverage in limited time. In cases where the lectures are manifestly producing little student learning, they should engender a *sense of humility* in the teacher and a reconsideration of the teaching mode. Indeed, it might be said that no teaching has taken place in a lecture unless at least one person, through that lecture, has acquired new insights and meanings. The quality of any teaching activity can be evaluated by the number of students who learned something significant from it.

The teacher must also be completely honest. *Honesty* is made explicit in many ways. The teacher who does not know the answer to a student's question should say so and further regard it as an opportunity (if the question deserves it) for significant collaborative learning. But honesty in a teacher goes beyond humility in scholarship and confessions of ignorance to outright admission of error. It also requires adherence to policies or guidelines set down for the conduct of a course. The teacher who asserts that attendance will not be checked and then penalizes those who do not attend simply reaffirms the suspicion in the student's mind that, to get a good grade, the learner must second-guess and comply with the professor's preferences. Honesty merges very quickly with *ethics* and *self-criticism,* both of which are essential to good teaching. Ethics is part of any relationship between a professional and his or her clients. But the teacher has a particular ethical obligation here since the student wants credit and a satisfactory grade and may see any teacher-imposed expectation or demand as a moral or physical threat such that compliance becomes obligatory.

The teacher who is properly humble about the nature of the instructional role will recognize that lectures, readings, discussions, laboratories, films, audiotapes, field trips, and travel are only means to motivate and enhance learning and to increase the richness, range, and integration of learning experiences. Variety in experience can be stimulating and change hard work into play. Without a clear focus on learning and the motivation for it, the extensive use of the technology of learning quickly degenerates into gadgetry and confusion.

Preparation of Teachers

The preceding discussion of desirable teacher characteristics and commitments has dealt primarily with those traits and values that are essential to teaching and are intrinsic to the character and personality of the teacher. It may be possible to modify or reinforce those traits by formal educational experiences, but such experiences are not likely to develop humility or honesty in people totally lacking in them. Nor is it likely that formal educational experiences will transform people into motivators and facilitators of learning unless some previous commitment already exists.

As for the preparation of teachers, it is now necessary to turn the discussion away from personality characteristics to the effects of formal educational experiences on teachers. First in importance is, unquestionably, the nature and structure of organized knowledge, especially in the discipline the individual proposes to teach. Unfortunately, much of the course work and instruction in graduate school is directed to learning the subject matter of a discipline rather than its essential characteristics and place in the total structure of organized knowledge. The prospective teacher who writes a doctoral dissertation on Chaucer is likely to have viewed that effort as an end in itself rather than as a means of acquiring knowledge of a particular author and of literary works that provide insights into the discipline of literature and what that discipline can tell us about living in complex modern society. In order to view an author's works in this broader framework, the prospective teacher needs to know something about the historical, philosophical, and religious context in which the works were written. The point here is not that one cannot fully appreciate *The Canterbury Tales* without some grasp of the underlying philosophical and religious commitments, but that any literature emerges out of a historical milieu, which includes philosophical and religious orientations. Education can be very specific and narrow for the expert; but, for the purposes of humanistic or liberal education, study of specific works is only a means to the development of appreciations and abilities that enable the learner to read literature as a source of pleasure, as scholarly refreshment, and as a resource for new insights about life. Viewed in this way, graduate study and research are seldom directly relevant to the nature of undergraduate liberal education and, in many ways, are antagonistic to it.

Besides disciplinary training, the formal preparation of teachers includes teaching skills and methods. Much of the research and writing on teaching methodology reveals a wasteland in which time and resources have been expended with little return. Professors in the substantive fields have generally accused educationists of being preoccupied with method to the exclusion of significant content. In those cases where teachers have become overly absorbed in the development of a particular teaching technique, they are likely to carry it to extremes and thereby jeopardize the outcomes that originally led to the introduction of the method. The array of teaching skills and methods includes contract learning, Personalized System of Instruction (PSI), Computer-Assisted Instruction (CAI), simulation, gaming, practical intern or field experiences, competency-based education, case studies, case problems, and case reports, as well as the more traditional patterns of lecture, discussion, seminar, laboratory, and other variations. Despite the enthusiasm of the progenitors of PSI, CAI, and others, our own observations lead us to believe that some of these highly systematized approaches with specific tasks and phases of accomplishment are no better than older classroom techniques that overemphasize factual information and eliminate circumstances for critical and creative thought. In fact, these individualized systems of instruction and computer-assisted instruction are, in many ways, not unlike the old-fashioned workbook and objective examinations.

Overdependence on any particular teaching-learning methodology discourages the development of independent learners and often excludes experiences that are realistic to the context of learning outside formal school situations. In addition, variety is essential in maintaining enthusiasm, and any program of instruction that forces the learner into the same type of activity day after day is likely to take on the character of a routine if not rote performance. Effective as some of these methodologies may be in providing continuous feedback and thereby stimulating and correcting learning as it proceeds, it seems neither possible nor desirable to stimulate and evaluate complex, integrative, value-based responses and behavior on a mechanical or electronic basis. Teachers need to learn something about the resources available to promote teaching and learning, but they need even more to learn the kind of assignments and challenges that will stimulate students to use these resources. College and university teachers have too long assumed that the important activities of a course are those that go on in the classroom under their direct supervision. In fact, the long-range impact of excellent teaching is much more associated with the continued pursuit of learning by students and adults outside the classroom.

Evaluation of Teachers

Additional preparation in teaching skills and methods is subsumed under test development and evaluation of student and teacher performance. Much of the evaluation of teaching has overemphasized the classroom performance of the teacher and has employed, because of their simplicity, teacher-rating forms. These forms are completed by students who may never have been exposed to good teaching and so have neither the expectations nor standards to apply to their ratings. Most institutions give limited recognition to student evaluation of teaching, regarding it as uninformed and, to some extent, irrelevant. Student evaluation of teaching is usually irrelevant because it is a cumulative summary of responses to individual statements that, no matter how cleverly contrived, become ambiguous as students react to them and have little relationship to the quality of learning that results from a particular course. Furthermore, student responses to some of the questions on the rating form are generally meaningless because the statements themselves are meaningless. What is the point of finding out that most students agree that the instructor made the objectives explicit when the objectives themselves are inadequate or inappropriate? Evaluation of teaching must start with finding out what the learners have done, what they are currently doing, and what they continue to do. This applies in a particular course or across the entire curricular program. By looking at what learners in a course have achieved up to a particular point, we can assess the significance of the experiences and the quality of the output. By looking at where students are directing their energies, we can determine their level of effort and enthusiasm and the particular emphases of the course and its instruction. By examining students' actions after they complete a course and program, we can determine long-term effectiveness. Obviously, the student who takes but one course in psychology, does no reading in that area afterward, and refers slightingly to psychology as a field of study must not have had a productive learning experience. In evaluating teaching, we should also know what attitudes students have toward learning, how these have been affected by particular experiences, and, after the completion of an educational program, how they feel about continuing learning on their own.

In the evaluation of teaching, it is essential to know the learners' motivations for learning. Are they imitating the teacher in content, diction, and gesture? Are they identifying with a charismatic personality and emulating behavior through a kind of conditioning or habituation? Are they being indoctrinated by subtle recognition and approval, obvious remarks, or disagreeable deprivals or punishment? Beyond this, what are the students learning, and what does the teacher recognize and reward? Is student learning specific to the discipline and major areas of knowledge? Or does the learning promote various modes of thought and recognize interconnections among disciplines in developing definitions, classes, measurements, proof, and values? In brief, what problems do teachers pose, and what responses do students give?

As part of the evaluation of teaching, we must learn how a department and an individual teacher evaluate success in teaching. By reviewing course outlines and syllabi, we can discover the criteria of success implied and the modifications that teachers have made in their approach to specific courses within recent years. In particular, we can learn what attempts a teacher has made to relate a course to other courses within the department and to other disciplines.

Another important evaluative component comprises the teacher's assessment of student effort and of student accomplishment. Finally, the teacher's standards and procedures used for determining grades and credits indicate both learning objectives and expected attainments. The use of a 200-item, true-false final examination in a general humanities course, as the sole basis for grading, confirms student criticism of inadequate evaluation of student learning.

A responsible teacher is concerned with the amount of interest and effort evidenced by each student in a course and provides for assignments and observations of students' work that give some estimate of their progress. Students should have some feedback on the quality of accomplishment relative to their efforts. A student with a high level of accomplishment who is exerting almost no effort probably should be given course credit and not be required to go to class. A student who shows almost no accomplishment despite many hours of effort is probably misplaced in the course, and that should be detected within the first few weeks. The assignment of a terminal grade and granting of credit involve a professional and social responsibility. In recent years, there has been a widely recognized tendency for teachers to give high grades, or at least passing ones, to students whether or not they deserve them, and to spend minimal time reviewing student materials and providing feedback. Evaluation, in the minds of too many teachers, has become terminative or culminative rather than informative, facilitative, and motivational. Accordingly, an evaluator should learn how much evidence a teacher uses for each student, how much time is spent in reviewing that evidence, how much feedback has been given to the student as a result of that review, and how much opportunity is provided for improvement. A teacher who simply averages a succession of grades from the first week through to the final week fails to recognize that some students, after a slow start and with proper assistance, may rise to a higher level of achievement, while others with unusually good backgrounds may, after a strong start, become lackadaisical.

Furthermore, the general emphasis on requirements limits the extent to which students can act on their own evaluations of teaching by choosing their instructors. Limitations on class or section size have the same effect. If classes are closely gauged to the number of students available, the poor teacher is likely to have essentially the same number of students as the good teacher. In addition, when the teacher's enthusiasm causes large numbers of students or unusual amounts of student time to be devoted to a course, there is likely to be a negative reaction among other faculty who regard popularity as evidence of poor quality and unusual student involvement as a distraction from their courses. The tendency to highlight the department course and the individual professor rather than learning virtually eliminates any attempt to determine significant impacts of the college education over time. As on a stairway, the student moves step by step from course to course and teacher to teacher, rather than progressing from a lower to a higher level of competency and insight.

There is no way teachers can promote significant learning without devoting more time to teaching than most teachers seem inclined to do at present. Many assumptions are made about how much reading is done by students, how many problems worked, or new learning situations mastered. But until the teaching strategy includes feedback from students to provide assurance that they can and do read materials, work problems, and increase in ability to deal with new situations, it must be assumed that the standards of performance under that teacher involve factual memorization, minimal understanding, and little student judgment.

To know whether someone is an effective teacher, it is necessary to find out what students have learned and what they are capable of learning as the result of their education. Meaningful learning requires appropriate and stimulating experiences. However, if education is truly a cumulative experience and if each teacher plans a course as a segment of that experience, it is, in most cases, nearly impossible to determine with certainty the additional knowledge gained, retained, and used from that particular course.

As has been asserted earlier, learning and teaching can be enjoyable. This does not mean to imply that either learning or teaching is so simple that it requires no continuing effort. Both fun and satisfaction disappear from the classroom when, day after day, the pattern of teacher performance or student behavior is rigidly specified. In these courses, opportunities for students to perform and be evaluated are tightly structured, both in behavior expected and in responses given.

In one sense, most teachers are playing games some of the time. Teachers talk about what they covered in their lecture, phrasing the report to imply that all except the most incorrigible students enjoyed and profited from the experience. Teachers talk about "my course" as though it were unique and given by the premier scholar in that field. Teachers blame poor performance in sequential courses on the sad preparation received in the courses of fellow professors. The performance and accomplishments of "A" students are readily accepted by departments and individual professors as evidence of their own excellent teaching, whereas failures and poor performance are often blamed on student indifference, student incapability, or indiscriminate admissions officers. These games, which discredit the higher education profession, are also played in business, government, and other walks of life. They are games that students readily perceive and well understand. Even among heads of church and government, there are many examples of ineptness, inflated ego, and unethical behavior. In the face of all this, it is not surprising that many colleges and universities have been driven to develop formal codes for the behavior of teachers.

Responsibilities of Teachers

Teaching is a profession with social, ethical, and moral responsibilities that are just as important to professional performance as scholarly competency. Various conceptions of the nature and responsibilities of teaching were presented in earlier chapters, especially Chapter Two. These responsibilities include motivation of students, development and adaptation of learning materials, and evaluation of student performance. Every profession acquires a few practitioners who are lacking in competency, good sense, or professional ethics. Although professional organizations recognize this problem, they have not dealt with it successfully. Professional associations are generally ineffective in reviewing and enforcing codes of professional practice. This is reflected, in recent years, by the increasing number of suits entered for malpractice, especially in medicine and law. The primary professional organizations for college and university professors are those of the particular disciplines, and the majority of them are focused upon advancement of the discipline through research.

The concept of academic freedom, which applies primarily to research, is often interpreted as granting complete teaching autonomy—in selecting course materials, interpreting them, and evaluating student accomplishment. Because of recurring and widespread concern about the quality of college teaching, some institutions have made repeated efforts to provide codes of teaching responsibilities that at least mention the most frequently expressed criticisms of college teaching and suggest ways to overcome them. The Code of Teaching Responsibility at Michigan State University was approved in 1976. This statement is not presented as an exemplar, but neither is it as inadequate as many other institutional codes.*

The teaching responsibilities of instructional staff members (herein referred to as instructors) are among those many areas of University life which have for generations been a part of the unwritten code of academicians. The provisions of such a code are so reasonable to learned and humane individuals that it may appear redundant or unnecessary to state them. However, the University conceives them to be so important that performance by instructors in meeting the provisions of this code shall be taken into consideration in determining salary increases, tenure, and promotion.

1. Instructors are responsible for ensuring that the content of the courses they teach is consistent with the course descriptions approved by the University Committee on Curriculum and the Academic Council. Instructors are also responsible for stating clearly to students in their classes the instructional objectives of each course at the beginning of each term. It is expected that the class activities will be directed toward the fulfillment of these objectives and that the bases upon which student performance is evaluated will be consistent with these objectives.
2. Instructors are responsible for informing students in their classes of any methods to be used in determining final course grades and of any special requirements of attendance which differ from the attendance policy of the University. Course grades will be determined by the instructor's assessment of each student's individual performance, judged by standards of academic achievement.
3. Examinations and other assignments submitted for grading during the term should be returned with sufficient prompt-

*"Code of Teaching Responsibility," *Faculty Handbook*, Michigan State University, East Lansing, Michigan, January 1981, pp. III-44, III-45, III-46.

ness to enhance the learning experience. Unclaimed final examination answers will be retained by the instructor for at least one term so that they may be reviewed by students who desire to do so. Examination questions are an integral part of course materials, and the decision whether to allow their retention by students is the responsibility of the instructor. Term papers and other comparable projects are the property of students who prepare them. They should be returned to students who ask for them and those which are not returned should be retained by the instructor for at least one term. Instructors who desire to retain a copy for their own files should state their intention to do so in order that students may prepare additional copies for themselves.

4. Instructors are expected to meet their classes regularly and at scheduled times. Instructors will notify their units if they are to be absent and if appropriate arrangements have not been made, so that suitable action may be taken by the unit if necessary.
5. Instructors of courses in which assistants are authorized to perform teaching or grading functions shall be responsible for acquainting such individuals with the provisions of this Code and for monitoring their compliance.
6. Instructors are expected to schedule and keep a reasonable number of office hours for student conferences. Office hours should be scheduled at times convenient to both students and instructors with the additional option of prearranged appointments for students when there are schedule conflicts. The minimum number of office hours is to be agreed upon by the teaching unit, and specific times should be a matter of common knowledge.
7. Instructors who are responsible for academic advising are expected to be in their offices at appropriate hours during pre-enrollment and enrollment periods. Arrangements shall also be made for advising during registration.

The preamble to this code indicates in the second sentence the reluctance many members of the faculty have about developing such statements. The following sections of the code exemplify quite clearly the reasons for that reluctance and the resultant difficulties in creating a meaningful code. Note that the code states "that performance by instructors in meeting the provisions of this code shall be taken into consideration in determining salary increases, tenure, and promotion." However, unless administrators from the departmental level upward accept the responsibility for evaluating teaching performance and related duties, there is no way in which the code can be enforced. And any attempt to enforce the code in circumstances in which there are no well-defined procedures, no clear standards for evaluation, and no penalties prescribed for violations is foredoomed. For example, section 1 in the code indicates that instructors are responsible for ensuring that the content of the courses they teach is consistent with course descriptions. One has only to cast an eye over the range of course descriptions to find that their lack of specificity makes it possible, in most cases, for an instructor to argue that whatever content is taught is consistent with the course description. To assert that instructors are responsible for stating the instructional objectives to students does nothing toward assuring good teaching so long as the objectives are determined by the instructor. Since much of teaching focuses on memorizable, factual content, those educators who are critical of such instruction and who believe that learning should focus more on values, judgments, and applications are placed in a difficult position. After all, facts are important.

The statement in Section 1 that "it is expected that the class activities will be directed toward the fulfillment of these objectives and that the bases upon which student performance is evaluated will be consistent with these objectives" is only a pious and essentially meaningless extension of the consistency specification. By whom is it expected that class activities will be directed toward the fulfillment of these objectives? Who will determine whether this is done and what actions can be taken when class activities are clearly not related to some of the course objectives?

Section 2 of the code indicates that instructors are responsible for informing students of the methods used in determining the final course grades. Superficially, this can be satisfied by specifying the weights attached to various requirements in the course, but the standards used and the extent of deviation from those standards are determined by an instructor's assessment, beyond which appeal is exceedingly difficult.

Section 3 of the code stipulates promptness in returning examinations and papers and is responsive to the recurring complaint of students that grading is often delayed two, three, or four weeks; however, the code provides no suggestion of a reasonable interval for grading, or procedures for reaching judgments about that interval. By implication, the code speaks in section 3 against an instructor's publishing student papers under his own name, with little or no credit to the students. One may note the variation in the phrasing of the several statements. Section 2: "Course grades *will be* determined by the instructor's assessment of each student's individual performance, judged by standards of academic achievement [italics added]" only states what almost certainly will happen, but the adequacy of that determination and the criteria for it are left unstated.

Section 4 alludes to the irresponsibility of some teachers who simply do not meet their classes regularly or who modify the scheduled time of classes to their own convenience. Section 5 makes the instructor responsible for informing teaching assistants of the code and for monitoring their compliance. It is curious that the code specifically requires the instructor to monitor the teaching assistants whereas no similar monitoring of the instructor is required by the department chairperson or designate. Section 6 advocates a reasonable number of office hours, their convenient scheduling, and agreement upon minimal office hours within a teaching unit. The vast majority of the faculty in most institutions probably make reasonable attempts to meet this obligation. Here, and in section 7, on availability for academic advising, an obligation is made clear, but there are no guidelines offered for meeting it and no penalty evoked for failure to do so.

This code is, like many others, a bland and ambiguous statement of the obvious, largely unknown or ignored by those to whom it is addressed. It is certainly not enforced and probably not enforceable in the existing form. Michigan State University also issued an earlier governing board statement of teacher responsibility, indicating the accountability of faculty members to the Code of Teaching Responsibility and stating clearly that the University will not pay salaries to teachers who fail to provide these services. The difficulty with implementing this penalty is that much time and effort are required to collect adequate evidence about faculty performance, and this effort itself may generate so much tension and ill will that its overall impact on teaching may be worse than that of the relatively few faculty members who ignore their responsibilities. When attempts are made to check irresponsible behavior in the face of inadequate specification of rules, there is often great difficulty in deciding that there has been any irresponsibility, and even more difficulty in determining whether the extent of the violation is such that a teacher should be required to change or be discharged. In our experience, the most successful attempts to obtain compliance with the code of teaching responsibilities have come about when a department chairperson, supported by a group of senior colleagues, has enforced policy standards. When teaching expectations are not clarified and enforced at the departmental level, it becomes virtually impossible for any significant action to be taken at higher levels. In addition, a code of teaching or any other responsibilities that indicates only that certain types of behavior must be *present* can lead to degeneration of teaching performance since no criteria are provided for evaluating the *quality* of that performance.

A few individuals are capable of effective learning through their own initiative and efforts. For most, significant learning depends upon the presence of stimulating teachers to define appropriate and interesting learning tasks and aid students conscientiously to develop the means for learning and self-evaluation. Teaching is the most important function in undergraduate education. Thus the definition of good teaching cannot be left to the individual teacher or department.

It is hoped that this review and reconsideration of the disciplines and their interrelationships, and their composite significance in individual lives and in society, will provide a framework in which the vigor, rigor, and fun of undergraduate education can be advanced.

Suggestions for Further Reading

Aleamoni, L. M. *The Usefulness of Student Evaluations in Improving College Teaching.* Urbana: Measurement and Research

Division, Office of Instructional Resources, University of Illinois, 1974.

Anderson, S. B., Ball, S., and Murphy, R. T. *Encyclopedia of Educational Evaluation: Concepts and Techniques for Evaluating Education and Training Programs.* San Francisco: Jossey-Bass, 1975.

Bergquist, W. H., and Phillips, S. R. *A Handbook for Faculty Development.* Washington, D.C.: The Council for the Advancement of Small Colleges, 1975.

Centra, J. A. (Ed.). *New Directions for Higher Education: Renewing and Evaluating Teaching,* no. 17. San Francisco: Jossey-Bass, 1977.

Curwin, R. L., and Fuhrmann, B. S. *Discovering Your Teaching Self: Humanistic Approaches to Effective Teaching.* Englewood Cliffs, N.J.: Prentice-Hall, 1975.

Doyle, K. O., Jr., and Crichton, L. I. "Student, Peer, and Self-Evaluation of College Instruction." *Journal of Educational Psychology,* 1978, *70* (5), 815-828.

Dressel, P. L. *Handbook of Academic Evaluation: Assessing Institutional Effectiveness, Student Progress, and Professional Performance for Decision Making in Higher Education.* San Francisco: Jossey-Bass, 1976.

Dressel, P. L. *A Degree for College Teachers: The Doctor of Arts.* Berkeley, Calif.: Carnegie Council on Policy Studies in Higher Education, 1977.

Gaff, J. G. *Toward Faculty Renewal: Advances in Faculty, Instructional, and Organizational Development.* San Francisco: Jossey-Bass, 1975.

Gaff, J. G. (Ed.). *New Directions for Higher Education: Institutional Renewal Through the Improvement of Teaching,* no. 24. San Francisco: Jossey-Bass, 1978.

Grasha, A. J. *Assessing and Developing Faculty Performance: Principles and Models.* Cincinnati, Ohio: Communication and Education Associates, 1977.

Koen, F. "The Preparation of College Teachers." In D. S. Dean, *Preservice Preparation of College Biology Teachers.* Washington, D.C.: Commission on Undergraduate Education in the Biological Sciences, American Institute of Biological Sciences, 1970.

Miller, R. I. *Developing Programs for Faculty Evaluation: A Sourcebook for Higher Education.* San Francisco: Jossey-Bass, 1974.

Pace, C. R. (Ed.). *New Directions for Higher Education: Evaluating Learning and Teaching,* no. 4. San Francisco: Jossey-Bass, 1973.

References

The following section contains those references suggested after each chapter and many others relevant to the concerns of this volume. There are also numerous references dealing with aspects of teaching not discussed herein but with related curriculum problems.

Abercrombie, M. L. J. *Aims and Techniques of Group Teaching.* London: Society for Research into Higher Education, 1974.

Albert, E. M. (Ed.). *The Teaching of Anthropology.* Berkeley: University of California Press, 1963.

Aleamoni, L. M. *The Usefulness of Student Evaluations in Improving College Teaching.* Urbana: Measurement and Research Division, Office of Instructional Resources, University of Illinois, 1974.

Anderson, J. "The Teacher as Model." *American Scholar,* 1961, *30,* 393-398, 400-401.

Anderson, O. R. "The Effects of Varying Structure in Science Content on the Acquisition of Science Knowledge." *Journal of Research in Science Teaching,* 1968, *5,* 361-364.

Anderson, O. R. *The Quantitative Analysis of Structure in Teaching.* New York: Teachers College Press, 1971.

Anderson, R. C., and others (Eds.). *Current Research on Instruction.* Englewood Cliffs, N.J.: Prentice-Hall, 1969.

Anderson, S. B., Ball, S., and Murphy, R. T. *Encyclopedia of*

Educational Evaluation: Concepts and Techniques for Evaluating Education and Training Programs. San Francisco: Jossey-Bass, 1975.

Applebee, A. N. *Tradition and Reform in the Teaching of English: A History.* Urbana, Ill.: National Council of Teachers of English, 1974.

Association of American Colleges and Council of Graduate Schools in the United States. *The Graduate Preparation of Scientists for Undergraduate Teaching in Liberal Arts Colleges and Universities.* Washington, D.C.: Association of American Colleges and Council of Graduate Schools in the United States, 1970.

Astin, A. W. *Four Critical Years: Effects of College on Beliefs, Attitudes, and Knowledge.* San Francisco: Jossey-Bass, 1977.

Ausubel, D. P. "Cognitive Structure and Transfer." In N. Entwistle and D. Hounsell (Eds.), *How Students Learn.* Readings in Higher Education, 1. Lancaster, England: Institute for Research and Development in Post-Compulsory Education, University of Lancaster, 1975.

Axelrod, J. *The University Teacher as Artist: Toward an Aesthetics of Teaching with Emphasis on the Humanities.* San Francisco: Jossey-Bass, 1973.

Baird, L. L. "Teaching Styles." *Journal of Educational Psychology,* 1973, *64* (1), 15-21.

Bandman, B., and Guttchen, R. S. (Eds.). *Philosophical Essays on Teaching.* Philadelphia: Lippincott, 1969.

Barzun, J. *Teacher in America.* Garden City, N.Y.: Doubleday, 1945.

Beard, C. A. *An Economic Interpretation of the Constitution of the United States.* New York: Macmillan, 1935.

Beard, R. *Teaching and Learning in Higher Education.* Harmondsworth, England: Penguin Books, 1972.

Belknap, R. L., and Kuhns, R. *Tradition and Innovation: General Education and the Reintegration of the University.* New York: Columbia University Press, 1977.

Bell, D. *The Reforming of General Education.* New York: Columbia University Press, 1966.

Bergquist, W. H., and Phillips, S. R. *A Handbook for Faculty*

Development. Washington, D.C.: The Council for the Advancement of Small Colleges, 1975.

Blackburn, R., and others. *Changing Practices in Undergraduate Education.* Berkeley, Calif.: Carnegie Council on Policy Studies in Higher Education, 1976.

Bligh, D. *What's the Use of Lectures?* Harmondsworth, England: Penguin Books, 1972.

Bloom, B. S. (Ed.). *Taxonomy of Educational Objectives: The Classification of Educational Goals.* Handbook I: *Cognitive Domain.* New York: Longmans, Green, 1956.

Bloom, B. S. *Human Characteristics and School Learning.* New York: McGraw-Hill, 1976.

Bloom, B. S., and Broder, L. J. *Problem Solving Processes of College Students.* Chicago: University of Chicago Press, 1950.

Bloom, B. S., Hastings, J. T., and Madaus, G. F. *Handbook on Formative and Summative Evaluation of Student Learning.* New York: McGraw-Hill, 1971.

Boulding, K. B. "The Task of the Teacher in the Social Sciences." In W. H. Morris (Ed.), *Effective College Teaching.* Washington, D.C.: American Association for Higher Education, 1970.

Bowen, H. R. *Investment in Learning: The Individual and Social Value of American Higher Education.* San Francisco: Jossey-Bass, 1977.

Briggs, L. J. *Sequencing of Instruction in Relation to Hierarchies of Competence.* Pittsburgh: American Institutes for Research, 1968.

Briggs, L. J. *Handbook of Procedures for the Design of Instruction.* Monograph No. 4. Pittsburgh: American Institutes for Research, 1970.

Brookes, E. H. "Through British Eyes." In R. H. Connery (Ed.), *Teaching Political Science: A Challenge to Higher Education.* Durham, N.C.: Duke University Press, 1965.

Brown, J. W., Lewis, R. B., and Harcleroad, F. F. *Audiovisual Instruction: Media and Methods.* New York: McGraw-Hill, 1969.

Bruner, J. S. *The Process of Education.* Cambridge, Mass.: Harvard University Press, 1962.

Bruner, J. S. *Toward a Theory of Instruction.* Cambridge, Mass.: Harvard University Press, 1966.

Buxton, T. H., and Prichard, K. W. (Eds.). *Excellence in University Teaching.* Columbia: University of South Carolina Press, 1975.

Carnegie Commission on Higher Education. *The Fourth Revolution: Instructional Technology in Higher Education.* New York: McGraw-Hill, 1972.

The Carnegie Foundation for the Advancement of Teaching. *Missions of the College Curriculum: A Contemporary Review with Suggestions.* San Francisco: Jossey-Bass, 1977.

Carpenter, P. *History Teaching: The Era Approach.* Cambridge, England: Cambridge University Press, 1964.

Centra, J. A. (Ed.). *New Directions for Higher Education: Renewing and Evaluating Teaching,* no. 17. San Francisco: Jossey-Bass, 1977.

Chickering, A. W. *Education and Identity.* San Francisco: Jossey-Bass, 1969.

Claxton, C. S., and Ralston, Y. *Learning Styles: Their Impact on Teaching and Administration.* AAHE-ERIC/Higher Education Research Report No. 10. Washington, D.C.: American Association for Higher Education, 1978.

Clayton, T. E. *Teaching and Learning—A Psychological Perspective.* Englewood Cliffs, N.J.: Prentice-Hall, 1965.

Cole, C. C., Jr. *To Improve Instruction.* AAHE-ERIC/Higher Education Research Report No. 2. Washington, D.C.: American Association for Higher Education, 1978.

Commager, H. S. *The Nature and Study of History.* Columbus, Ohio: Merrill, 1965.

Conant, J. B. (Ed.). *Harvard Case Histories in Experimental Science.* Cambridge, Mass.: Harvard University Press, 1957.

Connery, R. H. (Ed.). *Teaching Political Science: A Challenge to Higher Education.* Durham, N.C.: Duke University Press, 1965.

Cook, J. M., and Neville, R. F. *The Faculty as Teachers: A Perspective on Evaluation.* Washington, D.C.: ERIC Clearinghouse on Higher Education, George Washington University, 1971.

Council on Education in Geological Sciences. *Audio-Tutorial Instruction: A Strategy for Teaching Introductory College Geology.* Washington, D.C.: Council on Education in Geological Sciences, 1970.

Cronkhite, B. B. (Ed.). *A Handbook for College Teachers: An Informal Guide.* Cambridge, Mass.: Harvard University Press, 1950.

Cross, K. P. *Accent on Learning: Improving Instruction and Reshaping the Curriculum.* San Francisco: Jossey-Bass, 1976.

Curwin, R. L., and Fuhrmann, B. S. *Discovering Your Teaching Self: Humanistic Approaches to Effective Teaching.* Englewood Cliffs, N.J.: Prentice-Hall, 1975.

Davis, J. R. *Teaching Strategies for the College Classroom.* Boulder, Colo.: Westview Press, 1976.

Dean, D. S. *Preservice Preparation of College Biology Teachers: A Search for a Better Way.* Washington, D.C.: Commission on Undergraduate Education in the Biological Sciences, American Institute of Biological Sciences, 1970.

Denemark, G. W. "Concept Learning: Some Implications for Teaching." *Liberal Education,* 1965, *51,* 54-69.

Donald, D. *Charles Sumner and the Coming of the Civil War.* New York: Knopf, 1960.

Doyle, K. O., Jr., and Crichton, L. I. "Student, Peer, and Self-Evaluation of College Instruction." *Journal of Educational Psychology,* 1978, *70* (5), 815-828.

Dressel, P. L. *College and University Curriculum.* (2nd ed.) Berkeley, Calif.: McCutchan, 1971.

Dressel, P. L. *Handbook of Academic Evaluation: Assessing Institutional Effectiveness, Student Progress, and Professional Performance for Decision Making in Higher Education.* San Francisco: Jossey-Bass, 1976.

Dressel, P. L. *A Degree for College Teachers: The Doctor of Arts.* Berkeley, Calif.: Carnegie Council on Policy Studies in Higher Education, 1977.

Dressel, P. L. *Improving Degree Programs: A Guide to Curriculum Development, Administration, and Review.* San Francisco: Jossey-Bass, 1980.

Dressel, P. L., and Mayhew, L. B. *General Education: Explora-*

tions in Evaluation. Washington, D.C.: American Council on Education, 1954.

Dressel, P. L., and Mayhew, L. B. *Critical Analysis and Judgment in the Humanities.* Dubuque, Iowa: Brown, 1956.

Dressel, P. L., and Thompson, M. M. *Independent Study: A New Interpretation of Concepts, Practices, and Problems.* San Francisco: Jossey-Bass, 1973.

Duane, J. E. (Ed.). *Individualized Instruction—Programs and Materials.* Englewood Cliffs, N.J.: Educational Technology Publications, 1973.

Eble, K. E. *Professors as Teachers.* San Francisco: Jossey-Bass, 1972.

Eble, K. E. *The Craft of Teaching: A Guide to Mastering the Professor's Art.* San Francisco: Jossey-Bass, 1976.

Einstein, A., and Infeld, L. *The Evolution of Physics.* New York: Simon & Schuster, 1938.

Eiss, A. F., and Harbeck, M. B. *Behavioral Objectives in the Affective Domain.* Washington, D.C.: National Education Association, 1969.

Elton, G. R. *The Practice of History.* New York: Crowell, 1967.

Entwistle, N., and Hounsell, D. (Eds.). *How Students Learn.* Readings in Higher Education, 1. Lancaster, England: Institute for Research and Development in Post-Compulsory Education, University of Lancaster, 1975.

Eulau, H., and March, J. G. (Eds.). *Political Science.* Englewood Cliffs, N.J.: Prentice-Hall, 1969.

Fairchild, H. N., and Associates. *Religious Perspectives in College Teaching.* New York: Ronald Press, 1952.

Falk, B., and Lee, D. K. *The Assessment of University Teaching.* London: Society for Research into Higher Education, 1971.

Ford, G. W., and Pugno, L. (Eds.). *The Structure of Knowledge and the Curriculum.* Chicago: Rand McNally, 1964.

Gaff, J. G. *Toward Faculty Renewal: Advances in Faculty, Instructional, and Organizational Development.* San Francisco: Jossey-Bass, 1975.

Gaff, J. G. (Ed.). *New Directions for Higher Education: Institutional Renewal Through the Improvement of Teaching,* no. 24. San Francisco: Jossey-Bass, 1978.

Gagné, R. M. *The Conditions of Learning.* (2nd ed.) New York: Holt, Rinehart and Winston, 1970.

Gerber, J. C. (Ed.). *The College Teaching of English.* New York: Appleton-Century-Crofts, 1965.

Gibbons, M. *Individualized Instruction: A Descriptive Analysis.* New York: Teachers College Press, 1971.

Gibbs, G. I. *Handbook of Games and Simulation Exercises.* London: Spon, 1974.

Grant, B. M., and Hennings, D. G. *The Teacher Moves: An Analysis of Non-Verbal Activity.* New York: Teachers College Press, 1971.

Grasha, A. F. *Assessing and Developing Faculty Performance: Principles and Models.* Cincinnati, Ohio: Communication and Education Associates, 1977.

Green, T. F. "The Concept of Teaching." In D. Vandenberg (Ed.), *Teaching and Learning.* Urbana: University of Illinois Press, 1969.

Greene, T. M. "Philosophy." In H. N. Fairchild and Associates, *Religious Perspectives in College Teaching.* New York: Ronald Press, 1952.

Greene, T. M., and others. *Liberal Education Reexamined: Its Role in a Democracy.* New York: Harper & Row, 1943.

Grittner, F. M. *Teaching Foreign Languages.* New York: Harper & Row, 1969.

Gropper, G. L., and Glasgow, Z. *Criteria for the Selection and Use of Visuals in Instruction: A Workbook.* Englewood Cliffs, N.J.: Educational Technology Publications, 1971.

Handlin, O., and Handlin, M. F. *The American College and American Culture: Socialization as a Function of Higher Education.* New York: McGraw-Hill, 1970.

Hardy, N. T. "A Survey Designed to Refine an Inventory of Teaching Styles To Be Used by Individuals Preparing for College Teaching." Unpublished doctoral dissertation, Michigan State University, 1976.

Harvard Committee. *General Education in a Free Society.* Report of the Harvard Committee. Cambridge, Mass.: Harvard University Press, 1945.

Hawkes, J. *The Teaching of Writing to College Freshmen.* Stanford, Calif.: Graduate School, Stanford University, 1968.

Hill, W. F. *Learning Thru Discussion.* Beverly Hills, Calif.: Sage, 1972.

Hinds, E. A. "Parity and Time-Reversal Invariance in Atoms." *American Scientist,* 1981, *69* (4), 430-436.

Hong, H. (Ed.). *Integration in the Christian Liberal Arts College.* Northfield, Minn.: St. Olaf College Press, 1955.

Hyman, R. T. (Ed.). *Teaching: Vantage Points for Study.* Philadelphia: Lippincott, 1968.

Hyman, R. T. *Ways of Teaching.* Philadelphia: Lippincott, 1970.

Hyneman, C. S. "Some Crucial Learning Experiences." In R. H. Connery (Ed.), *Teaching Political Science: A Challenge to Higher Education.* Durham, N.C.: Duke University Press, 1965.

Institute of Society, Ethics, and the Life Sciences. *The Teaching of Ethics in Higher Education.* Hastings-on-Hudson, N.Y.: The Hastings Center, 1980.

Joint Council on Economic Education. *College Preparation for Teaching Economics.* New York: Joint Council on Economic Education, 1969.

Kaysen, C. (Ed.). *Content and Context: Essays on College Education.* New York: McGraw-Hill, 1973.

King, A. R., Jr., and Brownell, J. A. *The Curriculum and the Disciplines of Knowledge, A Theory of Curriculum Practice.* New York: Wiley, 1966.

Kitzhaber, A. R. *Themes, Theories, and Therapy: The Teaching of Writing in College.* New York: McGraw-Hill, 1961.

Knopf, K. A., and Stauss, J. H. (Eds.). *The Teaching of Elementary Economics.* New York: Holt, Rinehart and Winston, 1960.

Koen, F. "The Preparation of College Teachers." In D. S. Dean, *Preservice Preparation of College Biology Teachers.* Washington, D.C.: Commission on Undergraduate Education in the Biological Sciences, American Institute of Biological Sciences, 1970.

Krathwohl, D. R., Bloom, B. S., and Masia, B. B. *Taxonomy of Educational Objectives: The Classification of Educational Goals.* Handbook II: *Affective Domain.* New York: McKay, 1964.

Krislov, S. *A Laboratories Approach to Teaching Political Science.* Minneapolis: Department of Political Science, University of Minnesota, 1970.

Krug, M. M. *History and the Social Studies: New Approaches to the Teaching of Social Sciences.* Waltham, Mass.: Blaisdell, 1967.

Kruskal, W. *Mathematical Sciences and Social Sciences.* Englewood Cliffs, N.J.: Prentice-Hall, 1970.

Kuethe, J. L. *The Teaching-Learning Process.* Glenview, Ill.: Scott, Foresman, 1968.

Lado, R. *Language Teaching, A Scientific Approach.* New York: McGraw-Hill, 1964.

Layton, D. (Ed.). *University Teaching in Transition.* Edinburgh, Scotland: Oliver and Boyd, 1968.

Levine, A. *Handbook on Undergraduate Curriculum.* San Francisco: Jossey-Bass, 1978.

Lumsden, K. (Ed.). *New Developments in the Teaching of Economics.* Englewood Cliffs, N.J.: Prentice-Hall, 1972.

McKeachie, W. J. "Research on Teaching at the College and University Level." In N. G. Gage (Ed.), *Handbook of Research on Teaching.* Chicago: Rand McNally, 1963.

McKeachie, W. J. *Research on College Teaching: A Review.* Report No. 6. Washington, D.C.: ERIC Clearinghouse on Higher Education, George Washington University, 1970.

McLeish, J. *The Lecture Method.* Cambridge Monograph on Teaching Methods No. 1. Cambridge, England: Cambridge Institute of Education, 1968.

Mattfield, J. A. "Toward a New Synthesis in Curricular Patterns of Undergraduate Education." *Liberal Education,* 1975, *61* (4), 531-547.

Mayville, W. V. *Interdisciplinarity: The Mutable Paradigm.* AAHE-ERIC/Higher Education Research Report No. 9. Washington, D.C.: American Association for Higher Education, 1978.

Miller, R. I. *Evaluating Faculty Performance.* San Francisco: Jossey-Bass, 1972.

Miller, R. I. *Developing Programs for Faculty Education: A Sourcebook for Higher Education.* San Francisco: Jossey-Bass, 1974.

Milton, O., and Associates. *On College Teaching: A Guide to Contemporary Practices.* San Francisco: Jossey-Bass, 1978.

Morris, D. *The Naked Ape.* New York: Dell, 1967.

Nedelsky, L. *Science Teaching and Testing.* New York: Harcourt Brace Jovanovich, 1965.

New Directions for Teaching and Learning series. San Francisco: Jossey-Bass.

Pace, C. R. (Ed.). *New Directions for Higher Education: Evaluating Learning and Teaching,* no. 4. San Francisco: Jossey-Bass, 1973.

Perry, W. G., Jr. *Forms of Intellectual and Ethical Development in the College Years: A Scheme.* New York: Holt, Rinehart and Winston, 1968.

Phenix, P. H. *Realms of Meaning: A Philosophy of the Curriculum for General Education.* New York: McGraw-Hill, 1964.

Phenix, P. H. "The Play Element in Education." In R. T. Hyman (Ed.), *Teaching: Vantage Points for Study.* Philadelphia: Lippincott, 1968.

Posner, G. J., and Strike, K. A. "A Categorization Scheme for Principles of Sequencing Content." *Review of Educational Research,* 1976, *46* (4), 665-690.

Postlethwait, S. M., Novak, J., and Murray, H. T., Jr. *The Audio-Tutorial Approach to Learning.* Minneapolis: Burgess, 1970.

Pullias, E. V., Lockhard, A., and others. *Toward Excellence in College Teaching.* Dubuque, Iowa: Brown, 1964.

Rice, W. "A Proposal for the Abolition of Freshman English As It Is Now Commonly Taught from the College Curriculum." *College English,* 1960, *21,* 361-367.

Rorecek, J. S. (Ed.). *The Teaching of History.* New York: Philosophical Library, 1967.

Rudolph, F. *The American College and University: A History.* New York: Random House, 1965.

Rudolph, F. *Curriculum: A History of the American Undergraduate Course of Study Since 1636.* San Francisco: Jossey-Bass, 1977.

Russell, D. H. *Children's Thinking.* New York: Ginn, 1956.

Shubnikov, A. V., and Koptsik, V. A. *Symmetry in Science and Art.* (New York: Plenum Press, 1974. (Translated from Russian by G. D. Archard; edited by D. Harker.)

Simpson, E. J. "Educational Objectives in the Psychomotor Domain." In M. B. Kapfer (Ed.), *Behavioral Objectives in Curriculum Development.* Englewood Cliffs, N.J.: Educational Technology Publications, 1971.

Skinner, B. F. *The Technology of Teaching.* New York: Meredith, 1968.

Smith, A. H., and Fischer, J. L. (Eds.). *Anthropology.* Englewood Cliffs, N.J.: Prentice-Hall, 1970.

Soltis, J. F. "Education and the Concept of Knowledge." Inaugural Lecture as William Heard Kilpatrick Professor of Philosophy and Education, Teachers College, Columbia University, February 7, 1979.

Spencer, R. E. *The Role of Measurement and Evaluation in Instructional Technology.* Urbana: University of Illinois, 1968.

Stober, R. *The Nature of Historical Thinking.* Chapel Hill: University of North Carolina Press, 1967.

Stone, L. *The Past and the Present.* Boston: Routledge & Kegan Paul, 1981.

Taffe, E. J. *Geography.* Englewood Cliffs, N.J.: Prentice-Hall, 1970.

Taylor, H. S. "Physical Sciences." In H. N. Fairchild and Associates, *Religious Perspectives in College Teaching.* New York: Ronald Press, 1952.

Taylor, J. T., and Walford, R. *Simulation in the Classroom.* Harmondsworth, England: Penguin Books, 1972.

Toynbee, A. J. *A Study of History.* (6 vols.) London: Oxford University Press, 1959.

Travers, R. M. W. (Ed.). *Second Handbook of Research on Teaching.* A Project of the American Educational Research Association. Chicago: Rand McNally, 1973.

Tricart, J. *The Teaching of Geography at University Level.* London: Harrap, 1969.

Trillin, A. S., and Associates. *Teaching Basic Skills in College: A Guide to Objectives, Skills Assessment, Course Content, Teaching Methods, Support Services, and Administration.* San Francisco: Jossey-Bass, 1980.

Turner, F. J. *The Frontier in American History.* New York: Holt, Rinehart and Winston, 1920.

Umstattd, J. G. *College Teaching: Background, Theory and*

Practice. Washington, D.C.: University Press of Washington, D.C., 1964.

University of Chicago, Members of the Faculty. *The Idea and Practice of General Education.* Chicago: University of Chicago Press, 1950.

University of London Teaching Methods Unit. *Improving Teaching in Higher Education.* Leicester, England: Cavendish Press, 1976.

Wesley, E. G., and Adams, M. A. *Teaching Social Studies in Elementary Schools.* (rev. ed.) Boston: Heath, 1952.

Weyl, H. *Symmetry.* Princeton, N.J.: Princeton University Press, 1952.

Whitehead, A. N., and Russell, B. *Principia Mathematica.* New York: Cambridge University Press, 1915.

Wilson, R. S., and Hildebrand, M. *Effective University Teaching and Its Evaluation.* Berkeley: Center for Research and Development in Higher Education, University of California, 1970.

Wittich, W. A., and Schuller, C. F. *Instructional Technology, Its Nature and Use.* (5th ed.) New York: Harper & Row, 1973.

Wynne, J. P. *General Education in Theory and Practice.* New York: Bookman, 1952.

Zuckerman, D. W., and Horn, R. F. *The Guide to Simulation for Education and Training.* (2nd ed.) New York: Western, 1973.

Index